Fit and Fabric

from

Threads MAGAZINE

Fit and Fabric

from Threads MAGAZINE

The Taunton Press

Cover photo by Susan Kahn

Taunton
BOOKS & VIDEOS
for fellow enthusiasts

First printing: May 1991
Second printing: February 1992
Third printing: December 1996
Printed in the United States of America

A THREADS Book

THREADS magazine® is a trademark of The Taunton Press, Inc.
registered in the U.S. Patent and Trademark Office.

The Taunton Press
63 South Main Street
Box 5506
Newtown, CT 06470-5506

Library of Congress Cataloging-in-Publication Data

Fit and Fabric   :   from Threads magazine.
        p.   cm.
    ISBN 0-942391-81-0
    1. Sewing.   2. Clothing and dress.   I. Threads magazine
TT705.F48   1991   90-23683
646.4—dc20   CIP

Contents

Introduction

Sewing a garment that you'll love to wear means sewing one that fits your body. It means making those little changes to a commercial pattern that put the pockets where *your* hands fall, the crotch seams and waistline where they're comfortable for *you*. It also means understanding the fabric you've chosen so that you can get the results you want.

In this group of articles from the first four years of *Threads* magazine, we explore the exciting concepts of pattern, fit and fabric. Whether you want to design your own garments, adapt patterns or copy your favorite clothes; whether you're sewing with leather or lace; the advice and explanations from the sewers, designers and patternmakers included in this volume should help you make the clothes you can imagine — and make them fit, as well.

Betsy Levine, editor

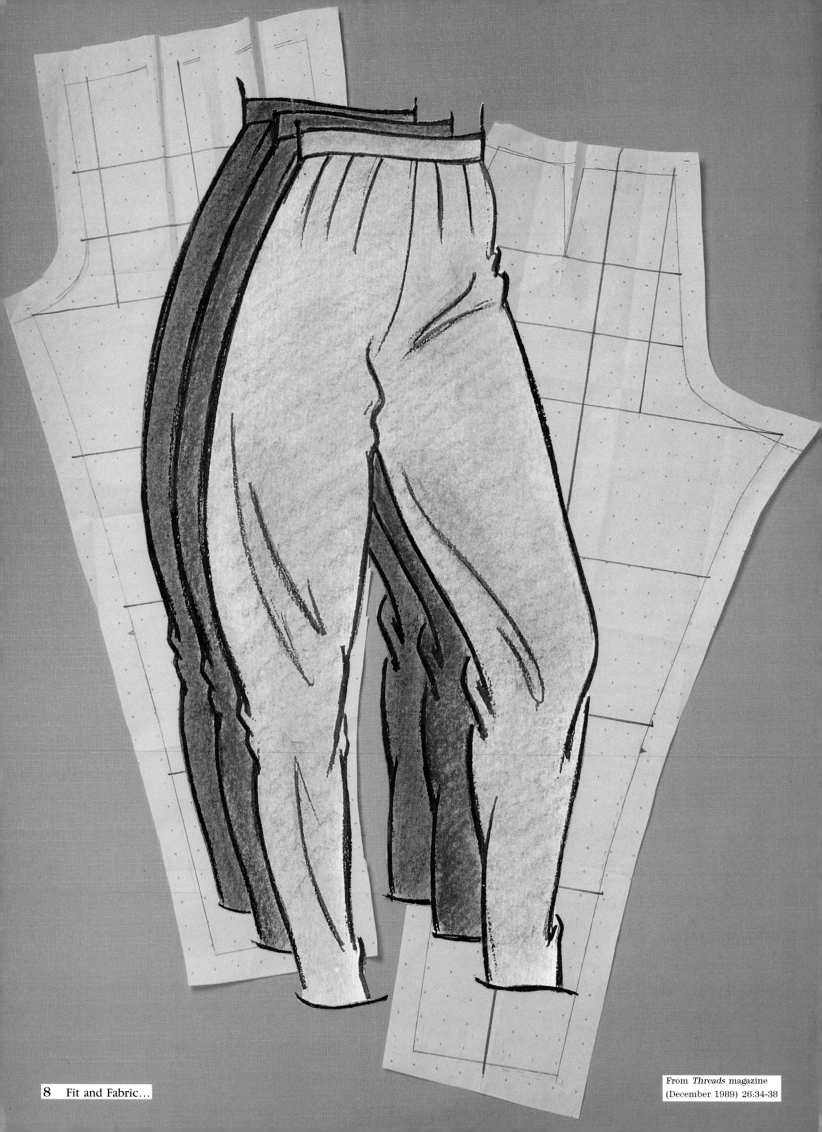

From *Threads* magazine
(December 1989) 26:34-38

Copy the Clothes You Love

Pants are an easy introduction

by Jann Jasper

do you have a favorite garment that's too worn to wear? Perhaps there's a vintage dress you'd like to reproduce. How about those store-bought pants that fit you better than any you've ever made? To make a pair just like them, read on.

You can make a pattern from an existing garment without taking it apart. And you can do it very accurately. It's much easier to start with a garment that can be smoothed out fairly flat, such as pants, so I'll use them to illustrate the concepts of copying a garment. A garment with a lot of shape built into the seams (e.g., a jacket or fitted dress) is more difficult to copy because it can't be flattened. Avoid complex garments on your first attempts. A garment with many pieces isn't necessarily more difficult to copy, but it's time-consuming because of all the pattern pieces involved.

Garments of very soft or unstable fabric; e.g., knits and wovens, may have been badly stretched or may have distorted grain lines. A stretched-out garment fits well because it has been forced out of its original shape. It's difficult to duplicate this precise fit in a brand-new garment, as you must estimate how and where to include the ease, so select something less worn for your first try.

You can make your pattern on muslin or paper, but paper distorts less. Any paper on which pencil markings are easily visible is fine. Pattern paper with horizontal and vertical lines of dots or letters to denote lengthwise and crosswise grains is ideal. Lightweight or medium-weight shipping paper is okay, but markings are a bit hard to see. Don't use newspaper; you can't see markings on it. Artist's tracing paper is brittle, and tissue paper tears. White shelf paper is good, but something less opaque is better.

Preparing the pants—Regardless of which garment you choose to copy, start by studying how it's made, both inside and out. Notice whether the fit and shape are provided by curved seams, darts, pleats, or all three; these features will be included in the paper pattern. How many pattern pieces will the

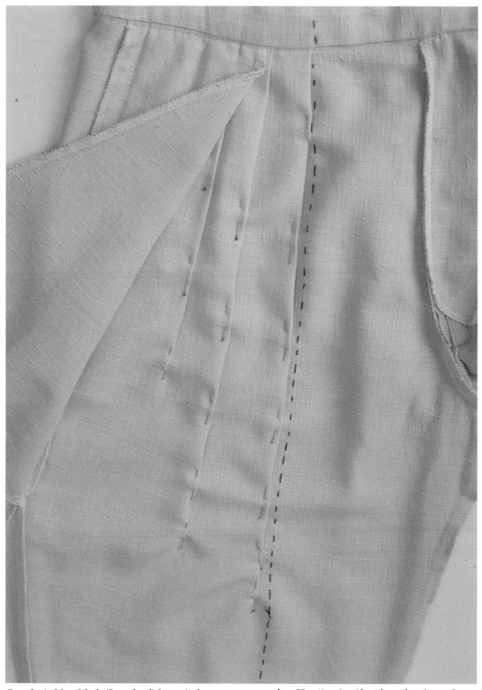

Comfortable old clothes don't have to be mere memories. Use the duplicating tips from Jann Jasper to make a pattern for new ones. Prepare pants for taking a pattern by closing and pinning all pleats, then thread-tracing the grain line (in brown on pants above).

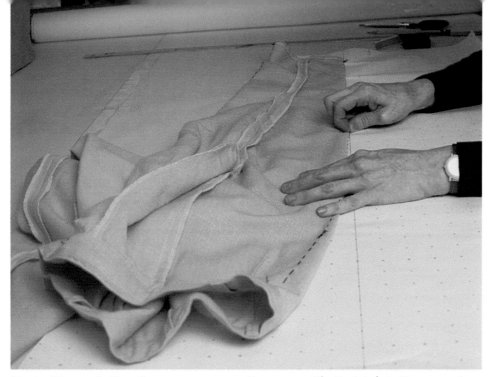

Start with a grain line. Draw one on your pattern paper. Pin the fabric to the paper along the grain line, rolling to match lines accurately.

garment need? If you want to include all the details, such as pockets or a fly front, note how they're constructed. Make sure you understand how the garment was assembled before you begin making the pattern.

The dimensions of pleats and darts must be measured in the garment, then transferred to the new pattern; they provide ease that's difficult to restore later if missed. Think of a pleat as a long dart; it may taper to an end at hip level, or its fullness may continue well down into the leg. Smooth and pin each pleat shut to its natural endpoint (photo, p. 9). You can insert a yardstick between the layers to avoid pinning the pleat to the back, which must remain free.

If your pants have an elasticized waist, and the elastic is inside a casing, you can easily remove the elastic and flatten the fabric. If the elastic is sewn into the waist, no preparation is necessary at this point.

Since fabric is malleable, especially in garments that have been worn and washed, you must keep the grain straight while you work. To do this, thread-trace the lengthwise grain on both the front and back of a pant leg down the center. On more complex garments you can also trace the crosswise grain. You'll leave this thread line in until you're finished; later, it will serve as a reference point for double-checking your pattern measurements against your pants measurements.

Turn the pants inside out and mark locations for pattern notches with safety pins (they won't fall out as you work) along the inseams and outseams near midleg. Pattern notches will help you match the pieces together and check their dimensions.

Tracing—It doesn't matter if you copy the front or back first; I'll start with the back. Cut pieces of paper wide enough and long enough for the front and back pant legs, and draw grain lines down the center the

full length. Lay the pants on a sheet of paper, with the wrong side of the part that you're working on against the paper. Match the thread-traced grain line to the line on the paper and pin the lines together from waist to hem (photo above). Check often to see that the grain line remains straight and that the pant leg is smoothed flat. Place pins several inches apart.

Then work from the pinned grain line toward the inseam and outseams and fold the pleats and darts into the paper (left photos, facing page). Measure from the thread-traced grain line along the cross grain to darts or pleats to find their exact locations, and mark the paper. Measure the pleat or dart width on the pants; then fold a pleat into your paper at the location marked. Make sure the fold in the paper is the same width and length as in the pants, or you'll change the fit.

The stitching line of a dart makes it easy to see how much fabric it contains. Insert a pin at the dart endpoint in the pants so you'll be able to feel for the point when marking the paper. Your sense of touch will help you smooth the fabric flat against the paper to check the location. Sometimes it's also helpful to flip the pants and paper over and place a press mitt or tailor's ham inside the dart area to hold out the curve and facilitate folding the dart smoothly.

Pin the darts and pleats of fabric and paper together. Flip the pants to the top again. Transfer the outseams, then the inseams (photo at top right, facing page); you'll add seam allowances later. Pin the fabric flat to the paper and mark the paper at the outseam from hem to waist, smoothing the fabric against the paper and checking that the fabric grain stays straight. I use short pencil marks rather than a continuous line; after I trace the pattern, I connect the marks into a smooth line. Then roll the pant leg

toward the inseam, and pin and mark it from hem to crotch. Cross-mark the paper at the safety pins that you've placed for notches, and mark the finished hem edge.

If the pants have gathers to the waist because elastic is sewn to the waistband, you probably won't be able to pin the pants all the way to the top. When you've pinned as close to the waistband as possible, stretch the waistband against a yardstick to measure the waist distance between the center and side seams. Mark this width on the paper pattern at the height of the waist. Locate the grain at the top of the side seam and follow it down 3 in. Measure out to the side seam; then make the paper pattern to determine the rough shape of the hip.

It's especially important when you're pinning the back of the pants to paper that the lengthwise and crosswise threads be at right angles through the entire crotch and hip area, as it's probably stretched from wear. Lay a square on the fabric to ensure this. You might not be able to completely straighten the stretched areas without having bubbles appear in the seat; those bubbles are the extra room you've built into the garment by wearing it.

The next step is to pin and mark the waist and crotch seams. Carefully mark the paper at the waist seamline, lifting the waistband off the paper if necessary to see it. If the waist is elasticized, stretch it out as you mark. Next, mark the crotch, lifting the seam allowance so you can see and mark the seamline. Once you've squared the grain, the back crotch seam and upper inseam will probably look wavy because the fabric has stretched, just as mine did (photo at bottom right, facing page); pat it into place to restore the crotch curve to that of the original pattern. If you flatten the curve and disregard the grain, it will be longer than on the original garment. The back is done, so unpin and repeat for the front.

Perfecting the pattern—After you've copied both the front and back, double-check the accuracy of your pattern by measuring it at several checkpoints and comparing it with the pants. Since fabric isn't rigid, it's normal to find that adjustments are necessary.

For reference, draw lines perpendicular to the grain line at the following locations on your pattern, as I did on mine (top photo, p. 11): high hip (4 in. below waist); hip (7 in. below waist); top of the inseam; midthigh; knee; midcalf; and hem. Pin-mark the corresponding points on the pants. On both front and back, compare the widths at these places and also the crotch depth and total crotch length.

Make any needed adjustments. When in doubt about which markings to follow, make the pattern looser rather than tighter. The crotch is a tricky and crucial area. If you've double-checked your pattern against the pants at the length from the waist to the top of the inseam and you've double-checked

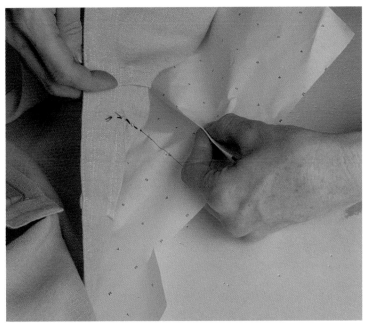

Locate dart positions. Pinch in the body of the dart.

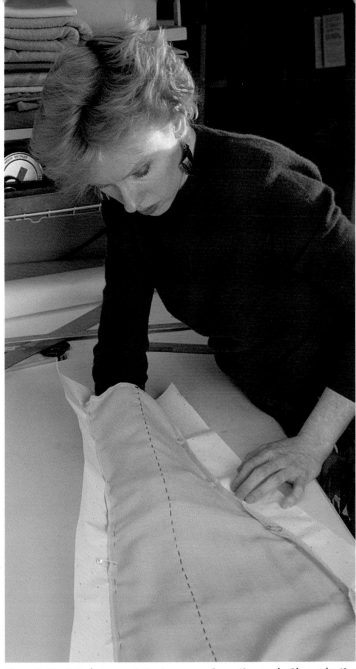

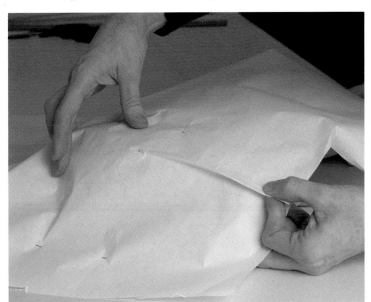

Fold the darts into the paper, using a pressing ham underneath to mimic body curves (above). Mark the dart legs, and pin the folded dart to the pants (below).

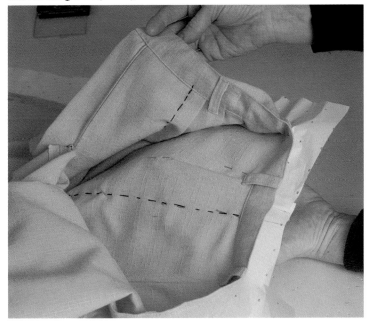

Smooth the fabric toward the leg seam from the grain line; pin the pants to the paper from hem to waist. Mark dots along the seamline; roll the leg if necessary to pin the inseam. Since the darts and pleats are pinned shut, the pants won't lie flat, but the fabric should lie smooth against the paper, as Jasper checks here.

Pin the crotch so the grain lines are straight. The fabric may ripple, but that's fine; an incorrectly pinned crotch may lie flat but result in a crotch line that's too long.

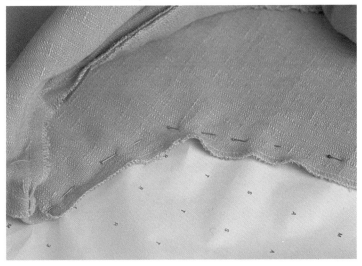

Check the length and width of the pattern against the original. As a reference for the hip area, draw horizontal lines perpendicular to the grain line on your pattern at high hip, inseam top, and midthigh. Then use a tape measure to check the width of areas that won't lie flat (above), such as the back.

Redraw the crotch curve (far left) and waist curve—green lines (near left)—so the front and back meet smoothly at the side seams and inseam. Differences are averaged by eye.

the leg width at the crotch, your total crotch length should also be correct. If you're not sure, widen the "hook" area (where the back crotch meets the inseam). Women usually need more width here anyway.

Also check the width and length of your closed pleats. Pleat length may seem irrelevant, since the pleats aren't stitched shut, but you've incorporated the amount of fullness they contain, and you'll need the fullness to reproduce the fit of the garment.

Since you've double-checked your measurements, your markings should fall into line with only minor deviations. Connect and blend the marks smoothly, using straight and curved rulers. Cut off any excess paper, leaving 1½-in. seam allowances.

Next, you'll check the lengths of the seamlines on the front and back patterns against each other and smooth out any jagged intersections at the hem, crotch, and waist. Starting with the back and front inseams, lap one edge over the other from the notch at midleg to hem and pin. Correct discrepancies in seam lengths by dividing the difference in half and drawing a new hem.

Repeat this process for the top half of the inseam. Measure the length from the notch at the midleg to the crotch; divide the difference by 2, and mark the front and back at the common length where the crotch line meets the inseam. Overlap the front and back at this mark, pin them together

for a few inches, and draw a smooth crotch curve (left photo, above).

Use the same procedure to match the outseam length, evening up the hem if necessary. Pin shut all darts and pleats and draw a smooth waist curve (right photo, above). The hip area will cup when you pin the seams together, and it's tricky to draw on something that's not lying flat, but this is the only way to prevent peaks or dips in the finished waist seam. Draw the waist seam in a smooth curve, connecting most of the dots and ignoring any that are way out of line.

To match curved seams, like the jodhpur-style outseams of my pants, place pins at the notch and hem. Hold the patterns up to the light—you can compare the two seam lengths and shapes in one step. If there's a discrepancy in the shapes, compromise to make them match.

After the pattern is trued and I've added details, such as the fly front, pocket opening, and waistband, I use ¾-in.-wide seam allowances everywhere, except at the crotch, where I use ½ in. Wider seam allowances in a curved area obscure the fit because, when the fabric is stitched, it won't lie flat. There are so many variations on closures and pockets that I won't go into them here, but an easy way to add them is to refer to a pants pattern that you have and transfer the appropriate parts to your new pattern.

The pattern is finished, but before you cut it in the real fabric, test it in muslin or a fabric that's close to the original weight or drape. No matter how careful you are, there will be some adjustments needed, especially on your first attempts. Don't use a fabric that's limp or very stiff; it won't give a true picture of your fit. Baste the inseams, outseams, and crotch seam, and baste on a waistband. Don't iron the muslin; it's too easily distorted. Try the pants on, wearing the appropriate undergarments and shoes. Pin the zipper opening shut and make sure you can comfortably close the waistband. Walk, bend, and sit to ensure that the pants are comfortable. Note any corrections (for help with fitting, see the pants-fitting articles on pp. 66-71) and transfer them back to the pattern.

With any new pattern, it's normal even for experienced patternmakers to go through a few muslins before getting it perfect. Don't be discouraged; the results will be well worth it; it's a good investment that you'll use over and over again. □

Jann Jasper shares tips on how to fine-tune a muslin in her article, "How to spot and correct three common pants-fitting problems," on pp. 70-71. She is a professional free-lance patternmaker and writer in New York City. Her favorite media are fabric and clothing.

Perfect Fit
A harmony between garment and body

by Alice Allen

Correct fit in clothes today doesn't mean what it used to. Yesterday's fashions of boned collars and whalebone corsets are a far cry from stretch fabrics, oversized bodices, and simplified construction. Yet, even today, we must conform the "cut of cloth" to the reality of our own proportions.

Proper fit means compatibility of body form and fashion silhouette. A perfectly fitting garment, of which the houndstooth dress at right is an example, is comfortable and free from tension wrinkles or excess fullness. The seam lines flatter the body's curves. The garment complements the body's contours—the hollow of the collarbone, the angle of the shoulder, and the bulges of the bust and hipline. Garment closures don't strain. Curves of cloth lie close to body curves; neckline and armscye do not gap. Vertical seams hang straight, and vertical and horizontal grain lines fall true. The garment hangs smoothly on the body. Overall, it is balanced—its proportions are pleasing, and it is flattering to the wearer.

The components of fit

To evaluate the fit of a garment, we look at it in terms of five areas: ease, line, set, grain, and balance.

Ease—Wearing ease is extra cloth in the circumferences of the garment to ensure comfort and mobility. The criterion for evaluating wearing ease is the question: "Does the garment provide adequate room for the movement required by its intended use?" The amount of ease depends on the type of garment and the fabric. Street clothes of woven fabric usually allow the following range of wearing ease:

Bustline—about 4 in. Can you pick up a ½-in. tuck in each quarter of shirt?
Back—½ in. to ¾ in. between shoulder blades.
Waist—1 in. Will a finger fit comfortably behind the waistband?
Hips—2 in. when standing. Can you pinch a ½-in. tuck at each side seam?

A garment must have enough ease to sit properly on the body and be comfortable, but not so much that it becomes distorted. Inadequate ease results in the fabric's pulling across the area that's tight, causing horizontal wrinkles above it. Excess ease results in bagginess.

The teal dress on page 14 and the blue-denim dress at the top of page 15 have inadequate wearing ease across the hips. The fabric of each skirt pulls across the hip area and rides up, causing wrinkles to form in the waist area. Increasing the width by letting out the side seams would solve these problems. Conversely, excessive ease causes the diagonal wrinkles in the shoulders of the pink dress at the bottom of page 15. Lowering the shoulders and narrowing the sleeves in the upper arm (corrections most easily made during garment construction) would solve the problem.

On the other hand, the classic, semifitted houndstooth dress, shown in the photo at right, has sufficient ease across the bust and hip to allow the wearer comfort and movement, yet not so much that the fabric bulges and bags. The garment's surface remains smooth, as the designer intended.

Another category of ease, designer ease, refers to the further adjustments in fullness that a designer chooses to make to a garment so that it's appealing to the eye. Every garment has designer ease. With designer ease, one creates a full skirt instead of a straight one; a balloon sleeve instead of a tailored, fitted one; a gathered bodice instead of a tight, darted one. Because of the flexibility in designer ease, the "rules" of perfect fit don't apply to every garment. They apply most directly to closely fitting garments but also provide reference points for the evaluation of garments that deviate from a fitted silhouette.

Line—Line refers to the visible structural and decorative lines of a garment. Structural lines include all seams that hold the garment together; decorative lines can be

Perfect fit means harmony between garment and body. A well-fitting garment, such as this houndstooth dress, is both comfortable and flattering to the wearer; its contours relate to the body's contours without being too tight and therefore unflattering.

part of the seaming (such as piping in a princess seam) or surface trim.

Vertical lines divide the body in half and should be plumb. From the shoulder line, the side seams of the bodice and skirt should fall straight between the tip of the ear and the middle of the ankle and hang perpendicular to the circumference seams and the floor. Circumference lines, which include neckline, armscye, waistline, wristline, and hemline, are generally perpendicular to the silhouette seams (the shoulder and side seams). The side seam of the skirt of the blue-denim dress curves back slightly at the base of the pocket as the result of inadequate ease across the hips. Letting out the side seams would release the tension and allow the seam to fall straight.

Structural lines should complement body-contour lines. The neckline seam should correspond to the base of the neck, with the neckline sitting up slightly in back, yet fitting comfortably. The armscye seam should correspond to the shoulder joint, forming an oval around the joint. The wrist seam should correspond to the wristbone; the sleeve should not pull when the arm is stretched. Note how the sleeves of the pink dress fall below the wrists.

The waistline seam should correspond to the waist indentation and be parallel to the floor, though slightly lower in back to fit the hollow of the back. The horizontal wrinkles at the waist of the teal dress destroy the garment's lines. Inadequate wearing ease at the waist, as well as excessive fabric from neck to hip are the causes. Inadequate wearing ease at the waist also causes the front button closing to gap, distorting an important vertical line.

Vertical design lines, such as tucks, pleats, and gores, should hang perpendicular to the floor. Curved details, such as yokes and soft collars, should be symmetrical, with graceful, smooth lines. If they are asymmetrical, the lines should flow gracefully from one side to the other, from top to bottom.

Set—Set refers to the overall smoothness of the garment to body contours. A garment with the proper set hangs comfortably on the body, without pulling or bagging. Set is closely dependent on adequate wearing ease distributed evenly across body curves and planes.

Excessive ease in the shoulder area of the pink dress (obvious from the diagonal folds falling from the shoulder) prevents the dress from hanging smoothly from the shoulders. Inadequate ease in the waist and hips of the teal and denim dresses (indicated by pulled seams and a gapping button closure) prevent these garments from hanging smoothly over the hips. In each case, the set of the garment has been destroyed by the wrong amount of ease in one area. The houndstooth dress, on the other hand, hangs smoothly on the model, neither pulling nor drooping at her shoulders, arms, bust, waist, or hips.

Grain—The fourth component of fit is grain. In woven cloth, the weft threads (the horizontal threads that run across a length of fabric) intersect the warp threads (the vertical threads that run the length of the fabric). The directions of these threads are the fabric's two grain directions. Garments are normally constructed so that the lengthwise grain (parallel to the warp threads) will be vertical, because the warp threads are usually stronger and heavier than the weft threads. Crosswise grain (parallel to the weft threads) is usually softer and more flexible, and so it goes around the body.

The vertical grain should be perpendicular to the floor at center front and back and from center-sleeve-cap dot to elbow line. The horizontal grain should be parallel to the floor at bust, chest, and hip levels and at the bustline level of the sleeve. Wherever the grain runs on the bias, it should be symmetrical on both sides of the body.

An undesirable slant to the crosswise grain and wrinkles or sagging directly above a body bulge or hollow often indicate an incorrect amount of ease. For example, in the teal dress, the vertical grain aligns with the center-front line but is distorted at the waist because of inadequate ease. To correct the grain, open the seam directly related to the bulge or hollow and adjust the ease. Letting out the teal dress's side seams at the waist would increase the ease and allow the grain to hang without distortion. Note that grain distortion can result from factors other than fit—failing to straighten the cloth prior to cutting, laying and cutting the pattern off grain, and failing to stay-stitch curved areas of necklines, collars, and waistlines.

Balance—The totality of fit is unified by balance. Relative to fashion, balance refers to compatibility among the parts of a design and to the design's overall pleasingness. A design is balanced when both sides are alike. In this case, the design is symmetrical, or formal. If the two sides are different, the design is asymmetrical, or informal. Both formal and informal designs will be balanced if the parts are harmonious and the design as a whole is becoming.

For a garment to be balanced on the human form, it is normally centered on the figure from front to back and side to side. Tightness, excess fabric, and diagonal wrin-

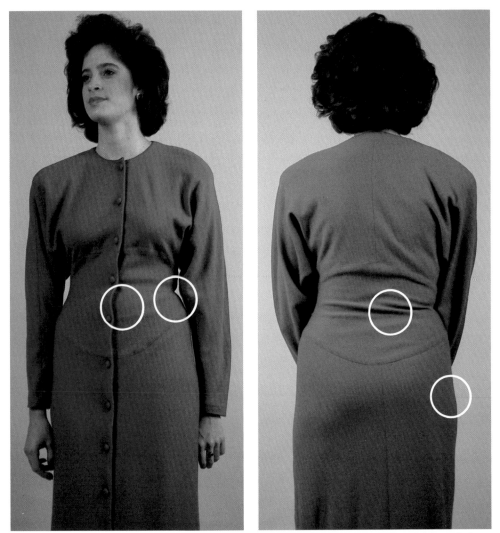

The front button closing gaps and the fabric pulls and wrinkles at the waist of this teal dress (left) because the dress is too tight around the waist—there isn't enough ease. Excess fabric in the back length also causes undesirable folds at the back (right). These problems destroy the garment's lines and set, distort the fabric grain, and draw negative attention to the waist area.

kles have been eliminated. The garment's curves (armscye, crotch, neckline) form smooth ovals and follow the body's natural contours. The vertical seams evenly divide the sides, the front, and the back. The horizontal lines are level across the body.

Perfect fit creates an attractive image. The houndstooth dress complements the model, conforming to, rather than overpowering or skimping, her shoulders, hips, bust, and arms. The front button closing is adequate and comfortable. The sleeves fall to the lower wristbone. The ease across the hip and bust provides comfort and allows unhindered movement. All construction components relate, adding to the garment's overall harmony. The well-fitting garment gives the wearer self-confidence and poise.

Analyzing fit

The steps for analyzing garment fit are the same whether the garment is one you are making or one you are contemplating buying. Naturally, it is easier to analyze and adjust fit during garment construction.

If you're sewing the garment, attach the major units early in the construction process so you can try it on. Baste the bodice and skirt at the shoulder and side seams. Stay-stitch curves. Put the bodice on, accurately aligning center front and center back. Baste the underarm sleeve seams and slip the sleeves on your arms, pinning them to the top-center point of the shoulders. Pin the skirt to the bodice parallel to the waistline seam, with the center front, center back, and side seams aligned.

Wear the same undergarments and shoes you'd wear with the garment. Try on the garment right side out so you can accurately see the relationships between body shape and dress parts. Then critique the garment's fit by asking yourself these questions:

Comfort—Can you sit, move, bend, or raise your arms easily? Consider the amount of ease at each body bulge. Is it adequate? Too much?

Seams—Do vertical seams hang straight, without pulling anywhere? Does the bodice droop vertically as the result of excess fabric width or pull taut because of inadequate width? Is the back smooth across the shoulders? Is the garment too long between the neck and waistline, causing horizontal wrinkles at the lower back? Are there horizontal wrinkles in front between the neck and bustline caused by excess fabric length?

Alignment—If the garment has a bustline dart, does the stitched line point to the fullest area, and is the point 1 in. from the apex? Are there excessive puckers at the point of the hip dart? If so, the dart length is inadequate and needs to be lengthened. Does the natural shoulder seam fall from the top center of the shoulder joint, neither slanting forward nor backward? Does the vertical grain hang straight at center

Because there isn't enough ease in the hip area, the fabric unflatteringly hugs the model's rump. A roll of fabric appears just below the back waist, and the side seam curves backward at the base of the pocket. Letting out the side seams would solve all three problems.

front and center back? Is the horizontal grain true at center-front and center-back waist, neck front, and base of armscye?

Closures—Check the accuracy of the relative positioning of buttons to buttonholes. Does the closure have adequate ease, or is there gapping and pulling? Does the zipper zip easily, without stress?

Collar—Is the collar balanced on the neck? In other words, is it snug against the neck in back? From the front, is each side symmetrical from left to right and up and down?

Sleeves—Bend your arm to check the length of long sleeves. Do they fall to just below the wristbone and have adequate ease through the elbow for normal movement? Fold your arms in front. Is the garment comfortable across the back, neither straining nor sagging through the shoulder?

Look the garment over for unwanted wrinkles and identify what's causing them. Look at the vertical and horizontal lines of the garment and assess their accuracy. They should be straight, smooth, and true.

Note obvious problems, but do not find too many nit-picky faults. Overfitting will cause other problems. First attack simple corrections—the ease and the lengths of the units. These adjustments will often solve the grain and alignment problems.

Always correct width problems by dividing the garment into equal parts and altering each part the same amount. For example, if a skirt is 1 in. too wide, narrow it by ¼ in. in each quarter (left back, right back, left front, and right front).

Remember, the successful fit of a garment is directly related to good dressmaking techniques: Cutting the pieces on grain; stay-stitching curves with the grain; accurately stitching seams; accurately stitching and pressing darts, tucks, and pleats. If these operations have been poorly executed, it is difficult to distinguish poor fit from poor construction. Poor fit in a garment means a lack of harmony between the clothing and the human body. Correct fit requires skillful coordination of pattern to fabric to body and results in clothing that is fashionable and flattering. □

Alice Allen, of Fort Worth, TX, is a sewing specialist for Bernina.

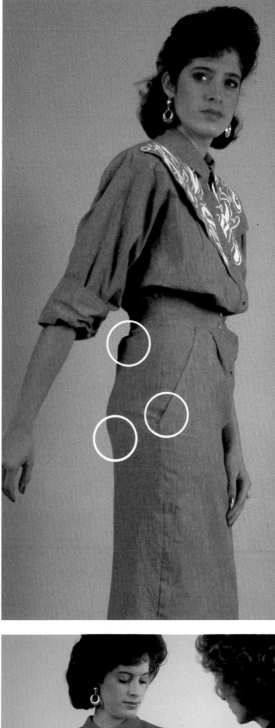

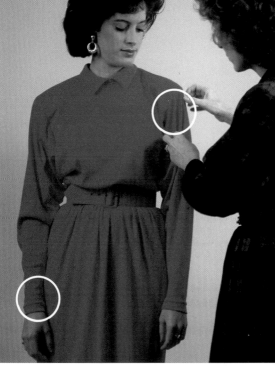

Alice Allen (right) adjusts the shoulder of this dress to eliminate the folds at the underarm and the diagonal wrinkles from underarm to neck, both caused by excess fabric in the width of the sleeves. The sleeves are also too long— they should fall just below the wristbone.

Playing with Darts

See for yourself why the dart is fashion's favorite weapon

By Deborah Abbott

ashions come and go, silhouettes change, technology advances, but the dart remains. Its manipulation is the basis of flat-pattern design. It may change its position and contour, but the dart is always there. Even in the unstructured, relatively shapeless styles popular today, one finds the dart—released, unstitched, but responsible for that casual mood.

The dart transforms a two-dimensional piece of fabric to fit a three-dimensional body. If a piece of fabric is draped over a body or dress form, fabric wrinkles will radiate from the most prominent point (the bust point in the front, the shoulder blades in the back). If you were to stitch closed these wedge-shaped folds of fabric, they would become darts, shaping the fabric over the body's curves.

The principle behind manipulating the dart is that it makes no difference where you position the dart. So long as it removes the wedge-shaped folds, and so long as the wedge or wedges point from a seamline toward the prominence, the shape of the cone of fabric and the fit will be the same, regardless of where the dart is. Only the outline of the pattern piece will change.

The basic bodice darts are the shoulder and waistline darts, but a dart can be shifted to the neckline, the armhole, the underarm, or the center front (or to any combination of these) without the size or the fit of the garment changing. Several darts can be combined into one large dart, as in the master bodice front shown in the left-hand drawing below, or, conversely, one large dart can be divided into many smaller darts, or even converted into a multitude of tucks. Darts can be released completely or transformed into gathers or pleats. Darts can be disguised in shirring or smocking. They can be concealed in a seamline, as in the classic Princess line. Thus, they can be decorative (as in pin tucks around a neckline), functional (creating fit over the bust),

One-quarter-scale master bodice

Use photocopies of these basic shapes for your experiments with dart manipulation. Usually, the bodice back is simply adjusted to match the front at side and shoulder seams, but it can be manipulated in the same way as the front.

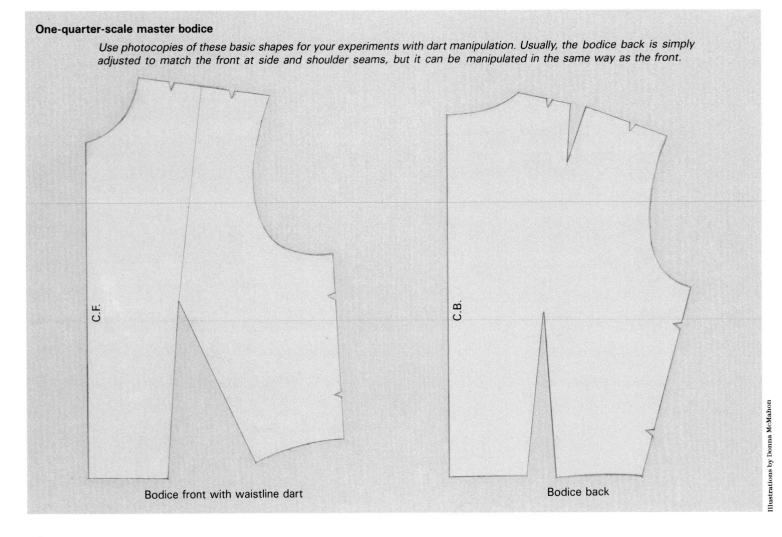

C.F.

Bodice front with waistline dart

C.B.

Bodice back

Illustrations by Donna McMahon

and structural (converted to a seam that holds the garment together).

"Why bother shifting darts yourself?" you ask. There are a multitude of well-designed and fashionable commercial patterns available. Although they are useful starting points, they can't consider the individual aspects of your figure, fabric, and needlework talents. Understanding how (and having the confidence) to change a commercial pattern to suit and interpret *your* intentions generates a satisfying freedom from the entire garment industry.

Dart decisions—Before you plunge in, I'll tell you why I love having mastered the dart and what kinds of things I consider when I take up my scissors. One's figure type determines the most flattering placement of fitting darts. The dress design may demand exact placement of certain darts in order for you to achieve the desired silhouette. One's own interests and skills may suggest one dart treatment over another. A smocker might smock a dart into gathers, while an embroiderer might create tucks with decorative threads. In order to display a lace insert, a lacemaker might convert two darts into a dart-equivalent seam, like the Princess seam described on page. 19. My primary concern is the relationship of the fabric to the dress design.

When selecting a dress design, and with it, its darts, I consider the fabric structure.

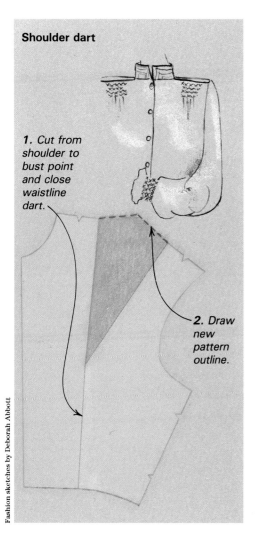

Shoulder dart

1. Cut from shoulder to bust point and close waistline dart.

2. Draw new pattern outline.

The pattern might call for knits only, but I may prefer to use a woven twill. I'll have to add fitting darts to allow for the lack of stretch in the woven fabric. I might have to add an opening if the original was meant to be slipped over the head. Perhaps the fitting darts can be concealed in the opening. If my fabric is lace or net, visible dart wedges in the transparent material may be distracting or unattractive. Maybe I can relocate the darts to an inconspicuous seam.

I consider the fabric weave. Twills drape beautifully, especially on the bias. A diagonal line is part of the fabric structure and, in heavier weights and most handwovens, is a strong visual element as well. A dart can be made to disapppear in that diagonal or to stand out at right angles. Satins and crepes have a smooth, stable structure, which is an ideal background for intricate seamlines and detailed stitching.

I consider the fabric finish. If I plan to wash the garment, I launder the fabric first. I have had a crisp raw silk turn limp, necessitating a change of plans. If the change in the fabric after washing or dry cleaning will alter the silhouette, it will often alter my choice of dart placement.

I consider the surface style or texture of my fabric. Light will reflect differently above and below the stitching line of a horizontal dart on a napped surface, such as velvet, corduroy, or terry cloth. To avoid the look of a blemished cloth, I would change that horizontal line to a vertical or diagonal line. Sewing with genuine leather and suede restricts my choice of pattern-piece size because animal skins come only so large. This in turn requires ingenious piecing with dart-equivalent seams. I avoid stitched darts in bulky fabrics (fake fur and prequilted fabrics, in addition to leathers), where the dart will not press flat.

I consider the pattern of the fabric. In small allover prints, most seamlines and dart lines disappear. In a striped or plaid fabric, the dart may disrupt a line, making it appear jagged, or it might form bold geometric graphics. Involved seaming and decorative dart lines are best displayed on a plain fabric, where a printed pattern is not competing with the styling lines.

Try it yourself—Just reading about the principle of the dart is no way to really understand it. It seems terribly abstract, and its usefulness unimaginable to a newcomer to flat-pattern design. So, for a minute, let's play with paper and scissors and bring some visual and tactile reality to this abstraction. Besides paper and scissors, you'll also need sharp pencils, Scotch tape, a ruler, paper for mounting (preferably a contrasting color), and a flat work space.

Make several copies of the quarter-scale-bodice front and back shown on the facing page. Use a separate bodice for each dart variation. I've found that drawing a page of quarter-scale bodices and making copies saves a lot of tracing. Lined paper will make

it easy for you to see how stripes are broken when you change the dart line, and graph paper will give you an idea of the effect on plaids. You can place the scale bodice diagonally on striped paper to simulate the bias cut and resulting chevrons. As you discover how much fun this exercise is, you will have little paper bodices strewn about the room.

In the quarter-scale bodice given here, you will notice that the dart goes directly to the bust point. This is so that the pattern can be slashed right to the point of pivot. On the garment, the stitched dart will be redrawn so that it ends within a 1-in. or 2-in. radius of the bust point (sometimes called the bust circle) because the actual bust is rounded, not cone-shaped. Redraw the darts to shorten them by sliding the point away from the bust along a line bisecting the dart.

The size of a dart is determined by the angle it makes at the bust point, not by its length. This is what permits us to shift darts around and to lengthen or shorten them as they hit the various seamlines. Ending a dart at the bust circle instead of at the point allows a little extra fullness by slightly enlarging the dart's angle, and it gives us some leeway to redirect the point of the dart to improve the design. Single darts usually look best when they point directly at the bust point; double darts can point to either side.

A good place to start playing is to make a *shoulder dart,* shown at left. Draw a line from the center of the shoulder to the bust point. Cut on the pencil line up to, but not through, the bust point, and then pivot the left-hand half of the pattern clockwise around the bust point to close the waist dart, as in the drawing. Note that although the position of the dart has been changed, the size and the fit of the bodice have not. All the fullness is now at the shoulder. There is so much fullness that a stitched dart will bulge awkwardly.

What alternatives are there? Divide the single dart into several smaller darts, as shown in the top-left drawing on page 18. Convert the darts into pleats by folding them closed but leaving them unstitched. I've updated an old shirt pattern by moving the traditional underarm fitting dart to the shoulder to form a Gibson pleat, set at right angles to the shoulder near the sleeve seam. Gather the dart closed instead of stitching it. For more fullness, split and spread the pattern, as shown in the top right drawing on page 18. The yoke eliminates fullness from the shoulder, keeping it all below the seam, where it's needed. Fullness can be smocked daintily for a silk blouse, or with lots of added fullness, shirred to drape off the shoulder. The shoulder dart can be left unstitched, creating a dropped shoulder. Split and spread the bodice back so the front and back shoulders match.

Divide the waistline dart into *two darts,* at shoulder and waistline, as shown in the

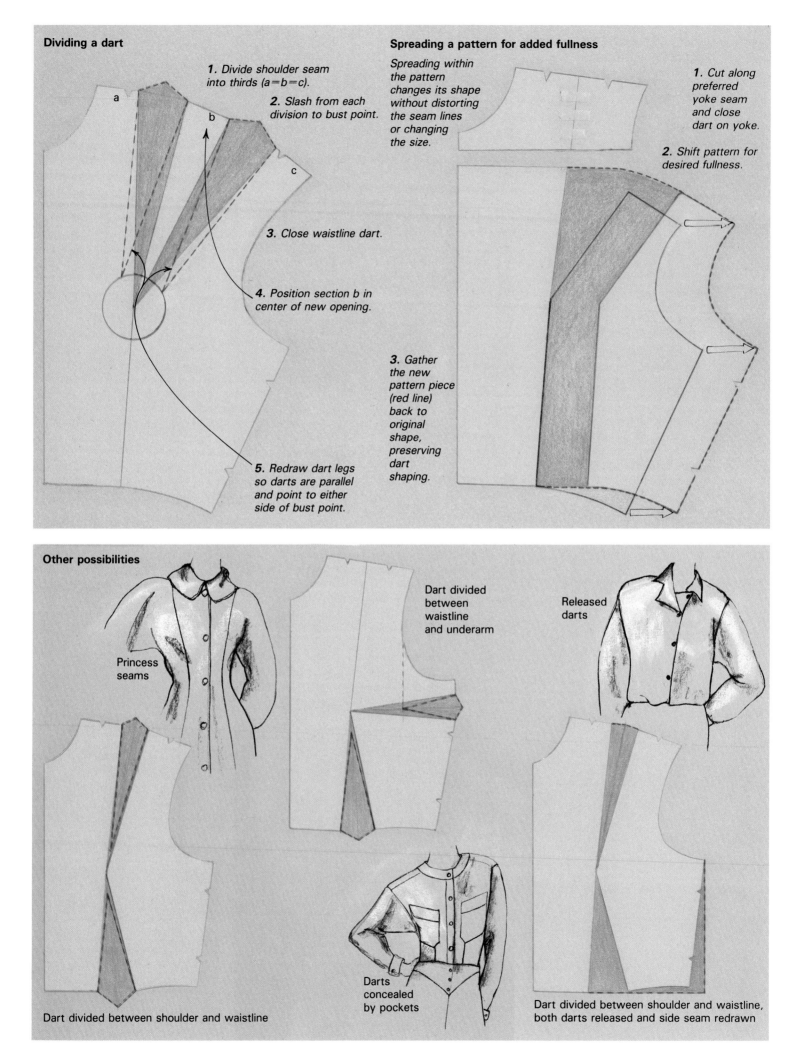

Dividing a dart

1. Divide shoulder seam into thirds (a=b=c).

2. Slash from each division to bust point.

3. Close waistline dart.

4. Position section b in center of new opening.

5. Redraw dart legs so darts are parallel and point to either side of bust point.

Spreading a pattern for added fullness

Spreading within the pattern changes its shape without distorting the seam lines or changing the size.

1. Cut along preferred yoke seam and close dart on yoke.

2. Shift pattern for desired fullness.

3. Gather the new pattern piece (red line) back to original shape, preserving dart shaping.

Other possibilities

Princess seams

Dart divided between shoulder and waistline

Dart divided between waistline and underarm

Darts concealed by pockets

Released darts

Dart divided between shoulder and waistline, both darts released and side seam redrawn bottom-left drawing, facing page. On another one-quarter-scale bodice, draw a line from the center of the shoulder to the bust point and slash as you did for the shoulder dart. Divide the fullness of the waistline dart between the waist and the shoulder, and then shorten the darts thus formed. Do two darts facing each other give you any ideas? Draw a line from the point of one dart to the point of the other dart; slash along the line and cut out the dart wedges. Now you have two pattern pieces that, when seamed together, conceal the darts: the classic Princess style. Because the Princess seam cuts through the entire length of the pattern, fabric can be molded to fit the body more smoothly than with a series of smaller darts.

Next, let's position the darts at the waistline and *underarm,* as in the center drawing on the facing page. The underarm dart is placed as high as possible under the arm without interfering with the armscye seam. It is a supplementary fitting dart and is used with a waistline dart. It is usually a short dart, designed to be hidden by the sleeve, tapering to end in line with the armscye. On another one-quarter-scale bodice, draw a line from the bust point to the position of the new dart under the arm (1¼ in. below the armscye seam on a life-size pattern). Cut along the pencil line. Partly close the waistline dart to form the new underarm dart. Redraw the darts to shorten them. Here is another familiar pattern piece: the bodice of a basic fitting shell from which a master pattern can be made.

A *released dart* is one that has been placed in an area and then allowed to flow without being stitched, as with both darts in the bottom-right drawing, facing page. Transfer any underarm fitting darts to another seamline before releasing them so that the back and front side seams are the same length. Releasing the darts and cutting and spreading the pattern create that loose-fitting look that is seen on runways today. Sometimes the pattern is simply expanded, and the darts are left intact to control the direction of the grain. The grain should usually be horizontal just above the largest circumference of the bust and over the shoulder blades in back.

Try some dart variations on your own. Draw a line from the bust point to the new position, cut, and reposition. By playing with the one-quarter-scale bodice, you will develop an understanding of, and confidence about, the way darts work. You will see why they cannot be ignored or eliminated from a dress pattern. Moreover, you will see how darts can be added to a pattern, giving shape and fit where there was none before.

When you feel that you have the confidence to cut with real fabric, use an old sheet for practice. Draw lines with Magic Marker on the sheet to simulate stripes and plaids so you will be able to see their positions change.

Source of inspiration—Your challenge as a designer is to invent variations of the basic dart, to create a becoming and comfortable garment, acceptable to today's fashion mood. Nothing can be quite as ordinary as a basic shoulder and waist dart or waist and underarm dart as they are used in a master block pattern or sloper. But the fledgling designer soon realizes that these are flattering, undistracting dart positions. Concocting interesting alternatives to this tried-and-true scheme is where designing departs from traditional dressmaking and tailoring. A shoulder dart is a good starting point—it draws the eye upward, which not only gives the appearance of height to the figure but centers attention on the face.

For some wonderful inspiration, browse through the fashions of the '30s and '40s, a time when intricate seaming was a hallmark of good design and skilled patternmaking. Check college and large city libraries for fashion and news periodicals, like *Life* and *Vogue,* as well as picture books of the well-known designers.

Ask your local fabric store for a pattern catalog that's about to be discarded. New catalogs are issued every three months, and most stores give away (or will sell for a modest sum) the old ones. Home-sewing patterns are modeled after ready-to-wear, which has increasingly yielded to the demands of a labor-intensive industry and competition from abroad. Current fashions are cut to fit loosely in styles that camouflage a multitude of figure faults, where accurate sizing is less important, and skilled labor less necessary. However, the dart is still visibly present, albeit not as manifest, especially in designer patterns and in better retail dress lines. Discerning how other designers have varied the basic dart will provide you with lots of ideas to draw on for your own designs and adaptations. □

Deborah Abbott is a fashion designer and weaver. When not manipulating darts, she designs and manufactures yarns and fabrics under the name Aurora Designs.

References

Armstrong, Helen Joseph. *Patternmaking for Fashion Design.* New York: Harper & Row, 1986.

Bane, Allyn. *Flat Pattern Design.* New York: McGraw-Hill, 1972 (out of print).

Hillhouse, Marion S., and Evelyn A. Mansfield. *Dress Design: Draping and Flat Pattern Making.* Boston: Houghton Mifflin, 1948.

Hollen, Norma R. *Pattern Making by the Flat-Pattern Method,* 5th ed. Minneapolis: Burgess, 1981.

Kopp, Ernestine. *Designing Apparel Through the Flat Pattern,* 5th ed. New York: Fairchild, 1981.

Wolfe, Mary Gorgen. *Clear-Cut Pattern Making (by the Flat Pattern Method).* New York: Macmillan, 1982.

Stanley Hostek on darts

Tailors think about darts in their own peculiar fashion, and it illuminates how darts work, in a way that's very different from a designer's approach. The dart, of course, remains the same. Tailors also point out that anything that is true of darts is true of manipulated fullness as well. Stanley Hostek gave me an impromptu lecture on darts while I was visiting him to photograph him at work. Here's the gist of it.—*David Coffin*

The dart's effect on fit

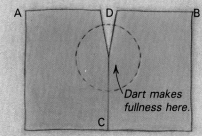

Adding a dart to a pattern piece makes the length of the piece across the dart short (A to B), and the length parallel to the dart longer (C to D), because the line from C to D now bends to cross the piece.

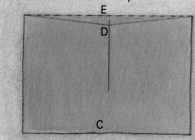

Smoothing out the join of the dart increases the length parallel to it even further (C to E).

The dart's effect on construction

The dart on the bias at left will be easier to bring to a smooth point than the one on the straight or cross grain at right.

The dart's visual effect

Angled waistline darts like the one on the left perceptually narrow the waist and emphasize the hips. The dart on the right will widen the waist and narrow the hips.

Draping a Blouse

A cowl-neck shirt from tissue to muslin to pattern

by Ellen Sperry

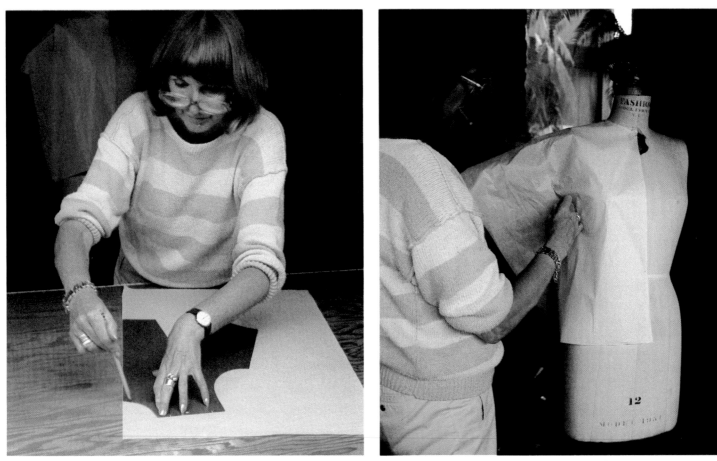

Ellen Sperry begins the draping procedure for her cowl-neck blouse by tracing her slopers on tissue. She aligns the center front of the half front bodice sloper with the edge of the tissue sheet and allows ample room on the other three sides for adjustments.

Sperry pins the half front to the form, aligning the center front. As she positions the shoulder seam and underarm eye, she marks any changes in the location of these points with a soft-lead pencil on the tissue. The underarm eye, for example, will have to be lowered and moved out.

anyone who has done enough sewing has perhaps thought it would be great to whip up something with a very different look in some gorgeous new fabric. Well, it's not such an outrageous thought. It can be done. But beware! Facility comes with experience. You must start somewhere, so bite the bullet and see how it's done.

I've just completed the draping and pattern work for a woven challis blouse with a draped cowl neckline for my fall collection. People work differently, of course, but my ideas always start flowing when I see the fabric. Then, according to what I

need for my collection, a form gradually materializes in my mind. In this case, it was a blouse with a big built-in cowl.

Tissue draping—I start draping in tissue paper. It's very unforgiving. It doesn't lend itself to much manipulation, and it doesn't stretch, so it's very apparent when the sleeve or cowl doesn't hang right. The tissue paper by its nature sets boundaries, thus creating a true preliminary pattern.

Using a full sheet of tissue for each, I trace a half front, a half back, and one sleeve piece from my blouse sloper, or pattern, which is actually a basic bodice pat-

tern (photo, above left). Most pattern companies sell basic patterns for a fitted dress or for pants. You can look for an approximation of the style you want, but select a pattern that closely fits the body. For a loose look, the sloper gives a point of reference from which to make your changes.

Next, I pin the whole traced tissue pieces on my dress form (photo, above right), centering the center front and back seams and noting the position of guidelines. I work at duplicating what's in my head. My greatest concern is the line of the cowl around the neck, but I'm also establishing the fullness of the top, the shoulder line, and the set

20   Fit and Fabric...

From *Threads* magazine (February 1986) 3:46-50

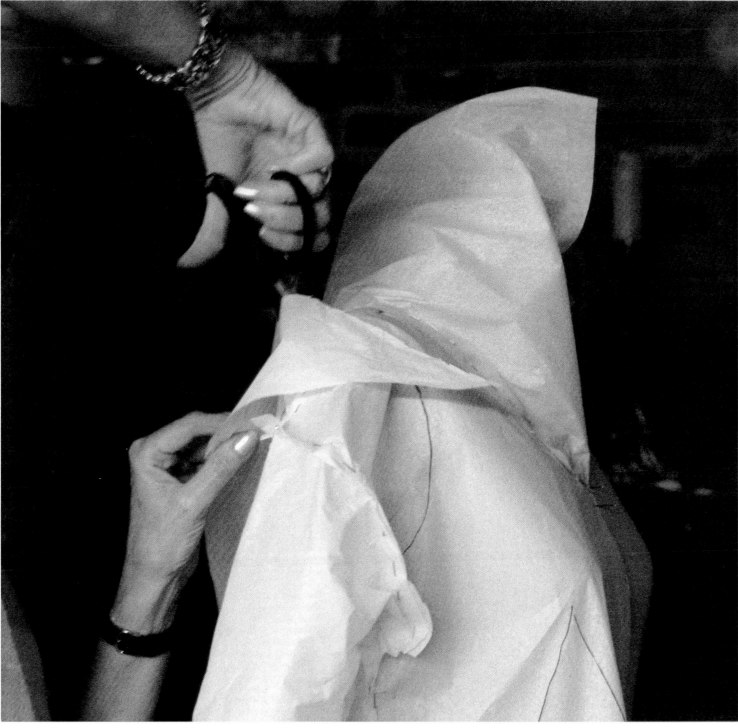

Sperry has pinned the half back to the half front, making sure that the shoulder seam falls directly over the guideline on the form. Then, after trimming the excess tissue and drawing in the line where the cowl should start, she pins a rectangular piece of tissue to that line, smoothing as she goes along and placing the pins on a curve where the tissue falls best. She then trims the tissue about 1 in. from the pinned line, leaving enough so that she will be able to see the shape while making any adjustments that may be needed.

and shape of the sleeves. After I pin the bodice on the form and arrive at the seam line for the neck (a deep V fore and aft), I drape and pin tissue paper for the cowl around the neck at the seam line, again using a full sheet, and trim the paper to shape at the neckline (photo above).

The resultant draped tissue for half a blouse becomes the preliminary pattern for cutting a muslin: After marking the seam lines by rubbing over the pins with the side of a pencil lead, remove the pins and smooth out the tissue pieces. With the pencil, straighten the lines at the shoulder, and down the side seam and hemline on both sleeve and blouse bottoms (photo at left, page 23). Check the side seams—on the sleeve and bodice—and the shoulder seams to make sure that the lengths match. You may have to square off the bottom edge or change the length (and radius) of a curve.

With a French curve, refine the curves of the armhole seam and cowl (photo at right, page 23). Aim for a smooth sweep in both the upper edge of the cowl and the seam line where it attaches to the bodice. Mark the point on the cowl where it meets the shoulder seam. This will be a stitching reference point. Do the same on the sleeve top at the point where it meets the shoul-

der seam. Then cut off all seam allowances along the drawn pencil lines. You now have the preliminary half tissue pattern.

Cutting a muslin—The next step is to cut a full muslin (medium weight) from the half tissue-paper pattern. If you have no muslin, use an old sheet. Fold the muslin in half lengthwise, and place the tissue pattern on the straight of the goods, with the center front of the bodice and cowl on the fold. Cut out the pieces, allowing an arbitrary 1-in. seam allowance on the other edges for any changes you find you may have to make. Now mark the center front

Sperry trims the top of the cowl and checks the drape of the tissue, above. There are still some adjustments to be made: She will make a note to extend the curve of the underarm seam out still more, and she will ease out some of the fullness in the shoulder seam before removing the tissue blouse from the form. At right, Sperry rubs over each pin with the side of a soft-lead pencil to mark her new seam lines.

The form

If you are really serious about designing your own clothes or clothes for others, it makes a great deal of sense to have a good dress form. Nothing I have seen in the home-sewing market comes close to a professional dress form. I say this for several important reasons. One, you need something absolutely solid and stable to push pins into—a form that will remain stable throughout its life. Two, you need a form that is true to established size measurements. Three, the professional form is absolutely symmetrical—one shoulder or hip isn't higher than the other. The kind of form you can buy that is custom-molded to the body is especially poor. It will accentuate any discrepancy in your body symmetry (we are not all size 10's), and the garment draped on it will further accentutate the discrepancy. Four, guidelines for your key body points and lines of measurement are established on the professional form according to standard measurements and proportions. These guidelines serve as a point of reference from which you

of the muslin cowl at the top and bottom edges and the point at the top of the sleeve where it meets the shoulder seam.

Pin the pieces together, and drape this full muslin on the form inside out. Now is the time to correct the fitting. Repin it and rub it to mark changes. Take it off the form and try it on. Move in it. Is it comfortable? Check the sleeve and body lengths, the look of the cowl. Trim the 1-in. seam allowance to ¼ in. at the upper edge of the cowl. See how the blouse conforms to your body, and make changes if needed. At this point I put the pinned blouse on the form right side out to check the drape and the

lines without looking at distracting seam allowances (photo at left, page 24).

Cut a muslin facing for the cowl, using the cowl tissue pattern as your guide. Allow ¼-in. seam allowances, ½ in. at center back. The facing should be about 3 in. wide in the back, extending to 5 in. in the front and long enough at the shoulder to be tacked on the inside at the shoulder seams.

From muslin to pattern—Pencil the seam lines on the muslin for a sewing guide, and sew the muslin blouse together with the stitch set at the largest gauge. Keep construction notes as you proceed so you'll

know how to reconstruct the final garment.

When the blouse is sewn together (don't bother to finish hems on sleeves and bottom), try it on for final fit. Check the drape of the cowl, and see how it fits with its facing sewn in. Would the cowl fall better if it were cut on the cross grain, or bias? Would you get better yardage by cutting on the cross grain? Refine the fit. Again note how it conforms to your body, keeping in mind the total look. Don't get bogged down in nitpicking! If changes are needed, pencil them on the muslin, rip, and resew according to changes. The large gauge stitches make this process far easier. For ease in

can proceed. That is, if your measurements, both height and width, vary slightly from standard form measurements, you know how much to add or subtract because these reference lines establish a constant.

I have an old form I bought when I graduated from design school. It's funny looking. Its shape is all girdled up! But most important, the measurements are in proportion. While it's a size 12, à la 1952 (all sizing has been "reevaluated" in the last 10 to 15 years), it provides a given to work with no matter what size is called for.

And, aside from all this, I'm terribly fond of my dress form. It has been by my side for over 30 years. It traveled to the South Pacific with me for two years. It lived through a typhoon with me. It has been drawn and painted upon by small children, it has had darts thrown at it, it has been knocked around considerably, and it always brings me good luck! What more could I ask? I would never dream of turning it in for an updated, curvaceous size 10.   —E. Sperry

The next step is to refine the tissue into a preliminary pattern. The shoulder and side seams are straightened with a ruler (above, left), and the neckline and armhole curves are smoothed out with a French curve (above). The tissue can then be trimmed on the seam lines. A full muslin with 1-in. seam allowances is then cut from this preliminary pattern.

construction, I changed from a one-piece back to a center back seam (there's already one in the cowl), thereby eliminating the need to fit a rounded seam into a deep V.

Now cut apart the muslin along stitched seam lines. Steam-press it, taking care not to stretch it. Lay it flat on pattern paper or bristol board, and station it with push pins. With a tracing wheel, trace the pattern pieces onto the paper, straightening out straight seams with a ruler and curved ones with a French curve. Add on the seam allowances—½ in. for sleeve, shoulder, side seams, and center back seam; ¼ in. for neckline and cowl facing. Cut the facing pattern from the pattern piece it's going to face. Grain lines should be noted on each pattern piece. Your final pattern check is to make sure the seams that are joined measure the same length. You now have a pattern from which to cut your blouse.

Lay the completed pattern on a large, flat surface, arranging it according to the established grain lines and the width of the fabric you plan to use. Make a cursory cutting diagram (see drawing on page 24). This process determines the amount of fabric needed and creates a cutting guide. If you work as I do, you already have your fabric or a good idea of what you'll use. Re-member, it has to be suitable for your garment. The weight, weave, and design on the fabric are all important to consider. For instance, if the fabric has little body, an interfacing will be needed in the cowl.

With the cutting diagram before you, place your pattern on the fabric, checking your grain, stripes, plaids, nap, etc. Now cut. Use the notes you made while constructing the muslin to sew the blouse together.

Ellen Sperry, a Rhode Island School of Design graduate and veteran of the garment industry, designs and produces women's clothing from her studio in Wilton, CT.

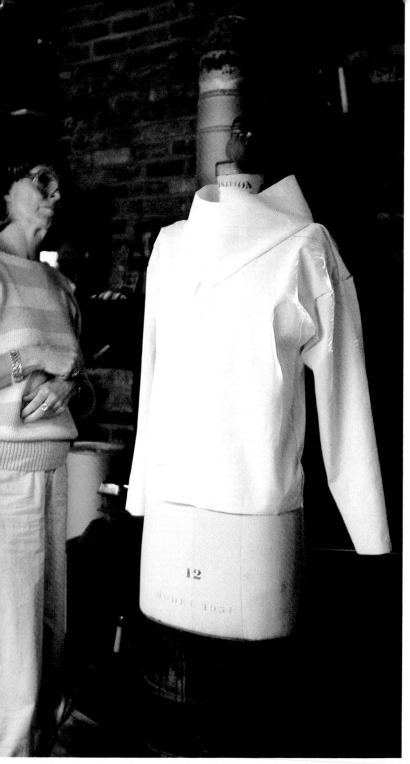

After a cowl facing has been cut and sewn in, the muslin blouse is sewn together and tried on. Now, before the blouse is cut apart at the seam lines and traced on pattern paper, last minute changes should be noted. Should the cowl be cut down another inch?

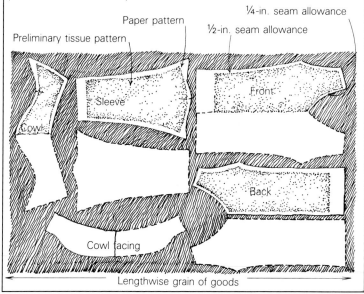

Layout of completed pattern pieces
This sketch is not to scale, but it shows the relationship of the preliminary pattern to the final pattern and the relationship of the pattern to the goods (for non-directional fabrics).

Paper pattern
¼-in. seam allowance
Preliminary tissue pattern
½-in. seam allowance
Cowl
Sleeve
Front
Back
Cowl facing

← Lengthwise grain of goods →

The pinned muslin was tried on the form inside out, then adjusted. Finally it is put on the form right side out so the lines and drape can be checked. Once again, any changes—new pin locations—are marked.

Sources for dress forms

Modern Model Form, *325 W. 38th St., New York, NY 10018.*
Manufactures and sells a full line of nonadjustable forms in 5 size ranges for dresses, suits, etc.; also miniature forms. Made of papier mâché, covered with cotton, jersey, cotton wadding, and Belgian linen. Average price, $310.

Wolf Form Co., *39 W. 19th St., New York, NY 10011.*
Manufactures and sells a full line of professional forms for dresses, sportswear, bathing suits, underwear, coats, etc., for women, men, children. Standard, large, and half-size forms, plus custom forms. Made of metal, canvas, papier mâché. Prices range from around $325 to $500.

Ardan/A.E. Arthur, *1704C Henry G. Lane St., Maryville, TN 37801.*
Ray Dancer, Inc., *7780 Quincy St., Willowbrook, IL 60521.*
Manufactures and distributes two adjustable lightweight solid-foam forms: Diana Deluxe, 3 sizes, with adjustable bust, waist, hip, waist/height, and shoulder/neck measurements, about $150; and Athena, 4 sizes, with bust, waist, and hip adjustments, about $120. Both have hemline gauge and basting attachment. Distributed through regional supply houses, such as Home Makers Supply Co. (2300 NE Broadway, Portland, OR 97232), and available at fabric chain stores.

Dritz Corporation, *Box 5028, Spartanburg, SC 29304.*
Manufactures "My Double" mesh form covered with laminated foam-backed nylon; waist adjustment; 2 sizes. Available at Singer, Sears, etc. Costs about $135.

Uniquely You, *8230-R Telegraph Rd., Odenton, MD 21113.*
Adjustable polyurethane dress and pants/skirt forms with poplin-polyester shell cover; 5 standard sizes (order by hip measurement) and 14 cover/shell sizes (order by bust measurement). Shell can be resewn to body measurement; form will compress accordingly. Sold by major chain stores. □

Ready for the Needle

Preshrinking and pressing prepare the fabric, and prepare you too

by David Page Coffin

a new length of cloth is a lovely thing. Possibilities radiate from it. You probably should have gotten more of it. If only you could just start laying out and cutting right now, but in its present elegant condition, your yardage is ready to be admired only. There's another kind of loveliness that the fabric will develop when it's ready to be sewn. As you bring out this quality in your fabric, you're getting yourself ready to sew with it because you'll begin to understand how this particular cloth needs to be handled. For all natural fibers, the process of preparing fabric for sewing starts with preshrinking.

The phenomenon of shrinkage has as much to do with fabric as a structure as it does with fiber as a substance. There are several distinct reasons fabric shrinks, and what's really going on bears little resemblance to the popular concept of shrinkage. Everybody knows that cotton shrinks, but actually cotton fibers don't shrink. It's cotton cloth that shrinks. In fact, no natural fiber shrinks, unless first stretched, and then the fibers are merely returning to their original shape, not getting smaller.

When wool cloth is washed, the fibers can cause a unique type of fabric shrinkage, called felting, which everyone has seen on a wool sweater or mitten that has gone through the washing machine. But even when wool cloth felts, the fibers themselves don't shrink. Wool fibers are covered with microscopic barbs, and when wet wool fibers are agitated together, the barbs catch on each other and won't easily let go, so the fabric mats to itself and gets irreversibly smaller. This type of shrinkage is called ***progressive,*** because it gets worse each time wool encounters felting conditions. Progressive shrinkage is not involved in preshrinking, except as something to avoid, which is why wool yardage should be dampened, not washed.

The technical, and more accurate, term for preshrinking is ***relaxation.*** It is the removal—by wetting—of stretch temporarily set into cloth while it was under tension during weaving. To various degrees, it applies to all fibers, and it can to some extent be reversed through restretching. This is what happens to your jeans in the wash: Although they stretch on your body, they get tight again each time you wash them.

All fabric is put under a lot of lengthwise tension by the weaving process itself. If the warp is an elastic fiber, like wool or silk, or a very tightly spun yarn, like crepe, the threads actually stretch. Once off the loom and wetted, the stretched threads unstretch, or relax—how much depends on how elastic they are. ***Compression*** is an aspect of relaxation shrinkage, in which the shape of the yarn, not its length, changes. Loom tensions hold the warp threads in a straighter line than the cross or weft threads.

When the tension is removed and the cloth is wetted, the straight warp threads start to bend over and under the weft, or compress—how much, depends on the weave: Tightly woven fabrics cannot compress as much as loosely woven ones. Once fabric has fully relaxed, no further shrinkage will occur, but sometimes this takes more than one washing.

The common element in all this is moisture, which softens the fibers and allows their shapes and positions to change. By the time washable fabrics reach the dryer, they have already been shrunk. Heat, either from a dryer or an iron, drives off moisture but then sets the threads in whatever shape they have while they dry—smooth or wrinkled, stretched or relaxed. This is why preshrinking is traditionally followed by pressing. I've found, as I explore the fabric, that it is often necessary to iron it as well.

Cottons (and most ***linens***) should be washed and machine-dried before they are cut out. Both are inelastic fibers, so washing or soaking relaxes the fabric a little but compresses it a lot. After washing and drying it, I iron—not press—the fabric to set it smooth. Ironing refinishes cotton and linen (reviving any natural gloss), but it also creates the stretched condition the fabric will have when ironed as a garment. If you were to carefully press the fabric to avoid any stretching, it would be so much more elastic than the seams that the gar-

Stretching cotton—Here's what happens to prewashed cotton when it's ironed. At left, below, cross-grain ironing has badly distorted the selvage. It's important to iron each section of cloth in both directions to prevent the diagonal wrinkles in the middle (center photo). To stretch the fabric and avoid the creases you can see at the bottom of the photo, pull a little tension into the cloth as you're ironing. At right, below, the woven plaid doesn't match on the ironed and unironed portions, because only the ironed portion has been stretched.

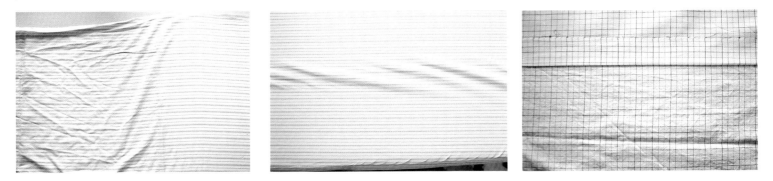

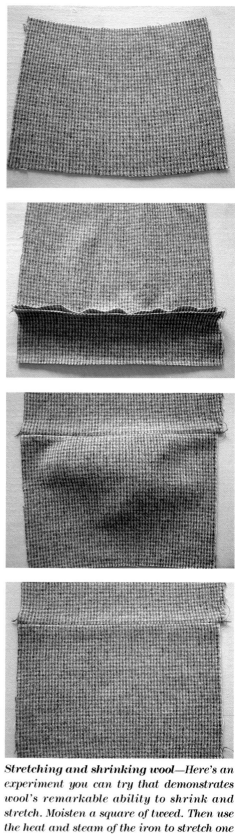

Stretching and shrinking wool—Here's an experiment you can try that demonstrates wool's remarkable ability to shrink and stretch. Moisten a square of tweed. Then use the heat and steam of the iron to stretch one edge and shrink the other. To stretch, pull the cloth while you iron it in the direction you want it to go. To shrink, slowly iron around the zone you wish to shrink in ever-decreasing half-circle arcs, allowing the heat to draw the cloth in (first photo). Ease the long edge to an unstretched scrap (second photo), making the bubble (third photo). Then shrink the ripples out of the seam allowance. Finally, stretch and shrink in reverse to return the whole thing to square (fourth photo). Try this with gabardine, and you'll see why you should do your first tailoring project in tweed.

ment would be hard to iron without creating wrinkles at the seam lines.

Now is also the time to pay attention to grain to ensure that the threads are straight and square to each other and that woven patterns line up. I align the selvages parallel to the length of the ironing board, spray the fabric with water, and iron until it's dry, sliding back and forth with the grain. I hold the iron in my right hand, while pulling the fabric straight and flat with my left hand.

Crinkled selvages may tempt you to iron cross grain, but this is disastrous because you're bound to stretch unevenly the more elastic weft yarns. You must stroke each section in both directions to stretch the whole piece of cloth evenly so that its woven patterns will match, as shown in the right-hand photo on page 25, and so that it will react uniformly to sewing, and later ironing. The stretching should be moderate, not to the extent that you remove all lengthwise elasticity, but stretch it you must. This is true ironing because you are moving the iron while it rests on the fabric, which inevitably moves the yarns. The downward pressure varies with the weight of the fabric and the weave: Lighter fabric, lighter pressure, but still ironing.

If the weave is open, loose, or textured, or if the fabric is very lightweight, you'll need to iron more delicately, or perhaps even press, with no sideways movement. I've come to trust my iron's high-heat settings for cotton and linen, though I do adjust them lower for thin fabric.

Silk is elastic, and so wetting both relaxes the fibers and compresses the weave. Iron with a light touch. Silk is more heat-sensitive than cotton and easy to overstretch. I start with lower heat than the dial suggests, adjusting up or down for thick or thin fabric. In *A Silkworker's Notebook* (Interweave Press, 1985), essential reading for anyone who works with a lot of silk, Cheryl Kolander states definitively: "Silk needs to be ironed unless a crinkly effect is part of the design or the piece is a soft handwoven that only needs a little fluffing up while drying." Her point is that it is easy to generalize about fibers, but the structure of the fabric and your own preferences must determine what you do. Kolander advises that you wash silk yardage in lukewarm water or steam it by holding above it a steam iron set for cotton. If you wet the silk, iron it before it completely dries out.

Wool is the preeminently pressable fiber. It is stretchable and absorbent, and it has a remarkable capacity to recover from the deforming stresses of manufacturing or daily wear. This recovery is aided by steam or even humidity, which is why the wrinkles work themselves out of wool garments that are hung in steam-filled bathrooms or allowed to relax a few days between wearings. These methods also work with silk and other animal fibers, though to a lesser extent.

The traditional method for relaxing wool cloth is called "London shrinking," in which, originally, whole bolts of yardage were rolled out overnight in fields (in London, of course) to allow the dew to dampen them and thus relax the loom stretch. The fabric was then hand-pressed with heavy irons and guaranteed "ready for the needle." These days, tailors ignore such guarantees, which occasionally appear on wool yardage, and pre-shrink anyway. They do it by folding the fabric between well-dampened sheets, allowing it to sit at least two hours to equalize the dampness, then laying it out to dry flat. Another way to dampen the fabric is to steam it without touching it with the iron. After the fabric has relaxed and dried, it should be steam-pressed to ensure against surprises during construction pressing, to straighten the grain, and to ensure that woven patterns match. Grain and pattern adjustments may require sliding the iron across the fabric to coax the yarns into place.

As with all fibers, the amount of manipulation possible with wool fabric is related to the structure of the yarn and the weave: The looser the weave and the softer the yarn, the more you can move it around. A good way to test wool for shrinkage is to align a corner of the cloth with a chalked right angle on the pressing surface. Apply steam and pressure, and see if the edges draw away from the lines. If they do, you must steam-press the whole piece; otherwise, construction pressing will cause shrinkage whether or not you want it. It's important that wool fabric not be pressed completely dry, or the fibers will be damaged. Always allow damp, just-pressed wool to dry out and cool before moving it, or it will stretch out of shape again.

Tailoring literature is full of references to stretching and shrinking in garment construction. Shoulder and sleeve ease are shrunk out, while chests and calves are stretched into fullness. Stanley Hostek of Tailor-Craft in Seattle, WA, describes the process succinctly: "To stretch: Moisten area, soften by applying heat from the iron, and as the pressure and weight of the iron hold one end, gently pull on the other while you move the iron from one end to the other. To shrink: Moisten area and slowly approach it in half-circle arcs, allowing the heat and moisture to shrink it in."

Stretching wool is thus very much an ironing process, almost identical to my method of stretching cotton yardage. Shrinking is more a matter of pressing on top of the wrinkles or bubbles that appear after the fabric has been positioned in the new shape wanted; you are actually packing the yarns in the weave more closely together. For precise shrinking of raw edges, the seam line could first be ease-stitched to the desired length. The processes of stretching and shrinking wool as applied to a pant leg are shown in the photos on the facing page.

Synthetic fibers are subject to the same loom tensions as natural fibers, of course,

Ironing fit into a pair of slacks—Couturier Fred Ungar of Los Angeles builds shape into a custom-made pant leg by taking advantage of wool's remarkable capacity to move under the iron. With the seams aligned directly on top of one another, Ungar positions the slight inward curve he wants along the front crease (above) and then shrinks out the excess length (top right). Next, he shapes the hip by stretching it to the back and sets the stretch with his shoe-covered iron, keeping the seams positioned together (bottom right).

but they are often permanently set in shape with heat and chemicals for easy care. This easy care is usually at the expense of easy manipulation: Shrinkage is not generally a problem, but ironing is. Most synthetics resist normal ironing and pressing, so I avoid them in garments that will need a lot of shaping or creasing.

The best way to approach the problems of preparing and pressing fabrics made all or in part with synthetic fibers is to find a reliable reference work that describes the character and care of the fibers you have. My favorite references are listed at right under "Further reading."

In general, you can safely assume that synthetics are more heat-sensitive than natural fibers and that you must test these fibers scrupulously, as they are not likely to forgive mishandling. Start cautiously with your iron settings, and reduce pressure by using a well-padded pressing surface. Most synthetics will melt before they burn, and the soleplate can flatten the melting fibers, irreversibly glazing them.

Rayon, which ranks with nylon and polyester as one of the most common synthetics, is the most variable because there are several types of rayon. Some varieties of rayon are not safely washable; other varieties are almost as sturdy as cotton. If your rayon or blend fabric is labeled *washable,* prewash a large swatch, and try pressing it before you plunge it all into the wash. You may still prefer to have it dry-cleaned in order to preserve the character that attracted you to it.

Nylon and **polyester** are both heat-treated for wrinkle-resistance and low shrinkage. Nonetheless, even as much as 50% synthetics in a wool blend is not enough to deter a tailor from preshrinking it in the usual way. The risk of not preshrinking, given

the nature of wool, is simply not worth the time saved.

The biggest danger to nylon and polyester presented by home laundering is that high dryer heat can set wrinkles into the fabric. It's almost impossible to iron them out or remove the heat-set creases at hems or on pant legs without also melting them.

If you're working with a poly/cotton blend, you can dampen such creases (or areas you want to crease) with a little bit of dilute white vinegar before pressing. The acid in the vinegar will dissolve some of the resins the factory used to finish the fabric, but the resin and the qualities it added will now be gone forever from that area. Do some testing on critical projects.

Most sewing texts feature a fabric-specific chart of iron settings and pressing advice. But by now I hope you can see that the "correct" procedure depends as much on your experience as you work with the fabric, and on your plans for it, as on anything else. Couturier and teacher Charles Kleibacker approaches almost every fabric, from silk crepes de chine to woolens, in fundamentally the same way, based on long experience. He preshrinks the yardage by steaming it from the wrong side on a well-padded commercial ironing board. He presses every square inch of fabric twice, once with steam and then dry. In most cases, he must lean heavily on his iron. All the while, he takes meticulous care to remove wrinkles and eliminate shrinkage.

Kleibacker emphasizes two points in his classes and seminars: Always honor the fabric, observing it carefully and letting it determine exactly how it is to be handled during pressing; and resist the temptation to send it out for "professional" steaming. You need to see and feel the fabric reacting to your iron, and it takes at least as much

time to find a cleaner who'll do the job and to fetch and carry the fabric as it does to do the job yourself.

Test how your fabric reacts to pressure, heat, moisture, and your tools. For fabrics new to you, buy a little extra. Don't rely on scraps; you can't cut out until you know how much shrinkage you'll get, which you can find out only by testing. Your test pieces should include all of the seam types and processes you plan to use, and each should be big enough so that you can compare unpressed with pressed sections. The time spent testing, preshrinking, and preparing the fabric for cutting is also time spent learning how your fabric behaves and how it can be manipulated. These tasks, rather than unwelcome chores before the sewing starts, can become pleasant periods of re-excitement with the fabric as you learn to bring it to the ideal condition for sewing. □

David Page Coffin is an associate editor of Threads *magazine. See his article on making shirt collars on pp. 33-39.*

Further reading

Hollen, Norma, and Jane Saddler. *Textiles,* 5th ed. New York: Macmillan, 1979. *A classic, well illustrated and in most public libraries.*

Ladbury, Ann. *Fabrics.* London: Sidgwick and Jackson, 1985. Distributed by Salem House Publishers, Topsfield, MA. *Essential equipment—the best fabric-handling reference for home sewers; dictionary format.*

Miller, Edward. *Textiles: Properties and Behaviour in Clothing Use.* London: B.T. Batsford, 1984. Distributed by David & Charles, North Pomfret, VT. *A readable textbook with lots of useful information for the home sewer.*

Getting Collars Straight
The shape is all in the curve

by Rebecca Nebesar

Collars are like hats. And these days collars are more like hats than hats because people hardly wear hats anymore. Collars are now the closest that our clothes get to our faces. By their very proximity, collars have earned the distinguished honor of conveying clues to the world about who we are, what we do, and what our attitudes are. From the clerical collar of a priest, to the blue collar of a worker, to the ruff of a clown, collars have achieved a kind of permanence and meaningfulness.

The right collar can improve our looks. A collar can be a focal point for an entire garment, leading the eye to the face, and it can give that *je ne sais quoi* to an otherwise pedestrian design.

Let's face it, though; collars are tricky. After years of working with them, I think I've figured them out, but I admit that I'm still somewhat in awe of them.

Collars are so closely wed to the shape and style of the neckline and the position of the neck relative to the body that it is impossible to understand them independently of these. For ease of comparison I'll base my explanations exclusively on collars that fit high, round necklines and that meet at the center front on a body with an average neck and good posture.

Collar basics

The properties of fabric—bias stretch, flexibility, stiffness, and drape—are essential to the functioning and beauty of a collar. The ideal collar material would be a fabric that bends and stretches equally in all directions when we want it to and stays firm and stable when we want it to. Alas, there is no such fabric. But by layering fabrics and finagling with the grains (as in plywood) and by trimming, stretching, and taping, we can create a composite fabric that approaches the ideal. We can combine the desirable properties of two fabrics (such as wool and hair canvas) by fusing them (ideally with pad-stitching, less than ideally with heat-sensitive adhesives). We can also use twill tape to stabilize; bones and starch to rigidify; and pressing, steaming, and hammering to smooth and flatten.

No amount of finagling will be enough, however, if the collar has edges of the wrong shape for the effect you're after, but a collar's edges aren't all created equal. The outer edges and points can be varied widely without basically affecting how the collar will sit on the garment. The key to that is in the edge that attaches to the garment.

The neckline edge—A collar always begins with a neckline. The neckline edge of the collar must be the same length as that of the garment, but there is a wide range of collar shapes. Some collars are *neck-based,* deriving their shapes from the shape of the neck. Others are *body-based,* deriving their shapes from the garment bodice. In the photos on the facing page and on page 32 the neckline edges of the pattern pieces are marked in purple, and roll lines are dotted.

A collar's neckline edge can be straight, convex (bowing out), or concave. A neck-based collar has a straight or convex neckline edge because it is cylindrical or slightly cone-shaped, while a body-based collar has a concave, often nearly circular, neckline edge because it is circular and flat. By varying the degree of curve, either convex or concave, you can control how the collar will rest in relation to the neck.

A straight neckline edge forms a simple cylindrical collar—it is the shape for simple bands and turtlenecks. The more convex the neckline edge is, the more the collar will hug the neck, as in a stand-up collar, or shirt collar.

The more nearly circular the neckline on a body-based collar is, the flatter the collar will lie. Straightening out the neckline edge will force the collar to stand up (when attached to a round neckline), creating a fold, or *roll,* as it curves around the neck.

A neck-based collar usually has an outer edge that is the same length as, or shorter than, the neckline edge. This holds the collar, and any roll it may have, close to the neck (top photos, facing page). A body-based collar has a long outer edge relative to the neckline edge. If it is shaped to stand and roll, the standing part of the collar always sits away from the neck at the roll line (bottom-left photo, facing page).

If you want a collar that combines aspects of both collar types—for example, a long outer edge and a high, close fit, as in a dress-shirt collar—you must cut the collar in two pieces: the *stand* (neck-based) and the *fall* (body-based), sewn together at the roll line. You can often achieve a more subtle fit, more flexibility in styling, and a more attractive layout for plaids or stripes when you cut collars in two pieces.

The roll line—How is it that collars roll so beautifully on a curve? Fabric! So flexible. But what really does the trick is having the roll line on the bias. When a collar, an undercollar, or its interfacing is cut with as much bias as possible on the roll line, the collar will not buckle where it bends. The more bias in the roll line, the graceful the roll. A roll line with a lot of bias is often supported with tape so it won't stretch too much. Many collars have some bias and some straight grain on the roll, which creates an inconsistent roll. You can compensate by cutting the interfacing and/or undercollar on a different grain.

Because even all-bias nonwoven interfacings tend to be stiffer than wovens, I prefer woven interfacings for collars. You can also enhance a good roll by cutting the upper collar slightly larger and easing it to the undercollar.

But how do you know exactly where the collar will roll? The position of the roll line on a neck-based collar usually doesn't depend on the shape of the collar. You can simply fold over the collar wherever you desire or let it roll as it will when the center-front opening folds back. But a body-based collar has a mind of its own. All else

Rebecca Nebesar blossoms in a bed of collars.

From *Threads* magazine (February 1988) 15:34-38

Neck-based collars are derived from the shape of the neck.

Stand-up collar

Bias-cut straight collar

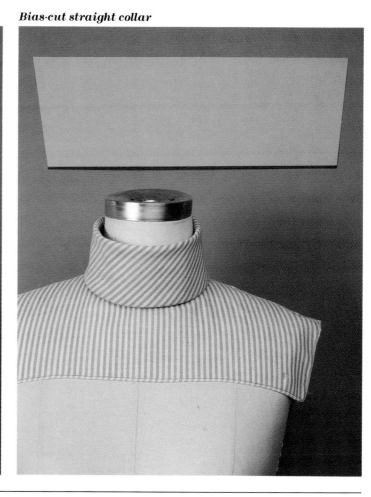

Body-based collars are derived from the shape of the bodice.

Roll collar

Flat collar

Sewing tips

My sewing methods are what work for me, and they are sometimes at odds with traditional sewing etiquette. I don't much believe in gadgets, and I think the sewing room needs more creativity and fewer rules. So, if it works, I do it, and if I can do it with what's at hand, so much the better.

The trickiest aspects of sewing a collar are making the points sharp—if there are points—controlling seam-allowance bulk, and connecting the often opposing curves of the neckline and collar.

To get the points sharp, I sew around them with small stitches. I've never found it helpful to make a diagonal stitch or two across the point, as some people suggest, but I trim away enough of the seam allowance so it won't buckle when folded inside the point. Frequently this involves cutting away very close to the seam. I don't like point turners; I can get most of the point out just by using my fingers. Then I use a pointed tool (I confess I use the tips of my scissors, but very gently) to work out the rest. When this fails, I use a pin to pull out the tip from the outside. Before turning, you could use a little glue or Fray-Check on the point to protect it from fraying during turning. *Always* be gentle.

Controlling seam-allowance bulk means knowing where to clip, and people tend to overdo it. It's often unnecessary to cut out actual V's. They're useful only on convex seam allowances. A simple slit is all that's needed for concave seam allowances, and after trimming, even slits are often superfluous. If you stitch shoulder and center-back seams only as far as the neckline seam and not into the seam allowance, you'll get an automatic clipped effect at those points.

Sewing a concave collar piece into a convex neckline requires understanding and care. Until you become familiar with what's going on, be sure to trace your seamlines entirely and mark all notches and dots clearly. Remember that it's the seamlines that match, not the edges of the seam allowances—they won't even come close. If you're a beginner, hand-baste the seam before you machine-stitch.

Where to put seam allowances is another common dilemma—press up, or down, or open? At one extreme, the flat collar, always clip the seam allowances, press down into the body neckline, and cover them with a facing or binding, which will be hidden by the collar. At the other extreme, the stand-up collar, trim or grade the seam allowances and press up into the collar. Press the seam allowances of all in-between collar styles either open or to one direction or the other, depending on how nearby the roll is. If it's in the way, press down; if not, press up. —R.N.

being equal, changing the curve of the neckline edge will change where the roll line will be. An accurate and illuminating method of establishing a curve for a body-based collar is described in "Making a body-based collar template" (facing page).

Neck-based collars

Simple *band* collars are rectangular and stand up but do not follow the shape of the neck. With a straight neckline edge and a straight outer edge equal in length or just slightly longer, the *straight collar cut on the bias*, shown at top right on page 29, is a wide variation on a band collar. It usually folds over upon itself to hide the neckline seam. When cut with a longer outer edge and much wider than the neck is long, the result is a simple cowl. There are many variations of cowl collars, mostly based on enlarged necklines.

The *stand-up collar,* shown at top left on page 29, has a convex neckline edge so it can taper in to follow the shape of the neck. A quick, adequate method of drafting this type of collar is to attach a 25-in.-long to 30-in.-long string to a pencil, and using this as a compass, to draw an arc the desired length for the neckline edge. Then you shorten the string to draw the outer edge parallel to, and inside, the first arc. The distance between the two arcs is the desired height of the stand. You can refine the shape a bit by flattening the curve an inch or so on either side of where it meets the shoulder line and dropping it about ⅛ in. at the center front. Metal or plastic bones often are sewn into casings on the under-collar side to keep the stand-up collar standing. There are also delicate thread-covered wires available for this purpose—especially nice for lace collars. Some looseness, or ease, is desirable in the fit, particularly for a man with a prominent Adam's apple.

Body-based collars

Flat collars and other body-based collars are easy to derive from basic bodice pattern pieces. To make a collar that doesn't roll up the neck, as in the photo at bottom right on page 29, lay the front and back bodice pattern pieces together along the shoulder, overlapping them about ⅝ in. at the armhole, as shown in the drawing at left. Draw a curved line in the desired shape of the collar the distance from the neckline that you want the width of the collar to be. This is your pattern, without seam allowances, for half the collar. Folding out a narrow wedge at the shoulder is essential. Without it, when the collar is sewn to the neckline edge, pressing the seam allowances down will force up a slight roll that will draw in the collar enough to cause it to ripple. Taking out the wedge flattens the collar's neckline edge just sufficiently to eliminate the ripple. The relationship between roll and straightening the neckline of the flat collar is the basis for the template described on the facing page. ⟹

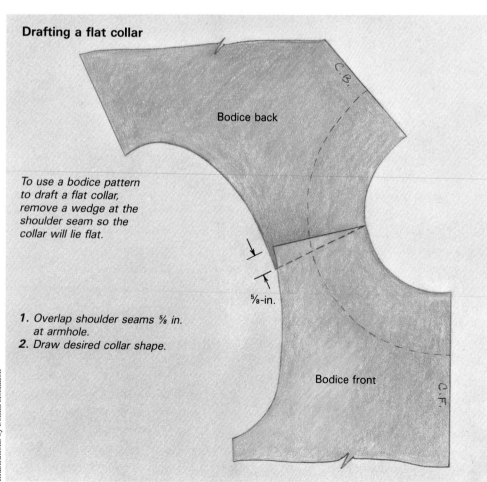

Drafting a flat collar

Bodice back

To use a bodice pattern to draft a flat collar, remove a wedge at the shoulder seam so the collar will lie flat.

⅝-in.

1. Overlap shoulder seams ⅝ in. at armhole.
2. Draw desired collar shape.

Bodice front

C.F.

Illustrations by Donna McMahon

Making a body-based collar template

Most untailored one-piece collars can be easily derived from basic front and back bodice patterns at the area around the neckline opening. You begin by making a template, using the bodice pieces as a base. Lay the pattern pieces together flat, attaching them at the shoulder seams. The template outline is simply a curve running from center front to center back, parallel to the neckline and a shoulder's width away, as shown in the left-hand drawing below. If you trace this shape onto paper or oaktag, you're on your way.

Here's how it works: Most collars equal the neckline edge in length but vary in curvature, width, and outer-edge length. The template permits you to manipulate the variables without changing the length of the neckline edge. You cut across the template and overlap the cut edges, pivoting at the neckline, thereby reducing the length of the outer edge and changing the curve of the neckline. With one template you can make all the patterns shown in the right-hand drawing below and all the patterns in between.

There is no absolutely correct way to make a template—I make mine by dividing the neckline edge into approximately equal sections, each about 1 in. long, with the center front and back as the end points and the shoulder point as one of the divisions. For my neckline, this works out to four sections in front and three in back. Then I extend the center-front and center-back lines until they

meet (see drawing at left, below) and draw lines radiating from that point to the outer edge of the template arc, through the divisions on the neckline edge.

For a paper template that I'm using only once or twice, I fold out wedges along the lines. For a permanent template, I use oaktag. I number the sections and cut them out. Next, I secure the neckline edge with button and carpet thread attached with masking tape, as shown in the photo below. Then, instead of folding out wedges, I just overlap the sections. Because of the thread, the neckline edge is always flexible and the correct length. As a final refinement, I add a bit of clear Con-Tact paper along the outside of the template so I can tape it closed and pull the tape off easily.

The more you overlap the wedges, the straighter the neckline curve becomes, and the more the finished collar will stand up before rolling over. For a flat collar (the one I advise you to try first), all you have to do is overlap the template at the shoulder division about ⅝ in. measured at the template's outer edge. This creates just enough roll in the collar, whatever its width, to allow it to lie flat when attached to the bodice. The collar's outer edge can be any shape you want.

For collars with more roll and more stand, and thus more template overlap, you have to use the other radiating lines and do some measuring, subtracting, and dividing. For a collar to be flattish in front and more standing in the back, you fold out more in the back and less

in the front. The variations are endless. You can produce a template for any neckline, not just a round one.

The challenge is to know just how wide and how straight to make a roll collar so that it sits where you want it on the body. Let's say I want a collar to rest about 2½ in. out on my shoulder but to have a roll about 1 in. up from the neck. That means that the actual collar should be about 3½ in. wide. The next thing I want to know is how long the outer edge should be.

I fold out the required ⅝ in. on the shoulder line, measure out along all the radiating lines, and mark off points at 2½ in. Then, with a measuring tape on its side, I measure the length around the template at the 2½-in. marks. This is the length my outer edge needs to become, but I need a 3½-in. collar. So I mark 3½ in. down the lines and find that length around the template. I subtract the length at 2½ in. from the one at 3½ in., and in this case I get a difference of 2¾ in. This is the total amount I need to fold out at each of the six radiating lines—a little less than ½ in. at each line, measured at the 3½-in. points. The new shape is the right width, has the right outer-edge length, and has a neckline edge that is somewhat less curved, but still equal in length to the garment neckline.

No system like this is foolproof. Always make a muslin from your pattern, and check it on the neckline before you cut into the final fabric and do finishing sewing. —R.N.

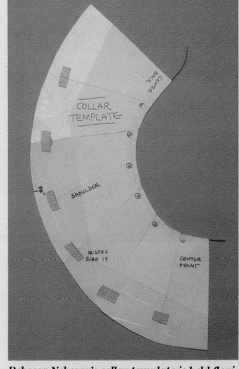

Rebecca Nebesar's collar template is held flexibly together along the neckline edge with button thread. She overlaps the wedges and tapes them in the shape she wants.

Drafting a template

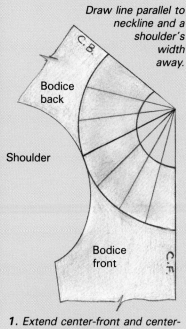

Draw line parallel to neckline and a shoulder's width away.

Bodice back

Shoulder

Bodice front

1. Extend center-front and center-back lines to meet.
2. Draw lines from intersection radiating out, through equal divisions on neckline, to outside of template.

Body-based collar shapes

The flatter the neckline edge, the more the collar will roll.

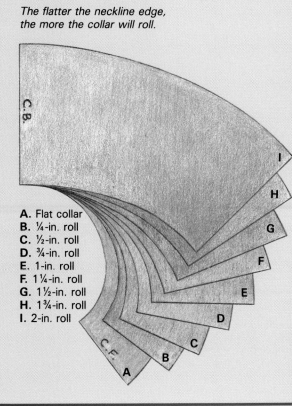

A. Flat collar
B. ¼-in. roll
C. ½-in. roll
D. ¾-in. roll
E. 1-in. roll
F. 1¼-in. roll
G. 1½-in. roll
H. 1¾-in. roll
I. 2-in. roll

Combination collars share elements of neck- and body-based collars. The convertible collar (top) has a shifting roll line, depending on whether it is worn open or closed. The tailored collar (bottom) is designed around the smooth transition from roll line to break line.

Convertible collar

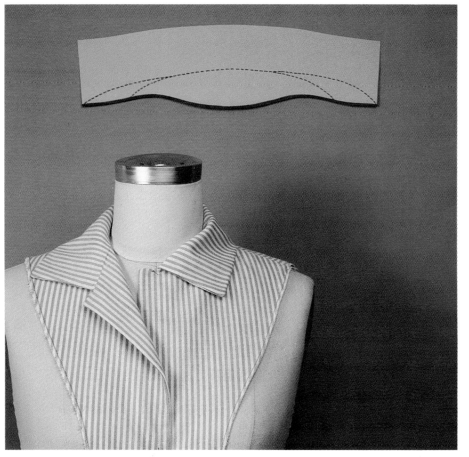

Tailored collar

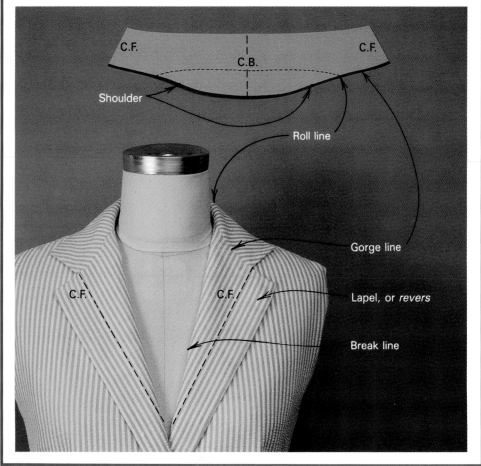

More complex collars

The *convertible collar* (top photo) gets its name because it can be worn buttoned or unbuttoned and folded back. It is a blend of body- and neck-based shapes. In its simplest form, its neckline edge is gently concave at the front and becomes slightly convex at the back, which gives it some stand. In other forms, more convexity, and thus more stand, is added to the neckline edge where you want the collar to have it (e.g., at the shoulder seams or in front). You must keep the curves smooth and the neckline edge at the center back at a right angle to the center-back seamline, or fold line.

The collar that probably has us the most awestruck is the *notched tailored collar* (bottom photo), which consists of a collar and a lapel. It is a type of convertible collar, designed to roll permanently and perfectly. It is neck-based with a convex neckline edge, like a stand-up collar, and wide enough that it can roll. Part of the body also rolls back to form the lapel, or *revers*. The neckline seam, where it is visible between the collar and lapel, is the gorge line (*gorge* is French for *throat*). Special attention is paid to fitting the collar smoothly to the gorge line. You can make many style variations by raising or lowering this line; lengthening or shortening it; or angling it up, down, or horizontally across the lapel. Other variations depend on how much stand you want and how long the break line is supposed to be. Careful construction is the key to success, and fabric fusing (pad-stitching) is at the core of the technique. This collar needs body, flexibility, drape, and firmness—a tall order.

The basic tailored collar has its undercollar and interfacing cut on the bias and the upper collar and lapel facing cut more on the straight grain. These pieces are usually not cut from the same pattern. The pad-stitching is done on the undercollar and the body, not on the parts that show, to give the subtle smoothness and shaping these collars are known for. Twill tape is often sewn along the body roll line, which is on a partial bias, to keep it from stretching. The sign of a well-made tailored collar is a perfectly smooth and continuous transition from collar to *revers* on the roll line.

* * *

Collars. To love them, you must understand them. They can be tricky to sew, but they're not hard to understand, and they're worth it. What would a bowtie be without a collar, or a leaf pin without a lapel? How would we recognize a pilgrim, Dracula in his cape, or the guy in the Bazooka comics with the red turtleneck up to his eyes? How dull and undifferentiated we'd be without collars! What symbolic meaning we'd miss! It's time we enjoyed them. □

See Rebecca Nebesar's article on three ways to make your own patterns on pp. 45-49. *Photos on pages 29, 31, and 32 by Michele Russell Slavinsky.*

A fine-quality shirt collar has no puckers on the inside or outside when the collar is shaped in a circle. Coffin often makes collars that can be detached from the shirts.

Making a Great Shirt Collar
Taut sewing's the key

by David Page Coffin

While investigating the construction of a fine-quality shirt with a stand collar, I developed collar-making procedures that will enable the home sewer to approach the results achieved by the elaborate machinery of the manufacturer. Stand collars, like the ones above, are most often found in men's dress shirts, but they are also used on women's shirts. A stand collar has a stand area, or collar band, separate from the collar area. The stand gives the collar its height. A fine-quality shirt has certain hallmarks. The collar is shaped so it curves around the neck without puckering. The edge seams are hidden under the edge of the collar, which rolls naturally at the roll line. The two collar points are exactly the same shape and length.

My objectives were to build shape or curve into the collar and its stand, to increase the accuracy of the sewing in order to ensure a perfectly symmetrical and precisely sized collar, and to keep seam bulk to a minimum. These concerns grew out of the unsatisfactory results I got when I followed pattern instructions or general sewing texts. After explaining the general techniques, I'll incorporate them into step-by-step instructions for making a stand collar.

The first technique I use is what I call taut sewing, required for many of the topstitching and construction steps in a collar. Taut sewing eliminates the common problem of additional length being eased into the bottom fabric layer by the action of the feed dogs, and it generally eliminates seam pucker. The technique, shown in the lower left photo on page 34, is to pull the layers of fabric equally and in opposite directions, from in front of, and behind, the needle while you're sewing, letting the feed dogs move the fabric under the presser foot. The needle won't be deflected if the tension is kept equal. If the hand behind the needle pulls too hard, the fabric moves faster than the feed dogs, and the stitch length increases; if the hand in front of the needle pulls too hard, the fabric moves too slowly, and the stitch length decreases. Long seams are sewn in sections, so the hands are never more than 12 in. apart. Practice on scrap fabric. Sew a few stitches and stop with the needle down. Now stretch the fabric gently and start sewing again, moving your hands evenly as the machine moves the fabric. You must still guide the seam accurately while stretching the fabric.

This technique is the basis for the next, which is to stretch one layer more than the other while you're sewing in order to build ease into the unstretched layer. Note that if you lay one piece of 2-in. by 12-in. on-grain cloth on top of another with all edges matching and hold the short ends together to make a circle, the inner strip buckles a little. If you were to add a layer or two of interfacing between them, the buckling would become severe. This is what happens to a flat collar when it curves around a neck. The principle is simply that one circle cannot fit inside another unless it is smaller; the inner circle (under collar) must be smaller than the outer circle (top collar), or it wrinkles. To achieve a smoothly curving collar, the smaller under collar is stretched to match the longer top collar; when it relaxes, the stretched under collar pulls the outer top collar into a circle.

To try this on your two pieces of cloth, first fold them in half and notch the midpoint of each. Then unfold and position them under the presser foot at the midpoint ¼ in. from one edge, and start to sew a seam toward one end. Stitch straight for about ½ in., and then stop with the needle down. Grab both pieces together at approximately the midpoint of the fabric, with the left hand behind the machine, and grab the bottom piece with the other hand in front of the machine. Now continue stitching, but pull only the bottom piece taut while allowing both to feed regularly, as in taut sewing. Try to keep both pieces aligned and the seam straight.

A more accurate way to do this is to trim the bottom piece ⅛ in. to ¼ in. at each end and, after stitching the first ½ in. from the midpoint, to stretch the bottom piece to match the top. This controls the amount of stretch you give. Try it both ways, however.

Whichever way you choose, you should be able to stretch the bottom piece at least ¼ in. to ⅜ in. by the time you are ½ in. from the end. Stop at this point, with the needle down, turn the corner, and sew the ends together, keeping them parallel. Now return to the midpoint so the stretched piece is still underneath, and do the same thing to the other end. You will be using the other side of the presser foot to guide your ¼-in. seam.

You should see a distinct curve built into what you've just made. Think of it as a rudimentary collar. Trim the seam allowances at the corners and turn it right side out.

Some readers may object that the longer piece should be on the bottom, not the top, to take advantage of the natural action of the feed dogs. I reverse this sensible procedure to ensure the precision of the seam line that eventually forms the collar shape. When sewing a collar, I stitch right along the edge of the interfacing (which has been glue-basted in position on the wrong side of the top collar), and so the top collar, the longer piece, must be on top where I can see it. To glue-baste, I use Baste and Sew Glue Stick by Fantastic Fit.

As you iron your collarlike construction after turning, you should notice several things. The under collar lies smooth, but the top collar is loose, even wrinkled. The short seams at the ends have a tendency to pull under toward the under collar. Even after heavy pressing, the curve remains. The finished collar is also slightly shorter than the original length of the pieces. All of these things result because the stretched under collar relaxes.

Of course, a collar not only curves around the neck, but it also folds over at the neckline. Thus, a curve is required along the short ends of the collar, at the roll line. Especially if the collar is a longer, pointed one, most of the curve (hence most of the stretching) should be in the 1 in. to 1½ in. nearest the collar stand (see step 7, page 37.) Therefore, when you make a real collar, after pivoting at the corner of the collar point, you will stitch straight, without stretching, until the last 1½ in. or so, and then stretch firmly and stitch right off the end. When you cannot grab the raw edge because it is too close to the presser foot, just press it down against the bed of the machine in order to resist the pull of the feed dogs, at the same time pulling both pieces from the back, as in the right-hand photo below. A straight seam here is much more important than a perfectly even stitch length.

As noted earlier, the finished collar will be slightly smaller than the original pieces. How then do you know how big to cut your collar pieces if sewing them together shortens the length? The answer depends on how much stretching of the under collar you do, how much interfacing you use, and how thick the shirting material is. You must make a sample, using fabric of the same or

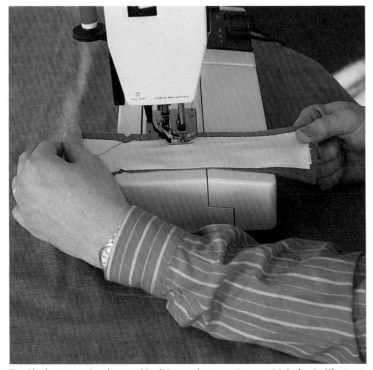

To eliminate puckering and build ease into one layer of fabric, Coffin taut-sews. Stitching along the edge of the interfacing ensures perfect shaping.

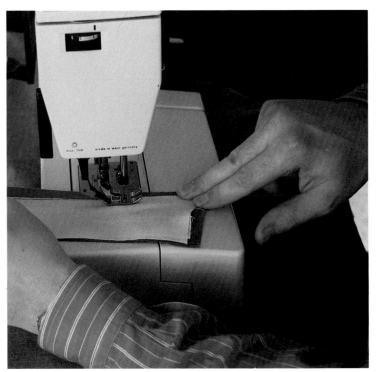

When there is too little fabric to hold, Coffin presses the fabric against the bed of the machine while still pulling from the back.

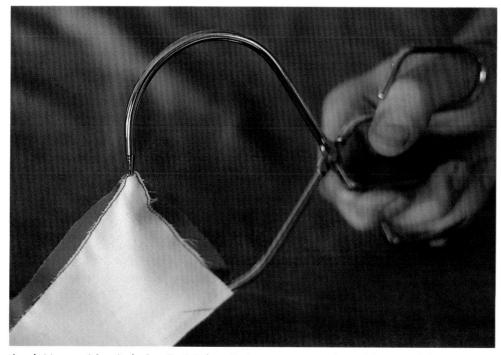

A point turner (above) pinches the fabric so that you can turn points without straining the fabric or poking through it. At right, Coffin wearing one of his shirts.

similar weight, and interface it. Measure before and after to determine how much smaller the finished product is than the original top collar, and then add this amount to your top-collar pattern. The amount of stretching you do, and thus the amount of curve, is a matter of personal choice. I feel you should stretch at least ⅛ in. but not more than ⅜ in. at each end. You can establish a fixed amount of stretching for all your cotton dress shirts and cut the under collar short by that amount on each end, centering the notches in the middle. When you make a shirt of a lighter- or heavier-weight fabric, make another sample collar.

When topstitching a collar into which ease has been built, you must also taut-sew. The best way is to start at one short end of the collar and stitch smoothly to the corner or around the curve on a round collar until you're about to stitch the long edge. Then pick up the ends and, stretching until the top layer is taut, stitch to the other corner, maintaining even pressure. Stop stretching, turn the corner, and sew off the other end. The challenge is to maintain an even stitch length while you are taut-sewing—practice helps.

These are the main applications of taut sewing for collars, but there are a few more techniques that will help make your collars perfect. When stitching the collar points, take from one to four stitches diagonally across the point before turning completely (drawing 7, page 37). The number depends on the thickness of your material and interfacing, and your stitch length, which should be quite short.

I construct the entire collar, and in fact the whole shirt, with the machine set at 1.5mm (18-22 stitches/in.), and .8mm or .9mm (approximately 30 stitches/in.) for points or curves of collars where the seam

allowances will be trimmed off. Short stitches are important when you're stretching seams, since a seam of short stitches stretches more than a seam of long stitches. I use 100% cotton DMC Machine Embroidery Thread—available from Treadle Art, 25834 Narbonne Ave., Lomita, CA 90717, (213) 534-5122—for all construction and topstitching when making a shirt. It matches the weight of the thread in a manufactured shirt, is appropriate with short stitches, and looks beautiful as topstitching.

When trimming a collar point, clip straight across the tip, parallel to the diagonal stitches, at most ¹⁄₁₆ in. away. Then trim away the sides so that there will be no overlap when the seam allowances are on the inside. Try to trim each collar point exactly the same, as identical construction at each step ensures that the points will look the same when the collar is finished.

A point turner, shown in the left-hand photo above, is a useful tool. It looks like a small pair of ice tongs and works in much the same way as commercial point-turning machines, pinching the fabric at the point between two fingers of metal. You can easily turn the collar right side out or back again without straining the fabric or poking through it. Point turners are available from Fashion Sources, Inc., 600 First Ave, Minneapolis, MN 55403, or Nancy's Notions, Box 683, Beaver Dam, WI 53916.

After you've turned a collar that has been eased together, the seam allowances will press more easily if you stretch the seams a bit as you iron to stretch out the wrinkles in the top collar. Once the collar is turned, spray it lightly with water to relax the stretch, and then iron the curve in. Creasing the edge of the top collar with the iron helps you position the seams. Keep checking the two points for similarity, and

press from the point toward the collar, avoiding wrinkles by curling the collar around the tip of a sleeve board or off the edge of the ironing board, as in the photo on page 37.

The best interfacing for an all-cotton shirt is also all cotton. The cheapest and most widely available option is bleached muslin, which closely resembles the nonfusible interfacing used in the manufacture of fine shirts. It can be used double for collars and single for the other interfaced parts of a shirt: the cuffs, collar stand, and front band. Any thoroughly preshrunk soft cotton will also do, including self-interfacing or scraps from other shirts, as long as no pattern or color shows through and you like the final thickness. A little polyester content would do no harm, but why gamble with a mixture of fibers?

A fusible interfacing will irreversibly alter the outer cloth and permanently remove from the wearer's choice any decision about collar stiffness and appearance. Since it is very difficult for home sewers to fuse completely, as they lack the huge presses of the factories, fusing directly to the top collared piece is like adding a time bomb to your shirt: It's only a matter of time before it becomes unstuck.

Now we're ready to make an actual collar with an attached stand. You can use any pattern for a stand collar, or you can take apart the collar from a favorite old shirt, as I've sometimes done.

David Page Coffin, a watercolor artist and custom shirtmaker, is the author of The Custom Shirt Book and Custom Making Neckties at Home. Both books are available from the author, 1708 Madison Ave., San Diego, CA 92116. Photos by Lisa Long, except as noted.

The collar

1. Using the collar pattern, cut interfacing to exact pattern shape, with a ⅝-in. seam allowance on top edge only (edge you'll sew to stand), and no seam allowance on other edges. Fold in half and cut ends together so they'll match exactly. If you want two layers of interfacing, use spray starch on one layer; lay the second piece on top; iron them together, being careful not to distort or stretch the fabric, and cut as one. Starching all the interfacing isn't a bad idea, as it makes it easier to handle and prevents raveling.

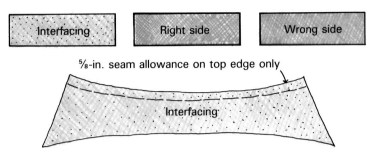

2. Using the collar pattern, cut two layers of shirting fabric (any of the fabrics usually used for shirts, including broadcloth, chambray, madras, oxford, and poplin). Allow a ⅝-in. seam allowance at the top edge and ¼-in. seam allowances at the other edges. Notch the midpoints at top and bottom.

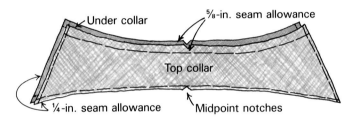

3. Lightly glue-baste all the edges of the interfacing, particularly the points and the front edge. Lay the interfacing on the wrong side of the top collar. Position carefully with regard to stripes or patterns, since you'll follow the outline of the interfacing exactly when stitching the collar.

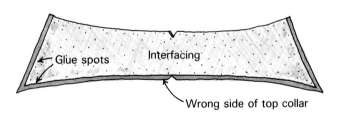

4. Trim the top and side edges of the under collar by the amount you've determined from your sample that you'll stretch back in. Almost ¼ in. is average for each side, and ⅛ in. to ¼ in. is average for the top, depending on the length of the collar points.

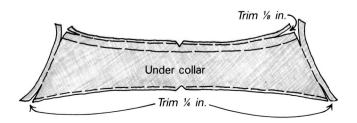

5. Make slots for the collar stays in the under collar, following one of the two methods illustrated below. Collar stays are not required on rounded, button-down, or pinned collars, or if you have your collars heavily starched. Starch and heavy pressing would cause the collar slots to show up on the front of the collar, which would be unattractive.

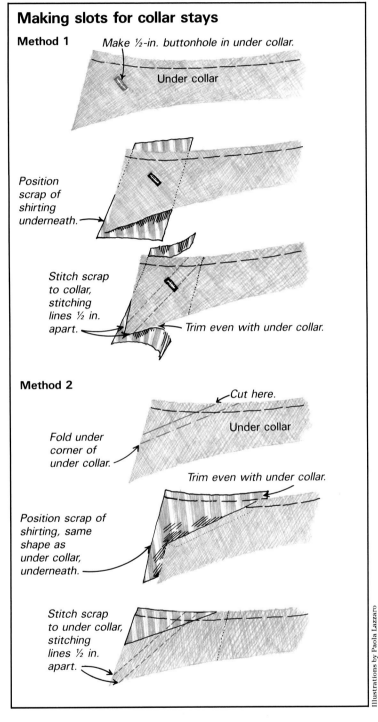

6. Align under collar and top collar at midpoint notches and along bottom edge, right sides together, interfacing on top.

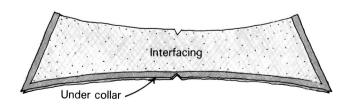

7. Stitch the top collar to the under collar, catching just the edges of the interfacing. Starting at midpoint notches on bottom edge, edgestitch interfacing for ½ in. Then taut-sew, stretching under collar to align with top collar and edgestitching interfacing until you reach the collar point. Take one or two diagonal stitches across point, turn, edgestitch side of collar until 1½ in. from top edge. Stop and lower needle. Stretch under collar to match top collar, hold down firmly on sewing machine bed in front of needle, and pull from behind, stitching along edge of interfacing exactly. Stitch other side exactly the same, duplicating any slight uncorrected shaping errors. Most important, keep the stitching on the front edges very straight.

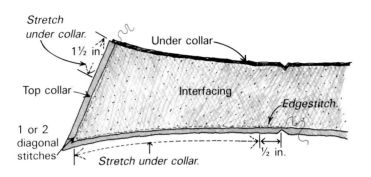

8. Trim seam allowances at collar points exactly the same way on each side. Press and stretch bottom edge flat. Press seam open on point presser, a wooden tool with a narrow pointed arm that slips into the point to be pressed. Turn collar right side out, shaping points carefully until they are as identical as possible.

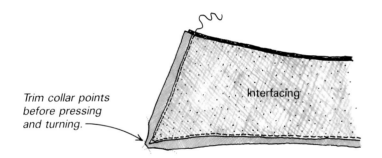

Trim collar points before pressing and turning.

9. With iron, carefully shape the collar, positioning seams just inside the edges. Start pressing at center back with top collar face down on ironing board. Then press points by placing on edge of sleeve board, with collar hanging off. Smooth any wrinkles. Shape collar in a circle, and press in the curve (see photo at right).

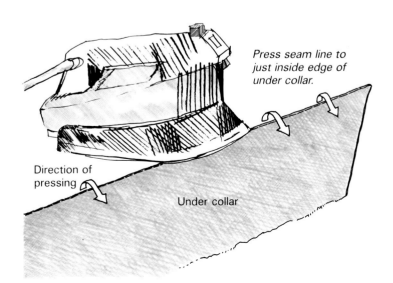

Press seam line to just inside edge of under collar.

Direction of pressing

Under collar

10. Once you are satisfied with the position of the edge seams and have pressed out all wrinkles, you're ready to topstitch. To topstitch, start at one raw edge and carefully stitch ¼ in. from the edge, stopping when the needle is ¼ in. from each side of collar point. With the needle down, pivot the collar and stitch for ½ in. or so. Then pick up the points of the collar and stretch taut so the top collar is flat against the under collar. Slowly and smoothly stitch to about ½ in. from the opposite point, stop stretching, pivot with needle lowered, and then stitch off the other raw end. This method preserves the curve in the collar and eliminates any puckering in the topstitching and the join in the back that would be caused by starting at midback and stitching toward either end.

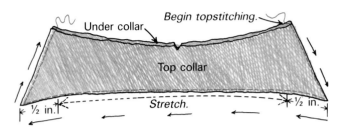

11. To shape the roll line, fold the ⅝-in. seam allowance of both the top collar and the under collar toward the under collar, and smooth the fullness in the under collar up toward the fold. The under collar should stick out slightly beyond the top collar. Iron this edge flat and hard when you are satisfied that enough of the fullness in the under collar has been taken out. You can use a tailor's ham (a firmly packed ham-shaped cushion that is used for shaping and pressing curves) to shape and check the collar. Make sure that the collar points are exactly the same length from fold to point and that the fold hits any pattern or stripe at the same point on both sides.

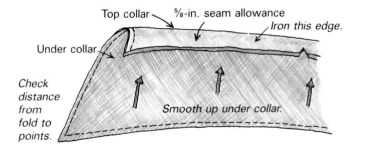

Top collar — ⅝-in. seam allowance
Iron this edge.
Under collar
Check distance from fold to points.
Smooth up under collar.

To shape the collar, Coffin presses it on a sleeve board, letting the collar hang off the edge.

12. When you are satisfied with the shape, position the collar under the presser foot with the needle at far left (or use zipper foot), and to hold the fold in place, machine-baste the seam allowances together approximately ⅛ in. (but no less) from the fold (see photo below). Trim seam allowances to ¼ in. from fold. The collar is now ready to be attached to the collar stand.

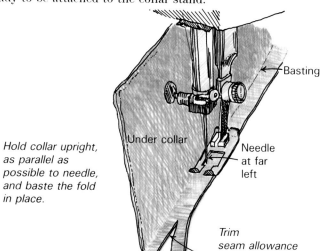

Hold collar upright, as parallel as possible to needle, and baste the fold in place.

13. Cut two pieces of shirting for collar stand and collar-stand facing, and one piece of interfacing. Lightly glue-baste interfacing to wrong side of stand. I allow ¼-in. seam allowances on collar-stand edges, collar-stand facing edges, and interfacing edges, but you could use ⅝-in. seam allowances and trim the seams later.

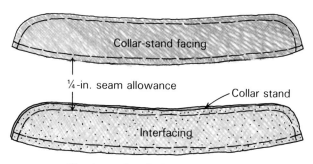

Glue-baste interfacing to collar stand.

After folding the seam allowances, smoothing out the under collar's fullness, and pressing the fold, Coffin sews the fold in place. Photo by author.

14. Stitch the collar stand to the right side of the neck edge, then the collar-stand facing to the wrong side of the neck edge, clipping the neckline edge as necessary. Stretch the collar-stand facing just as you did with the under collar. Stitch from center back toward ends, but not beyond the front edges of the shirt.

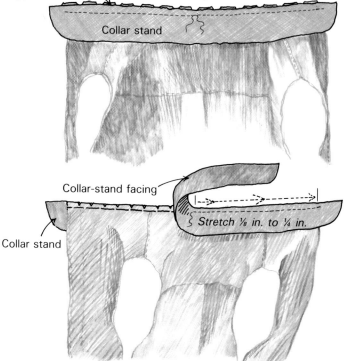

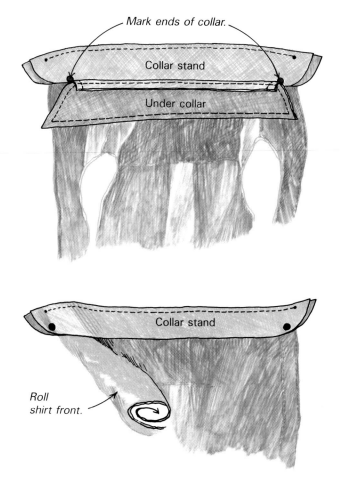

15. Center the collar on the stand and mark the end points. Remove the collar. Roll the shirt fronts until you can bring the top edges of the collar stand together to the marks for the collar.

16. With the machine set at approximately 30 stitches/in., stitch the ends of the stand in the shape you want, and stop at the points just marked. You may want to trace this shape on each end to make them identical. Don't backstitch. Trim the seam allowances, and turn collar stand right side out.

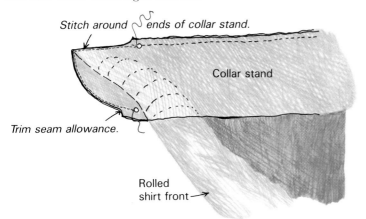

Stitch around ends of collar stand.

Collar stand

Trim seam allowance.

Rolled shirt front

17. Turn the collar stand and facing right side out. Try the shirt on, pinning the front and the stand comfortably closed and checking that any pattern on the front matches as it should. Center the collar on the stand and re-mark with chalk or a washable marker where the collar ends meet the stand. Take the shirt off and clip the seam allowances of the collar-stand facing at these two points.

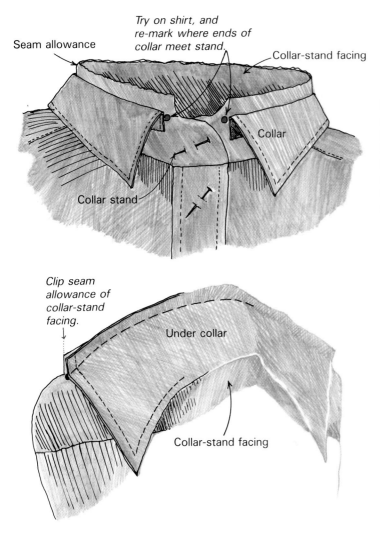

Seam allowance

Try on shirt, and re-mark where ends of collar meet stand.

Collar-stand facing

Collar

Collar stand

Clip seam allowance of collar-stand facing.

Under collar

Collar-stand facing

18. Stitch the collar to the collar-stand facing at the raw edge with a ¼-in. seam, without catching the seam allowance of the collar stand in the stitching.

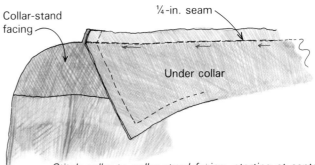

Collar-stand facing

¼-in. seam

Under collar

Stitch collar to collar-stand facing, starting at center and stitching to ends, without catching collar stand.

19. Press under the seam allowance of the collar stand, and glue-baste if necessary, to just cover the seam made in the previous step. This folded edge will be slightly full.

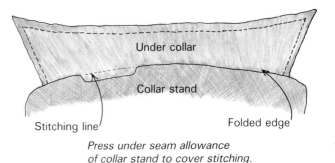

Under collar

Collar stand

Stitching line

Folded edge

Press under seam allowance of collar stand to cover stitching.

20. With collar-stand facing and upper collar on top and pressed edge of collar stand underneath, edgestitch around collar-stand facing, starting at the yoke shoulder seam and stitching around the end. Edgestitching should be close to edge of collar-stand facing, except where collar is attached. Here, edgestitching drops down slightly to ensure that pressed edge of collar stand is being caught in stitching. Stretch collar-stand facing to ease in fullness of collar stand. □

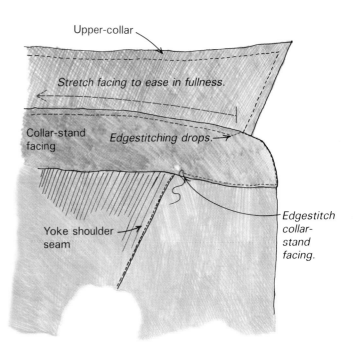

Upper-collar

Stretch facing to ease in fullness.

Collar-stand facing

Edgestitching drops.

Yoke shoulder seam

Edgestitch collar-stand facing.

Plaid Basics

A primer on symmetry and proportion among the tartans and the tattersalls

by Grace Callaway

Plaids are always among the most tempting of the fabrics offered each season for the delight of sewers, and there's no reason to resist them if you're willing to follow a few simple guidelines. You'll need to consider how different plaids will relate to your figure, your garment pattern, and your sewing skills.

Plaids and the figure—Patterned fabrics create optical illusions when made into garments and worn. The boldest elements of patterns become focal points, so keep them away from figure parts you want to de-emphasize. The more obvious the pattern of a plaid, whether because of its size, its color, or both, the more carefully you'll need to position the pattern repeats on your figure. Placement is less critical for small patterns and for patterns in pale, muted, or low-contrast colors, where individual pattern elements have less impact.

Prominent horizontal designs make the body appear wider, while dominant vertical patterns give an appearance of height. Study the fabric to determine the design's most dominant lines. The usual placement for the dominant vertical line is at the center front, the center back, and the center of each sleeve. Place the dominant horizontal lines where they will flatter your figure most. Conventionally, one avoids placing dominant horizontals or the focal points of a pattern at the bust, hips, or waist, but flat hips can be made to look rounder if a dominant horizontal line is placed there.

Types of plaids—Whether bold or subdued, all plaids fall into two main categories: even and uneven. An even plaid is exactly symmetrical around a centerline. It repeats its pattern, both in shape and color, as a mirror image, whether you study it crosswise or lengthwise. An uneven plaid has asymmetrical variations of spacing or color within its design, either vertically, horizontally, or vertically and horizontally. See the drawings below for examples of the various types.

Even plaids provide the most matching options. Because they are the same on both sides of a centerline, you can lay pattern pieces in either direction, unless the fabric has a nap. If the repeat is exactly square, you can cut out small pattern pieces on the cross grain in a pinch, but perfectly square plaids are unusual. Most even plaids have rectangular repeats. Pattern pieces that cross the figure in one piece, like collars and yokes, will always match at each end when centered on an even plaid.

Uneven plaids must be cut all in one direction, whether napped or not, if they are to match. When a plaid is uneven lengthwise, the pattern moves in one direction; it won't be identical on both sides of a center-front or center-back opening or seam. However, in some cases, you can arrange uneven-lengthwise-only plaids so the right and left sides mirror one another around the centerline. First, make sure you have separate pattern pieces for each side, clearly marked "right" and "left." If your fabric

Slip-basting to preserve a careful plaid-matching job: Cutting the sleeve on the cross grain and slightly adjusting the shoulder seams to be identical simplified the matching challenge with this fabric.

Types of plaid symmetry

Even, crosswise and lengthwise, not square

Even in pattern, uneven in color, both ways

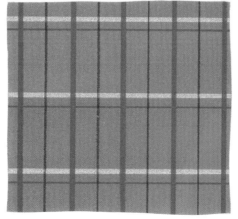

Uneven, crosswise only

Uneven, crosswise and lengthwise

From *Threads* magazine (June 1988) 17:26-30

Designing with plaid

by Deborah Abbott

Woven cloth, and especially plaid, is an orderly creation. Its geometric regularity is at odds with the curves of the human form. Out of this confusion of plaid on the body I make an attempt at order. I decide where the plaid's strength is and what its dominant line is. Where on the body will the dominant line work best? I can echo the rhythm of the plaid with brisk, staccato lines cut on the straight grain, or I can mold those lines to the body curves by cutting on the bias. Bias for a silk chiffon, straight for a suit-weight wool…but why not a bias-plaid suit? I sketch silhouette lines on stick figures and experiment with the direction of the plaid's strongest stripe.

Ideas start to grow. I mix lengthwise and bias grains in the same garment. I cut a dress with bias sleeves and skirt, contrasted by a straight-of-grain bodice, softening the silhouette physically with the bias drape and visually with a diagonal pattern and avoiding complex matching at the seams. I drape the bodice and sleeves as one on the bias and pair it with a skirt on the straight. I use the bias for both bodice and skirt and then trim the whole with cuffs, collar, front bands, and belt all cut on the straight, isolating the most vivid section of plaid for emphasis. I mix sizes of plaids. The skirt plaid is large and bold; the jacket plaid is smaller, more controlled. I mix two plaids. I cut the cuffs and yoke, and maybe half the front in the smaller plaid, the rest in the large plaid. I get playful. I add a hip wrap in a third plaid, in black and white. I think of patchwork, of the beauty of regular repeats of unmatched patterns, and of randomness. I cut small plaid shapes and piece them together so that the dominant stripe zigzags across the new cloth.

I make diamonds by seaming two pieces of bias-cut fabric, meeting at the same angle. I can put them on the shoulders and let them run down the arms. Or I can make an insert of diamonds that encircles the hips or an insert like a zigzag splashing across the body, contained by the straight-of-grain.

I try disguising the plaid. Around the hips or across the back, I fold pleats from one repeat to another, hiding the underneath part of the plaid. As the garment moves, color bursts from between the pleats. I change the dominant line by embroidering with a heavy yarn over a minor stripe. I add dimension. I get excited by the power to alter the fabricmaker's arrangement. I create my own patterns and add my own emphasis with needle and yarn. I outline whole repeats, or only certain squares, making a check pattern on a plaid background. I outline just the rectangles on the shoulders.

I use the plaid as an accent: sleeves and collar only in plaid. I line a coat with a brilliant plaid; cuffs turn up and collar turns back to display the pattern. Reversible, the plaid turns back to reveal serene color. I cut plaid fabric in bias strips to bind an edge; neat triangles curve around the squares and rectangles of the plaid. I throw a large square or rectangle of one plaid over an outfit of another plaid: The fabric expresses itself in its own folds and corrugations. It is again self-sufficient.

The ideas start to bear fruit. I choose the ones I'll use on this garment, storing the rest in my file under "Plaids—ideas." Here, with pages from magazines and newspapers, and with my sketches and notes, a treasure trove awaits my next project.

Deborah Abbott is a fashion designer and weaver. See her article on manipulating darts on pp. 16-19.

Plaid sewing tips

by Margaret Islander

Matching plaids on the sewing machine can be discouraging. To discover after sewing that your carefully pinned and basted layers have shifted anyway is enough to drive plaids from your repertoire forever. Here's an industrial technique that explains both the cause of the problem and the remedy, and it uses no pinning or basting. Practice with a few strips of scrap plaid and see if this method doesn't restore your enthusiasm.

Place two pieces right sides together on the machine, with the plaids matched. Lower the needle, *then* the foot. Lowering the foot first would set in motion the very difficulty you're trying to overcome: The top layer of fabric would be forced toward you by the foot, while the feed dogs would grab the lower layer and draw it in the opposite direction. Lowering the needle first holds everything in place until you start stitching.

Make a few stitches and stop with the needle down. Match the layers at the next bold line of the plaid. The lines in between will take care of themselves. Grab the lower layer with your right hand—thumb underneath, fingers on top—and tip up your hand, as shown in the drawing at right. With your left hand, pick up the top layer; with your index finger, force the top bold stripe slightly away from the lower matching stripe, toward the needle. This will form a small ripple in the top layer. Continue stitching almost to your fingers. Then release the ripple, allowing the stripe to fall into place exactly on top of the lower one. Adjust the next bold stripe as before, and continue this way to the end of the seam.

Of course, complete accuracy depends on correctly judging the amount you need to offset the top layer from the bottom layer. The heavier the fabric, and the farther apart the bold

Matching plaids without pins

Offset top layer slightly toward needle at a dominant line, and release only when you get to machine foot.

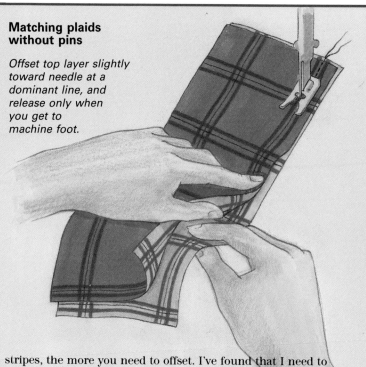

stripes, the more you need to offset. I've found that I need to offset lightweight fabrics about ¹⁄₁₆ in., medium-weight fabrics about ⅛ in., and heavyweight fabrics about ¼ in. It's important to practice with a sample of the actual fabric you'll be using.

I've used the same technique even for intricately shaped yokes and deep curves, but I do occasionally resort to a machine version of slip-basting by hand for complex seams. To try it yourself, press under the seam allowance on the yoke or ⇨

is reversible, cut one half of the garment with its pattern face down, and the second half face up. Flip one to make a pair. If the fabric isn't reversible, but has no nap, cut both halves face up but in opposite directions top to bottom, and rotate one to make a pair. And make sure before you cut, with either method, that the garment centers are positioned along identical pattern lines, and crosswise lines match, or the mirror effect will not be perfect.

Pattern selection—For any plaid to match perfectly across a seam, the seams must be the same length and shape, and they must lie at equal angles across the fabric. Obviously, this doesn't happen often, except in some gored or gathered skirts. But if you select a pattern with only a few simple seams (preferably straight), no darts, and few stitched details, you'll have little trouble matching all types of plaids. Stitched tucks, darts, pleats, princess seams, and the like create inevitable distortions in plaids. Use a simple pattern, and let the plaid itself supply the fashion interest. Most of the time you can be guided by the pattern envelope. If it says on the back that the pattern is not recommended for plaids, it means that there are major seams or details that will make matching plaids impossible. For the easiest time, look for patterns illustrated in plaid. If your plans are more adventurous, consider the suggestions in "Designing with plaid," facing page.

Buying and preparing the fabric—Extra fabric is required for matching plaids. Follow the "with nap" or "without nap" directions appropriate to your chosen plaid, along with these rules of thumb: For even plaids, allow one extra pattern repeat (the distance between dominant crosswise lines) for each major pattern piece. For uneven plaids, allow two pattern repeats for each major pattern piece, and then round up to the nearest half yard.

Preshrink and press your plaid just as you would any other fabric—the same way you plan to care for the finished garment. Be especially careful not to stretch it off-grain when removing the wrinkles. If you find the fabric is slightly off-grain, correct it. See p. 25 for more information on preshrinking and preparing plaid fabric to ensure perfect matching. If your fabric is more than slightly off-grain, see if you can return it. Before you buy printed plaids, check them carefully to make sure they are printed on-grain.

Preparing the pattern—A common sewing tip for plaids is to cut out half the garment pieces with the paper pattern and to use the cut cloth flipped over for the remaining pieces. I've found this to be a bad idea because cut fabric can easily stretch off-grain, in which case you won't get a true shape for the second piece you cut. You're also likely to cut the second piece slightly larger than the first one.

For the most exact match, cut the garment from a single layer of fabric, no matter how simple the plaid, and have a separate pattern piece for each garment section. It is difficult to be sure the bottom layer is exactly aligned with the top when the fabric is folded in half. Trace extra pieces from tissue paper for each pattern piece that will be cut out more than once. Pieces that are to be cut on a fold should be extended into one whole piece. Having a separate pattern piece for each garment section makes it easy to see if you have enough fabric for your garment. You'll be less likely to cut two left halves, and you'll be able to confirm the match of the design more easily.

Extend the lengthwise grain lines all the way to the edges of the pattern pieces. This makes vertical placement easier. Using a right angle, draw crosswise grain lines on all pattern pieces, extending them to the edges of the pieces. Try to place the crosswise grain lines in exactly the same position on corresponding pattern pieces. Draw these crosswise grain lines below any horizontal darts, since it is impossible to match plaids both above and below darts.

When bust darts are very deep or shaped so they'll cause a lot of distortion of the plaid, move them to the shoulders and convert them to gathers (see the article "Making Your Own Sloper" on pp. 114-119 and books on flat-pattern design).

Plaids must be matched at the seamline rather than at the cutting line. You'll need curve and pin it in place on the matching piece, with the seam edges aligned. Thread your machine with contrasting thread, and set the stitch to zigzag about ¼ in., or 4mm, for both length and width. Loosen the upper tension two or three points to allow for easy removal of the threads later. From the right side of the garment, carefully zigzag on the garment beside the folded edge of the yoke, catching just the edge with a tiny bite of the zigzag, as shown in the left-hand drawing below.

Rethread your machine with matching thread and reset the tension. Then open the two layers so they're right sides together. You'll see dots of color from the zigzag stitches just along the creased seamline. Stitch along this line, remove the contrast stitching, and press open, clipping the seam allowances when necessary.

Always check a sample of your material first to see if thread or needle marks will show after you remove the zigzag basting. If they do, you'll have to slip-baste by hand. Also, your machine is still operating as described in the first technique: The foot is pushing the fabric toward you, while the feed dogs pull back the lower layer, in spite of your basting. So be sure to push the top layer a little forward of the lower layer with your left index finger as you stitch, releasing it as the foot approaches.

Margaret Islander is the founder of Islander Sewing Systems. She has produced two videos that describe her industrial shortcuts for home sewers, available from her at Box 5216, Grants Pass, OR 97527.

Machine-basting plaid seams

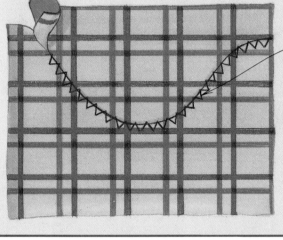

Zigzag on bottom layer of fabric, barely catching folded top layer.

Fold layers right sides together and sew along line of zigzag stitches.

Illustrations by Robert LaPointe

to draw in the seamlines on the extra pattern pieces you traced. When the pattern pieces are in place, fold back the pattern seam allowances to be sure there is a match of the design at the stitching line. An alternative is to remove the seam allowances on all pieces. As long as you are careful to allow for them when you cut out, this method will give you the clearest view of your fabric for the easiest match. Mark the seam allowances with a double-wheeled tracing wheel, or use a rotary cutter with a seam-width guide to cut out the pieces.

Pattern placement—The dominant vertical line usually is placed at the centers of the major garment sections. With some fabrics, however, vertical lines will match at the side seams only if the front and back are the same width or are both even multiples of the width repeat. Perhaps you can make them match by slightly widening the back or front or by adding a little to one side and subtracting it from the other. Try positioning the center equally between dominant verticals. If nothing helps, match the centers and live with the sides.

Crosswise grain lines should be placed on the same horizontal line of the design. If you have placed the crosswise grain lines accurately on corresponding pieces, the top and bottom corners of each piece will be on the same line as well, unless there are horizontal darts between the top and bottom edges.

When making pants, place the lengthwise grain line (the crease) on the most dominant vertical line of the design for the front and back pieces. This will provide the most balanced overall effect, which is more important than matching at the side seams. Straight-leg pants are easier to match and more attractive in plaids than tapered or bell-bottom pants.

Skirts with panels that are the same size and shape are easy to match. All seams will match if you arrange the center of each panel on the same lengthwise line and the crosswise grain lines on the same horizontal lines. If the garment has a curved hemline, place the least dominant horizontal line there. Very flared skirts, such as circle or modified circle skirts, generally don't lend themselves to plaids. Gathered, tiered, and other straight-panel skirt designs are more suitable.

Cutting and marking—When you're satisfied with your pattern layout, check it once again to be sure everything is correct. Are all pairs mirror images instead of clones? Are dominant vertical lines centered or placed so they don't make the garment look out of balance? Have you moved darts to the shoulders and converted them to gathers? Have you placed the hemline to minimize distortion? Are dominant horizontal lines placed in the most flattering locations for your figure? Does the design match at all key points?

If you've marked your grain lines accurately, there'll be little need to cut notches. Matching of the seamlines will be according to the lines of the plaid. For points that need an extra mark, like front-sleeve or armhole notches, or centers, cut a ¼-in. snip in the seam allowance. For internal markings, use tailors' tacks or chalk markers. Dressmaker's tracing-paper marks are difficult to see on many plaids.

Stitching—There are several ways to hold the seamlines together for stitching so that the design doesn't shift as you sew. Pinning works well on small plaids and gingham checks. Slip-basting is more secure, so it's better when there is a long pattern repeat. To slip-baste, fold under and press one seam allowance, match garment pieces on the seamlines, and use a few pins to hold them together. Baste at the seamline with a short running stitch, catching just the fold of the top layer, as shown in the photo on p. 40. On some fabrics, you can replace thread basting with glue stick or basting tape. See "Plaid sewing tips," p. 43, for a few alternate methods that will increase your sewing skills when you're working with plaid. □

Grace Callaway is a professor of home economics at Georgia College. See her other articles about making circle skirts with gathers, gores, and tiers (pp. 63-65) and perfect-fit swimsuits (pp. 78-83).

The Drafter, the Draper, the Flat Patternmaker

Three ways to make your own sewing patterns

by Rebecca Lanxner Nebesar

have you ever become slightly annoyed when, after you've come up with a strong idea to sew something, you can't get started without first journeying to the fabric store for a pattern, only to find that nothing quite resembles your idea? Making your own patterns is not beyond your reach. Patternmaking is not a mysterious talent possessed by the blessed few, as many people seem to feel; nor is it a science as much as it is an art. Experimenting freely and being open to serendipity and the infinite variety of fibers, fabrics, styles, and levels of fit are what's important.

If you're familiar with sewing and have used commercial patterns and altered them for fit or style, you can design and make original patterns. You just need to know what you are getting into and how to get started. And, you must practice. Making patterns is a challenge, and it's exciting. You'll feel such freedom. I remember the day it dawned on me that I could make anything—it was extraordinary.

The three methods—There are three basic methods of patternmaking: the flat-pattern method, draping, and drafting. Each has advantages and disadvantages, and there is a method for everyone. Vionnet did it one way, Chanel another. I borrow from all methods, depending on the project.

The **flat-pattern method** generates new shapes from a sloper, a basic pattern on stiff paper with no seam allowances. With this method, you trace the sloper onto plain paper, draw new style lines on the tracing, and cut the paper on the lines. From there, you can move the fitting darts anywhere within the pattern, or you can convert them to gathers, pleats, tucks, fitting seams, etc., simply by closing the darts and slashing and spreading the pattern. You can add fullness and change the style lines by splitting the pattern into several parts. You

then cut the resulting pattern in muslin or the final fabric.

The flat-pattern method can be used to create any design. It is a good starting point for patternmaking, especially if you have trouble visualizing shapes or are sewing for a hard-to-fit body. It requires the fewest tools of all the methods—oaktag, paper, scissors, tape, ruler, French curve, muslin, thread—and the least amount of skill. If you have lengthened or shortened a commercial pattern on the indicated line, you have already had some experience. And because you work with a sloper that already fits, you do not have to be very concerned with measurements.

A disadvantage of the flat-pattern method is that paper and cardboard don't have the same properties as fabric. Fabric has mysterious ways that aren't always predictable, such as the way bias areas can stretch.

Draping is manipulating fabric on a dress form or live model to produce the desired garment. The process is sculptural, artistic, and the least technical of the three methods. Draped garments are often the most original. The successful draper has a good eye and is dexterous. The tools for draping include muslin, a dress form, pins, scissors, a pencil, and a measuring tape.

Essentially, cloth is cut in rectangular shapes to the approximate sizes of individual pattern pieces. These pieces are pinned to the dress form and to each other and then adjusted and trimmed until the desired garment appears on the form.

The advantage of draping is that all work is done in fabric, whether it be a cheap muslin, a knit, or the final fabric. The solid dimensions of the body don't have to be imagined; they are there to be touched and fit. (Bias-cut styles must be draped to take full advantage of the fabric's potential.) A disadvantage of draping is its dependence on the dress form. Unless you have a lot of space, owning more than one dress form

can make a workroom a bit crowded. Also, if you have to travel and can't take it with you, you may be unable to work.

Drafting is drawing a pattern on paper, aided by body measurements and various tools. It requires an understanding of the relative proportions of body parts and experience with pattern shapes. The tools include gridded pattern paper or plain paper, rulers, a protractor, a hip curve, a French curve, a tailor's square, a compass, a pencil, and an eraser. Although it can be creative, drafting is the least straightforward and the most complicated patternmaking method. It is primarily used in the tailoring business and the ready-to-wear garment industry to create perfectly fitted, standardized patterns, which are then graded, or scaled, to various sizes.

Drafting's value is greatest when regular, precise, fitted garments are desired. Once a given pattern is mastered, it can easily, quickly, and accurately be drafted to another person's measurements. The techniques for drawing lines are good to learn and can be applied to the other patternmaking methods for redrawing seam lines and darts crisply and clearly. The disadvantage is that the drafter generally needs a good mind for math, especially fractions and geometry.

How to get started—Relax and empty your mind of pattern clutter, and start with the basics. Think of clothes in terms of simple shapes. If you can first learn how cloth cut in different shapes behaves when draped on the body, your understanding of clothes will expand. You will approach your first project with more confidence and a clearer image of what you are after. This image is of invaluable help, and the ability to see it is probably the most important skill to develop. You must know what you want either beforehand—perhaps from a sketch or a photo—or sometime during the process, when

Rebecca Nebesar designed each of these garments, using a different patternmaking technique. She drafted the pattern for the blouse at left, used the flat-pattern method for the blouse at center, and draped the dress at right directly on the mannequin.

Tips on sewing order

After you've made your pattern, you'll have to sew your garment together. Sewing order is pretty logical, so if you think through the steps, you won't sew yourself into a Möbius strip. A general sewing reference book will help with the trickier details.

1. Work flat for as long as possible. Attach pockets and other internal details on separate pattern pieces.

2. Work on the body first, starting with the back. Do not connect the side seams.

3. Prepare closures: zippers, button plackets, etc.

4. For the bodice, sew the shoulder seams, then the neck finishing (collar, facing, or binding).

5. Determine whether the sleeves should be set in or whether they can be attached flat before the side and underarm seams are closed. (Sleeves with high caps and garments with fitted bodices should be constructed by the set-in method.) Sew.

6. For skirts and pants, attach waistbands after you've made length and width adjustments.

7. Hem the lower edge(s) of the garment.

you see the draped shape on the dress form or the pattern piece on the table and say, "That's it!"

The next two exercises will show you how much you already know, as well as what you do not understand. For the first exercise, cut the following shapes, as large as you can, from fabric scraps or cheap fabric: a long rectangle, a short rectangle, a square, a circle, a half circle, a quarter circle, and an eighth circle. Play with these shapes for a while. Fold, roll, and gather them; twist them and pleat them; drape them over objects. Be creative. Try cutting more than one of each shape and putting them together.

What do the shapes remind you of? What kind of pattern pieces could they be? List possibilities for each shape. Think about what small cuts you would have to make to improve their functioning as pattern pieces, and try them.

For the second exercise, get out a few of your commercial-pattern packages. Place them picture side up in front of yourself. On a piece of paper, sketch what each pattern piece should look like. Then compare your drawings with those on the instruction sheet. How did you do?

Now that you've loosened up, go shopping. You'll need a stock of inexpensive fabric. You can often pick up sale fabric and remnants for less than $1/yd. If you make a mistake in cheap fabric (call it a learning experience for goodness' sake!), you won't be all that discouraged.

Next, look through your patterns (which are ideally all in one place) for basic or classical shapes—a straight sleeve, a plain skirt or slacks, standard-shaped collars, a princess-seam shift. Weed out the ones you don't use or that are so styled that they aren't adaptable. From the basic patterns, collect the ones you use frequently, either because they fit well and look good or because they are not too tricky to sew, and store them in a convenient location. Once you've learned a few patternmaking skills, these patterns can save you time and money because the pieces are often interchangeable and easily updated. Pattern companies themselves reuse old patterns, making only slight design changes and updating the look with new fashion drawings.

Aren't you tired of handling those fragile, taped-up, wrinkled old tissue patterns you've practically worn to death? By making slopers of frequently used patterns, you'll solve that problem, and at the same time you'll get some practice making patterns. You'll also have a starting point to try flat patternmaking. Work with patterns that fit well or have alterations already indicated.

Use stiff paper that's thick enough so you can use the edge as a drawing guide, but not so heavy that you can't cut it with household utility shears. Oaktag, which is available in various sizes at art-supply stores, is good to use. A 36-in. by 24-in. sheet should run about 50 cents.

Flat patternmaking

1. Trace the sloper onto paper and draw the new style line—in this case, the yoke line. 2. Cut the pattern out; then cut it apart along the yoke line. Tape the darts closed. Mark where notches should go. 3. To add fullness below the yoke, slash the lower pattern section vertically in several places, including through the bust point. Spread the sections apart to add the desired fullness. The yoke section is unchanged. 4. Trace the new pattern sections onto clean paper. Straighten and smooth the pattern lines. Add seam allowances and notches, and label the pattern.

To transfer a pattern to oaktag, use a tracing wheel and tracing paper or carbon paper, or use a needle wheel without the tracing paper. If you are planning to generate new patterns by the flat-pattern method, omit all of the seam allowances from your slopers. Label the important areas (center front, notches, etc.), and draw the straight grain line. Punch holes with an awl for the key internal marks, such as pocket and button positions. Cut around the outline and cut the darts away. To use your sloper as is for a pattern, just trace around it with chalk directly onto the cloth, or transfer the pattern to paper and pin the paper to the cloth. Add seam allowances when you cut the cloth.

An exercise in flat patternmaking—To try your hand at flat patternmaking, trace a basic bodice sloper onto paper. Now try changing the style of the pattern. For example, turn it into a gathered, yoked blouse, as shown in the photos at right. Draw the lines of the yoke and cut on the line. Tape the darts closed. The lower part of the pattern will no longer lie flat. Slash the pattern lengthwise in several places and spread the pieces apart to add fullness and to flatten out the sections. Trace the two new pattern sections onto a clean sheet of paper, straightening and smoothing the lines. Add seam allowances all around.

An exercise in draping—To get started draping, you'll need a few yards of fabric you don't mind ruining, pins, scissors, and a dress form or a person to drape on. A dress form is an invaluable adjunct to any workshop. There are three types: solid, cast-iron stand forms, such as the Wolf Form (Wolf Form Co., 39 W. 19th St., New York, NY 10011, [212] 255-4508) and Superior Form (Superior Model Forms Corp., 545 8th Ave., New York, NY 10018, [212] 947-3633); cloth-covered, foam-rubber, individually adaptable forms, such as Uniquely You (8230-R Telegraph Rd., Odenton, MD 21113, 1-800-822-6622); and adjustable forms, such as Athena (Ardan/A.E. Arthur, 1704C Henry G. Lane St., Maryville, TN 37801, [615] 977-7110) and Childaw (Reliable Sewing Machine, 378 Page St., Box 742, Stoughton, MA 02072, [617] 341-3991), which are made in sections that can be adjusted with

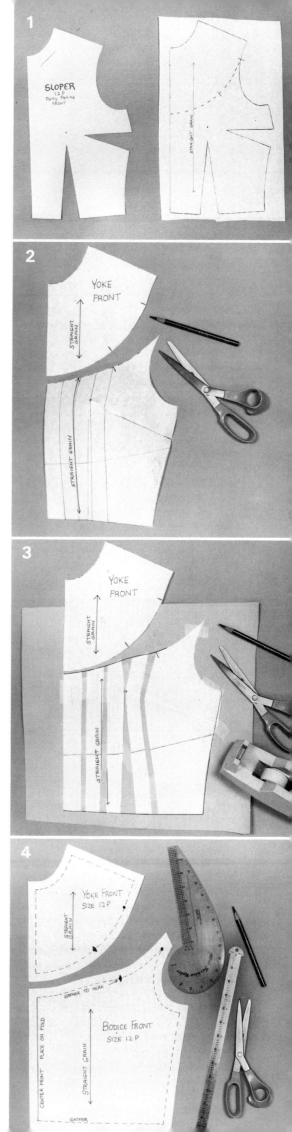

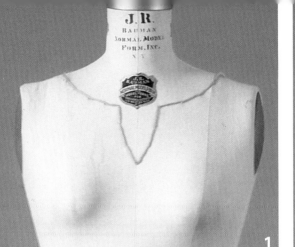

1

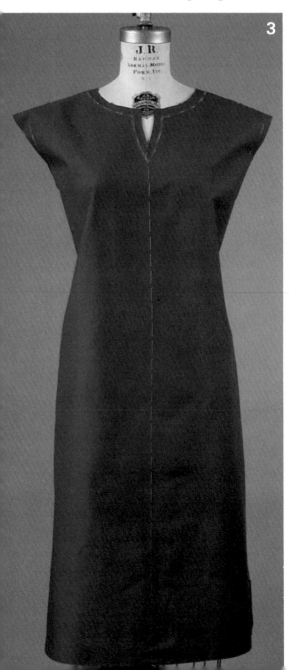

2

Draping

1. *Pin yarn to the dress form along the new style lines. Measure the form for the lengths and widths of the pattern pieces, and cut the fabric 2 in. to 3 in. longer and wider.* 2. *Pin the fabric on the form, aligning the straight grain with the center-front line of the form.* 3. *Pin the fabric to the form in the desired garment shape, adjusting it until you're satisfied with the shape. Cut away excess fabric as you work. Mark the seam lines with chalk while the fabric is on the form.* 4. *Take the fabric off the form and press it smooth. True the seam lines with curves and straight edges.*

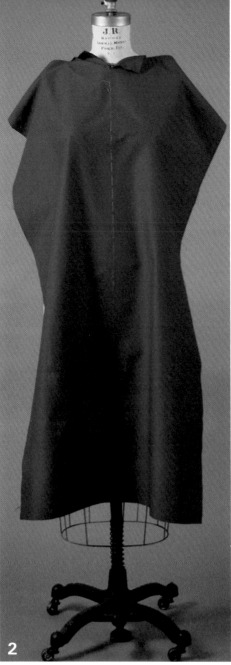

3

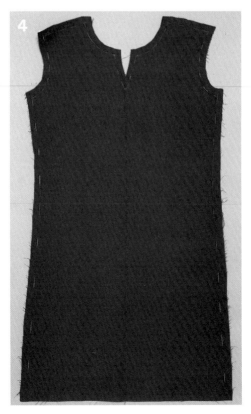

4

screws to individual measurements. For draping, the adjustable forms are the least accommodating because of gaps in the surface, but a strong fabric cover can be custom-made to fit over them. To create variations in body shape, a nonadjustable dress form can be padded with batting and covered with lightweight cloth. A good dress form has seams in the basic reference places, such as center front and back, sides, and shoulders. The seams are often raised so that they are perceptible through a layer or two of draped cloth.

Always begin with an idea of what you want, and try to imagine what the general shapes should be. Try draping the dress shown in the photos at left. Pin narrow tape, ribbon, braid, string, yarn, etc., to the dress form along the major style lines, and measure the form for the approximate lengths and widths of the pattern pieces. Paying attention to which direction you want the lengthwise and crosswise grains to run, cut the fabric pieces 2 in. to 3 in. longer and wider than the measurements. Pin the fabric on the form, placing the pins counter to the pull of the fabric so that they are secure. When draping, always try to have the grain running smoothly. It is sometimes helpful to pin the fabric on the straight grain. Don't be afraid to readjust. Cut away the extra fabric as you work, but only when you are pretty sure of the shapes, and leave generous seam allowances. Mark the seam lines with chalk while the fabric is still on the form. Then remove the fabric from the form and press it smooth. True the seam lines with curves and straight edges.

Exercises in drafting—Although drafting can be complicated, it's not hard to draft a pattern for something simple, geometric, and fairly loose-fitting. Some pattern pieces are little more than rectangles with tiny nicks cut out or circles with smaller circles cut out. Try sketching a full-size pattern piece loosely and freely in pencil. Keep the body measurements handy and remember what you know about pattern shapes, such as that the shoulder seam slants down from the neck to the shoulder, and the back of the neck is higher than the front. For the final shape, start with a vertical line at the center front or back. Then draw the main perpendiculars off it for waistline, hemline, or neckline. It is usually necessary to draw just half the pattern with the center front or back either on a fold or seamed. True up the lines with drafting tools.

Now, for more precise drafting, try the simple dolman-sleeved bodice shown on the facing page. First draw a small, rough sketch of what you imagine the pattern shape will be. Take the body measurements you'll need and mark them on the sketch. In this case, measure the center-front (CF) neck to the waist, neck edge at shoulder to the waist, neck edge at shoulder to the wrist, wrist circumference, waist circum-

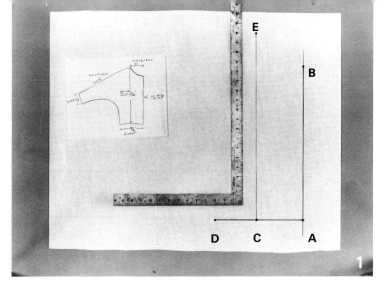

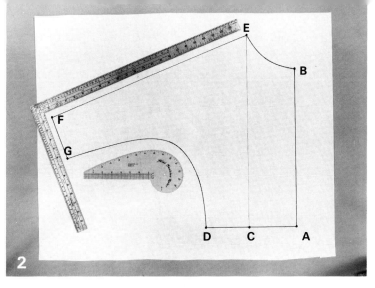

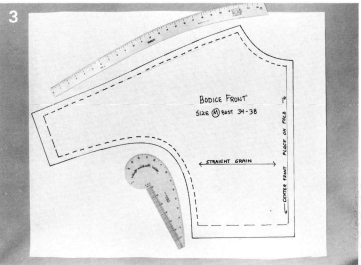

Drafting

1. Sketch the pattern and take the necessary body measurements: center-front (CF) neck to waist, waist, CF to neck edge at shoulder (perpendicular to center front), neck edge at shoulder to waist, neck edge to wrist, and wrist. With a tailor's square, draw a vertical line for the center front about 4 in. longer than the CF-neck-to-waist measurement, then a perpendicular line near the bottom of it for the waist. Mark point A, measure up the CF-to-waist measurement, and mark point B. Mark point C, using the CF-to-neck-edge-at-shoulder measurement, and point D, using one quarter of the waist measurement. Mark point E at the neck edge, measuring up from the waist. 2. Draw a straight over-the-shoulder line (E to F), using the neck-edge-to-wrist measurement, at 66° from line C-E. Draw the wrist line perpendicular to line E-F, and mark point G one half of the wrist measurement from F. Draw the curves for the neckline and underarm line, using a French curve and/or hip curve. 3. Refine the over-the-shoulder line to curve out slightly at the end of the shoulder. Add seam allowances, mark the straight grain, and label the pattern. The pattern for the blouse back is identical, except that the CF neck point is about 1 ¼ in. higher.

ference, and center front to the neck edge at the shoulder, measured perpendicularly from the center-front line. The measurements should reflect the style and ease of the particular garment. For example, if you want the neckline to fall 1 in. below your collarbone, take the center-front-neck-to-waist measurement from this point.

You'll need a piece of paper about 7 in. longer than the neck-edge-at-shoulder-to-waist measurement and 2 in. to 3 in. wider than the distance from center front to wrist. Using your tailor's square, draw a vertical line for the center front and a perpendicular line near the bottom of it for the waist. Then mark the points that correspond to your measurements by measuring from the center-front line. Mark the point of the center-front neck (B), using the neck-to-waist measurement; mark the shoulder point (E), using the neck-edge-to-waist and the center-front-to-neck-edge-at-shoulder measurements. Mark the remaining points, and continue as shown in the photos.

Some guidelines—Whether you get involved in flat patternmaking, draping, or drafting, you should keep the following guidelines in mind.

• Sew an original pattern in muslin first.
• When two pattern pieces connect, the corners that meet must form a straight line (or as close to straight as possible if the line is curved, as in a neckline).

• Curves should be smooth, with no irregular dips or bulges. Double-check them against a hip curve or French curve. Another way to check is by eyeing them from table level, much as you would check to see if a piece of wood is warped.
• If two hanging pieces, as in a skirt, are joined on the bias, their degrees of bias must be equal in order for the seam to hang straight.
• The fitting of curves, such as in the hip area of the side seam, should be gradual. For example, when you're fitting a large-hipped, small-waisted woman, you must distribute the curves in the seams, darts, and ease, not just at the sides.
• Keep the center-front and center-back seams straight. Although there are exceptions to this rule, you can achieve perfect fit if you stick to it, and it is probably best to learn this way.
• The two sides of a dart must be equal in length. The seam edge from which a dart originates must bow out so that the angle of each dart line to the seam line is 90°.
• To achieve a straight look over a curved body part, you must often curve the pattern pieces, as for example, in a princess seam from the shoulder.
• Don't forget to add seam allowances! □

Rebecca Lanxner Nebesar, a graduate of Cornell College of Human Ecology, is a patternmaker and designer in Canaan, NY.

Further reading

The best way to learn any of these patternmaking methods is through classes where you get hands-on experience. Most state universities have home-economics departments that teach these skills, and any city with a garment industry usually has a fashion institute or trade school with patternmaking courses. The following books are good reference sources.

Armstrong, Helen Joseph. *Patternmaking for Fashion Design.* New York: Harper & Row, 1987.

Bray, Natalie. *Dress Pattern Designing: The Basic Principles of Cut and Fit,* 5th ed. London: Collins, 1986.

Bray, Natalie. *More Dress Pattern Designing,* 4th ed. London: Collins, 1986.

Brockman, Helen L. *The Theory of Fashion Design.* New York: John Wiley and Sons, 1965 (out of print).

Hollen, Norma R. *Pattern Making by the Flat Pattern Method,* 5th ed. Minneapolis: Burgess, 1972.

Jaffe, Hilde, and Nurie Relis. *Draping for Fashion Design.* Reston, VA: Reston, 1975.

Kopp, Ernestine, et al. *How to Draft Basic Patterns,* 3rd ed. New York: Fairchild, 1984.

McCunn, Donald H. *How to Make Sewing Patterns,* rev. ed. San Francisco: Design Enterprises of San Francisco, 1977.

Practical Smocking

A fitting approach to fullness in garment design and embellishment

by Elizabeth Mattfield

Smocking, the delight of doting grandmothers and a technique for texturing every imaginable surface, was once an integral part of the countryman's work smock.

In 18th-century England, smocking was added to simpler overshirts to control fullness without creating tight, binding garments. During this time, virtually all fabrics were handwoven and precious, and the rectangle was the standard form for pattern cutters. Smocking provided a way to make the top of the shirt front or back smaller so it would fit on the shoulders, while leaving some elasticity and increasing the garment's warmth. The smock was a male garment, and the British countryman had an everyday smock to keep him warm and clean at his work, plus his Sunday dress smock. Early smocks were handmade by female relatives or specialists, and some are known to have passed through several generations.

Smocks became less desirable by the middle of the 19th century. Their fullness made them unsafe around dangerous farm machinery at the same time that machine-made cloth was becoming cheap and available. Although the smock hung on as a ceremonial garment for a while, the younger generation eventually rejected it and its traditional, rural connotations.

Meanwhile, attempts by middle-class observers of rural life to revive smocks had brought them to the attention of the fashion world. In the late 19th century, smocked garments were fashionable for women and children, and women's magazines told diligent housewives how to add smocking to any uncluttered surfaces remaining in their Victorian homes. Smocking has maintained its popularity in children's clothes and wan-

Elizabeth Mattfield used cable and trellis smocking for ease and interest on the front and sleeve cap of her silk blouse.

From *Threads* magazine (October 1988) 19:36-39

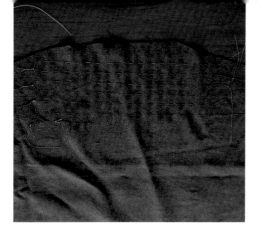

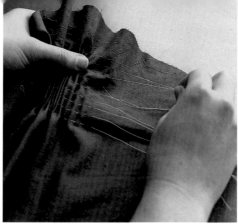

Mattfield has stitched through the rows of iron-on smocking dots that she applied to the wrong side of her material.

Next, she pulls very gently on the end of each of the threads to produce the pleats she will use for smocking.

To protect the finished smocking, she trims the front seam allowance and binds it with the yoke seam allowance in a false French seam.

ders in and out of style for adult clothing and household decoration. But smocking is in need of rehabilitation. It has been overused for decorative effects, particularly in precut panels that contribute neither to fullness nor ease in a garment.

I was introduced to smocking through baby dresses and fancy cushion covers. I became enamored of the technique, but I didn't know any girl babies or want elaborate pillows, and I didn't need a workman's smock either. So I began trying to figure out how and where smocking could be used appropriately as an integral part of contemporary adult garments instead of merely as surface decoration.

Smocking controls fullness and adds elasticity, and the smocked areas provide some insulation. It seemed to me that if one or more of these characteristics wasn't a part of the garment design, smocking wasn't being appropriately used, and I've tried to incorporate these features in my work.

Style considerations—There are a number of commercial patterns for smocked garments in addition to books with instructions for making smocked garments. You can also adapt a commercial pattern or design one. I recommend using a commercial pattern or book project for your first smocking, unless you're accustomed to making your own patterns. Whether you're choosing a pattern or designing one, several factors are important for making a garment that uses smocking appropriately and attractively. You can learn a lot from making Folkwear's English work smock, and the envelope is fascinating reading.

When you've seen how smocking affects yardage and hang and you understand the constraints that it imposes, you'll find it much easier to design new patterns or adapt existing ones, as I did for my smocked blouse at left (see photos above and drawings at right).

Make sure the smocking is placed where its bulk and weight won't be a problem. One of my early projects was a man's shirt that nearly strangled the wearer because the weight of the smocking and extra fullness of material fell behind the shoulder and dragged the shirt back. This wouldn't

have been a problem if the fabric had been very lightweight or if some of the smocking had fallen in front to balance better.

I've seen sketches of smocked skirts, and a smocked-waist dress is a lovely idea, but few women look good with the emphasis and extra bulk at their middles, so I probably won't ever make either.

Smocking is also somewhat elastic. This characteristic is valuable in allowing extra ease for movement, but it also means that there's a potential for smocking to droop and sag out of shape if it doesn't run horizontally when worn. Therefore, rectangular shapes are the most convenient for smocking. The smocking should run straight on the grain of the material to hang well; curves are difficult to work with. Other pieces of the garment can be curved, of course, unless you're making an authentic smock.

Designing with smocking—There are many more possible stitches for smocking than those shown on pp. 52 and 53. They vary in visual effect and elasticity. I recommend using embroidery thread for the smocking. Cotton for cotton, silk for silk, wool for wool, etc., will make garment care easier. But cotton also works well on preshrunk goods of other fibers, and a brand like DMC comes in sufficient colors to match or contrast nearly any material.

The color of the smocking thread and the amount visible in the stitches used are major design features. I prefer monochromatic effects, which I think look subtle and rich, but whatever effect is desired, the choice of smocking stitches and color is worth serious consideration at the design stage.

When you're choosing materials, the hand of the fabric is important. A fairly crisp fabric works up easier and looks nicer than a limp one. Very heavy fabric is hard to work with and bulky when smocked. A medium-weight crisp cotton or linen is a good first choice. Remember that the smocked area will pull up to about one-third its flat width, so patterns will have to be slashed to allow room (see drawings at right). If you forget that, you may be looking for little people to give your work to.

You must pleat and gather the area to be smocked very carefully (see photos above)

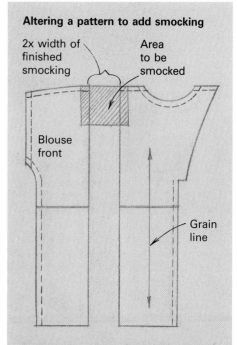

Altering a pattern to add smocking

2x width of finished smocking

Area to be smocked

Blouse front

Grain line

Cut pattern all the way down where smocking and additional fullness are desired, and spread pieces to twice width of planned smocking.

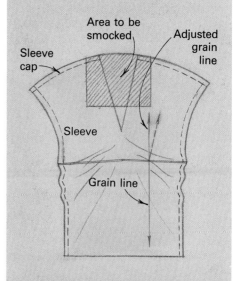

Area to be smocked

Adjusted grain line

Sleeve cap

Sleeve

Grain line

Cut a "dart" to add a little smocking without fullness. Spread pattern to twice width of smocking and taper to nothing below panel. Correct side seams by raising shoulder line ½ in.

before you can begin the actual smocking. You can either do this by hand or you can use a pleating machine. The information on the process is given at right. Illustrated smocking books are also useful for showing technical details, even if you don't accept the author's design decisions.

After smocking the garment, you'll cut and assemble almost as usual. If the top of the smocked area will be in a seam, leave the top gathering thread in place until you've sewn the seam to keep the gathering even. Make sure that all smocking threads end in a firm knot or in backstitches that can't be seen. If possible, enclose all raw edges in false French seams or seam tape (see right photo, p. 51). The added bulk of the smocking may make this difficult, but the seam finish will strengthen and protect the smocked area, as well as improve the garment's appearance.

There are a number of ways to use smocking that make it a functional part of modern garments. First, of course, are overshirts, smocks, blouses, or men's shirts. Smocking can go on the shoulder, it can replace the yoke, it can go below the yoke (front or back), or it can be put on sleeves or cuffs. It can be a small panel in front, at sleeve tops, at cuffs, or at all three places, as shown in the photo on p. 48. A peasant blouse is beautiful with the front, back, and sleeve tops gathered at a smocked neck yoke. You can smock a dress in any of the places suggested for blouses. Smocked-waist dresses or skirts or harem pants smocked at the ankles might be perfect on someone you know. Smocking at the neck is practical for maternity dresses, nightgowns, slips, and camisoles. It makes an apron or a sunbonnet fancy.

When you're adapting or creating smocked garments for yourself, you'll find that you'll be much more successful solving many of the design problems if you remember the functional origins of smocking in the English countryman's overshirt. Smocking isn't for everything, but it's ideal in a lot of modern adult clothes. □

Elizabeth Mattfield lives in Long Beach, a tiny town on the Pacific coast in Washington. A graduate student in archaeology, she smocks and knits to keep her sanity.

Further reading

Douglas, Sarah. *The Pleater Manual,* 1986. Available from The Smocking Bonnet, Box 555, Cooksville, MD 21723.

Durand, Dianne. *Smocking: Techniques, Projects, & Designs.* New York: Dover, 1979.

Holland, Allyne. "Graphing Techniques." *The Smocking Arts,* issue 26 (Winter 1986), pp. 14-16.

McCarn, Ellen. *Ellen McCarn on English Smocking,* 1986. Available from The Smocking Bonnet, Box 555, Cooksville, MD 21723.

Smocking techniques   by Debbie Ott

Smocking is the process of working embroidery stitches to secure pleats in gathered fabric. The pleats can be formed as the smocking is done or prior to stitching. Smocking stitches can be worked over preformed pleats for a crisp, formal appearance. Softer, less defined gathers form when the pleating is done during smocking.

Steps in a smocking project—Once you've chosen the floss and fabric for your project, test-gather a strip of the fabric to determine the fullness desired. Then calculate how much flat fabric will be needed, as explained below, or use a pattern designed for smocking where the calculations have already been done.

Next, preshrink and press the fabric to prepare it. Since it's easier to gather along a straight edge, either rip your material along the edge or pull a thread to cut along, and iron it again.

If you're gathering by hand, iron or baste smocking dots (tissue-paper transfers come with commercial patterns or can be bought separately) onto the wrong side of the fabric in the area to be smocked, or count threads. Then gather the fabric, tie off the gathering threads, spread the fabric, and steam-set it. If you plan to pleat while stitching,

mark dots on the fabric if necessary; and if you're machine-gathering, follow the manufacturer's directions.

When you've finished smocking, remove the gathering threads or wash the fabric to remove the dots, spread the smocking to the desired width, and pin it down to steam-set it. When the smocking is completely dry, construct the project.

Pleating the fabric—Before cutting, make a pleating sample to figure out the appropriate ratio of flat to gathered fabric for your material. Medium-weight broadcloth in the flat state needs to be three times the width of the smocked area—a ratio of 3:1. Thus, a 15-in.-wide smocked area needs 45 in. of flat fabric. Lightweight fabrics, such as batiste and many silks, will use a ratio of 4:1; heavier fabrics, such as challis, pinwale corduroy, and lightweight denim, might use ratios of 2½:1 or even 2:1. If you pleat by hand, you can use almost any fabric. Pleating machines pleat only a certain range of fabric weights.

To gather by hand for preformed pleats, you can use purchased smocking dots, which you iron or baste onto the *wrong* side of the fabric. They're usually indelible, so before you apply them, test the fabric to make sure they won't show

Smocking stitches

Outline stitch
Bring needle up at left of first pleat and insert from right to left through each subsequent pleat. Keep thread above needle for outline stitch and below needle for stem stitch.

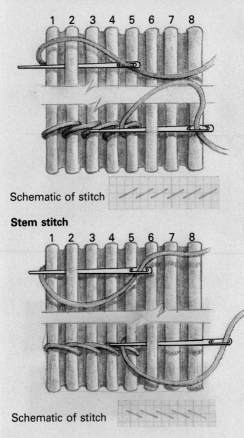

Schematic of stitch

Stem stitch

Schematic of stitch

Cable stitch
Bring needle up at left of first pleat and, with thread below needle, insert right to left through second pleat to form down cable. Form up cable through next pleat by keeping thread above needle. Alternate cables across row.

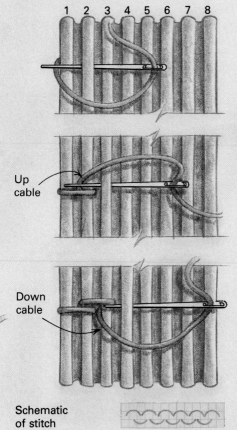

Up cable

Down cable

Schematic of stitch

through. If the fabric is sheer, baste the dot tissue to the wrong side, and remove it after you've gathered the dots.

Use quilting thread because of its strength, and pick up the dots by inserting the needle into one side of the dot and pulling it out the other. After you've picked up all the dots, each row on its own thread, gather the fabric to form pleats. You can pleat an even-weave fabric, such as that available for counted cross-stitch, by counting threads (pick up four threads every ten threads, for example).

Steam the pleats before and after smocking (when you've removed the gathering threads) to set them, especially with lightweight or slippery fabric. Hold the steaming iron above the pleats until the fabric feels damp.

When the pleats have dried, spread them out to measure about one inch less than the desired finished width. Tie the gathering threads together in pairs to secure them during stitching. If the top or bottom edge is to be sewn to another piece of fabric, leave that gathering thread single so it can be used to keep the pleats aligned during construction.

To form pleats while stitching, you must mark the right side of the fabric. If you want to iron on smocking dots, make sure they'll wash out first, or baste them to the fabric. You can also mark dots on your fabric with a water-soluble fabric-marking pen and a ruler. For lightweight fabric, the dots and rows should be every ³⁄₁₆ in.; for medium-weight fabric, every ¼ in.; and for heavyweight fabric, every ⁵⁄₁₆ in. If you use dotted or gingham fabric, you can work the stitches over the dots or the intersections. Wash out the dots after smocking and before steam-setting.

Smocking stitches—Many of the stitches used in smocking are formed with a backward-forward motion similar to that used to make a backstitch. There are two design categories of smocking stitches: geometric and decorative. Geometric stitches, which are used to create abstract designs, are traditional and tend to be more elastic. Some of the commonly used stitches are shown on this page and the next. They include stem/outline, cable, wave, trellis, feather, and Vandyke.

Decorative stitches are less elastic. They include daisy stitch, satin stitch, French knot, bullion stitch, and picture smocking, which stacks cable stitches in rows to create areas of color.

Stitching hints—The gathering thread in prepleated fabric marks the rows for smocking. But rows can also be visually subdivided. I like to use two strands of cotton embroidery floss for geometric designs with a #8 crewel needle and three or four strands for picture smocking with a #6 or #7 needle. But smocking stitches can be formed with almost any type of thread or string, as long as the strands don't drift apart after being pulled repeatedly through the fabric. Your needle should make a hole just large enough for the thread to pass through.

The needle moves horizontally through the pleats, parallel to the gathering threads, except for the feather stitch, where it moves diagonally. Work the stitches over the top third of the preformed pleats. For right-handers, the needle enters the right side of the pleat and exits on the left, and the smocking progresses from left to right. The two stitches that go the other way are feather and Vandyke. Left-handers should reverse these directions.

As a rule of thumb, when the stitching is progressing upward, the thread stays below the needle; when it's progressing downward, the thread stays above it. However, work a down cable with the thread below the needle, and an up cable with the thread above. Be consistent; pick up the same amount of pleat with each stitch and gently snug up the stitches so the pleats sit nicely side by side.

Debbie Ott is a weaver and spinner in Manitoba, Canada, who also enjoys smocking, particularly on christening gowns and Christmas ornaments.

Wave stitch
Work a down cable on row 2. Keeping thread below, insert needle through pleat 3 on row 1.

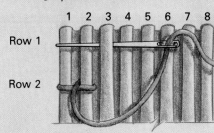

Move thread above needle and complete up cable on row 1.

Keeping thread above needle, insert through pleat 5 on row 2, and bring thread below needle to complete a down cable. Repeat these steps to form up cables on row 1 and down cables on row 2.

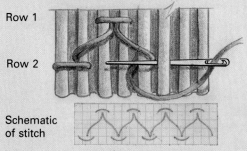

Schematic of stitch

Trellis stitch
For a two-step trellis, work a down cable on row 2. Insert needle through pleat 3 ½ row up; then work an up cable on row 1. Insert needle through pleat 6 ½ row down; then work a down cable on row 2.

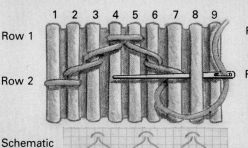

Schematic of stitch

Feather stitch
Work from right to left, angling needle upward and moving down by ¼-row increments. Then angle down and move up at same rate, as shown. Work over one old and one new pleat each time.

Schematic of stitch

Vandyke stitch
Working from right to left, begin in second pleat from edge. Work stitch over two rows, using one old and one new pleat each time, as shown.

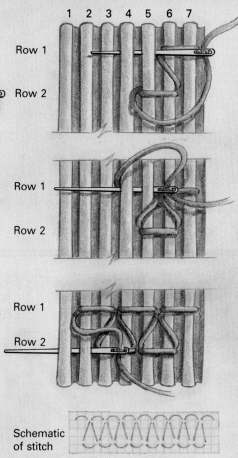

Schematic of stitch

The Poetry of Sleeves

Shaping and sewing cloth to fit the arm

by Rebecca Lanxner Nebesar

the poetry of sleeves is indisputable. Sleeves move with the body. They reach out to touch. They embrace. They are active extensions of ourselves. They fray at the elbows. They express joy, victory. With lace at the cuff they add a frivolous touch; left alone, a serious tone. They can be wings to fly on or straight-jacket strings to tie on.

Classic sleeves are classic for good reason. They work. They are timeless. But every age invents or reinvents. New fabrics, occupations, and uses challenge us to reach beyond the classics to find new forms that will become the classics of the future.

There are no hard and fast rules about sleeves. But there are three generalizations that are just about always true: Sleeves must have two holes, one for the arm to go in and one for it to go out; the tighter the fit, the more shaping in the cut is necessary; the sleeve-cap seam line should be at least as long or longer than the armscye seam line (the armscye is the garment opening to which the sleeve is sewn).

With knits, however, these rules are of limited value. Each garment, each armscye, and each sleeve design present unique requirements. For example, a ribbed knit has so much more give in the width than in the length that a well-cut, well-fitted sleeve can have a cap seam line that's shorter than the armscye, and the sleeve may require little shaping in the cut. Books that tell you exactly how to position the French curve when drafting a sleeve pattern are far too rigid, as each situation is different.

I'll use the basic fitted sleeve to explain the parts of a sleeve and how they work together. Once you understand the mechanics of the basic sleeve, you can experiment with other shapes. The drawing at top left on page 26 identifies the parts of a sleeve.

The cap—The sleeve cap is the section of the sleeve above the underarm line—the area that fits the upper arm, especially as it relates to the armscye. The arm is not flat; it is full and rounded. The cap must be shaped to fit the curve of the shoulder and the deltoid muscle of the upper arm and allow arm movement. Since darts in a sleeve cap would be distracting, ease is added to the cap to shape it. The cap seam line is made longer than the armscye, and the extra fabric is pulled in (eased) to create the appropriate roundness for the upper arm. Ease works especially well on sleeve caps because the cap seam line is cut on the bias, and so it responds beautifully and discreetly to easing. How much longer you make the cap seam line than the armscye depends on individual measurements and the desired fit. Generally 1 in. to 2 in. extra length in the cap is adequate for a fitted sleeve, but more or less is possible. Too much ease will create a gathered, puffy shoulder area, inappropriate for a classic fitted sleeve. To reduce the ease, trim down the cap a bit. Too little ease will cause the cap to pull across the deltoid muscle and will pinch, throwing off the fit of the body of the garment. To remedy this, recut the entire sleeve, unless you have left generous seam allowances (always a good idea), in which case just sew a narrower seam.

There are two axioms concerning sleeve caps that almost always hold true. First, the smaller the angle of the arm to the body in the garment's styling (for example a suit jacket versus a T-shirt), the longer the cap seam line must be, and vice versa (see drawing at right, page 56.). When the arm is hanging down, the distance from the wrist to the shoulder is about 5 in. to 7 in. longer than that from the wrist to the underarm. Thus, a garment styled with the sleeve close to the body has the extra length in the cap. When the arm is raised to a T position, these two distances are approximately equal, and a garment styled with the sleeve outstretched has no cap. Second, the closer the shoulder line is to the body (for example a raglan shoulder as opposed to an extended padded shoulder), the longer the cap seam line must be and the more ease it must have, and vice versa.

The back slope of the cap on a basic fitted sleeve is more gradual than the front slope. We pull forward on the sleeve more than backward, and the gradual curve gives the extra width needed in the back. On most people, too gradual a front slope generates an unsightly blip where the cap line hits the cap seam line, just before the sleeve slips out of sight under the arm.

Break points—If you use commercial patterns, you're familiar with the front (single) and back (double) notches on a sleeve's shoulder seam. These notches are at the break points. Above a line connecting the notches (the cap line) is the part of the sleeve that shapes the sleeve cap. Below the notches is the area of the sleeve cap that fits the underarm. When you raise your arm, the garment's break-point area remains relatively stable, whereas the cap area folds together, and the underarm area is pulled. In this way, the break points are pivot points. In a sleeve pattern, the curve of the cap changes from convex to concave at the break points; the S curve shifts direction, or "breaks," at these points. On a basic fitted sleeve these points are about a third of the way up the cap from the underarm line, and the front break point is slightly lower than the back one.

Gussets—A gusset is a piece of fabric incorporating bias stretch that is usually inserted into a slash or a seam under the arm. It adds fabric below the break points and allows a full range of arm movements without wreaking havoc in the hang of the garment body. It also prevents stress on the underarm seams and arms.

There are basically three types of gussets—square, football-shaped, and built-in—although there are variations. The drawing at bottom left on page 56 shows these basic types. The football-shaped gusset and built-in gusset both take into account that the break points are pivot points. As long as the gusset extends from the front break point to the back break point, the sleeve won't bind, and the fit of the sleeve cap will remain undisturbed. Too short a gusset won't work. The width of the gusset

(continued on page 58)

From *Threads* magazine (February 1987) 9:24-29

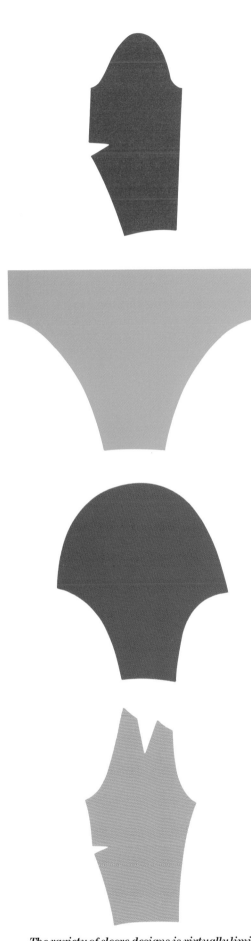

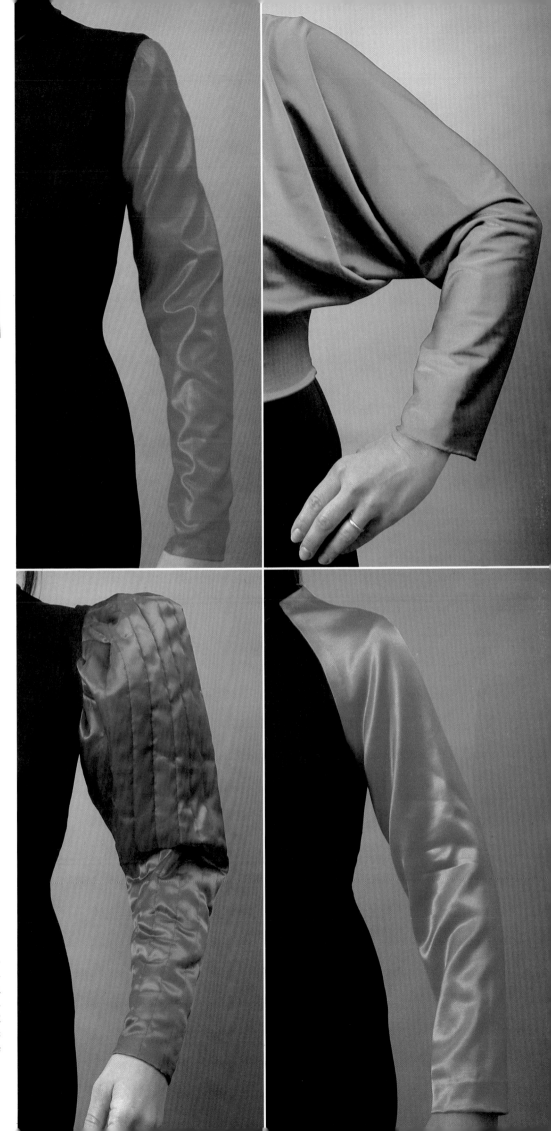

The variety of sleeve designs is virtually limitless. A few of the classic sleeves and the patterns from which they were shaped include a basic fitted sleeve (top-left photo and top pattern), a dolman sleeve (top-right photo and second pattern), a gigot sleeve (bottom-left photo and third pattern), and a raglan sleeve (bottom-right photo and fourth pattern).

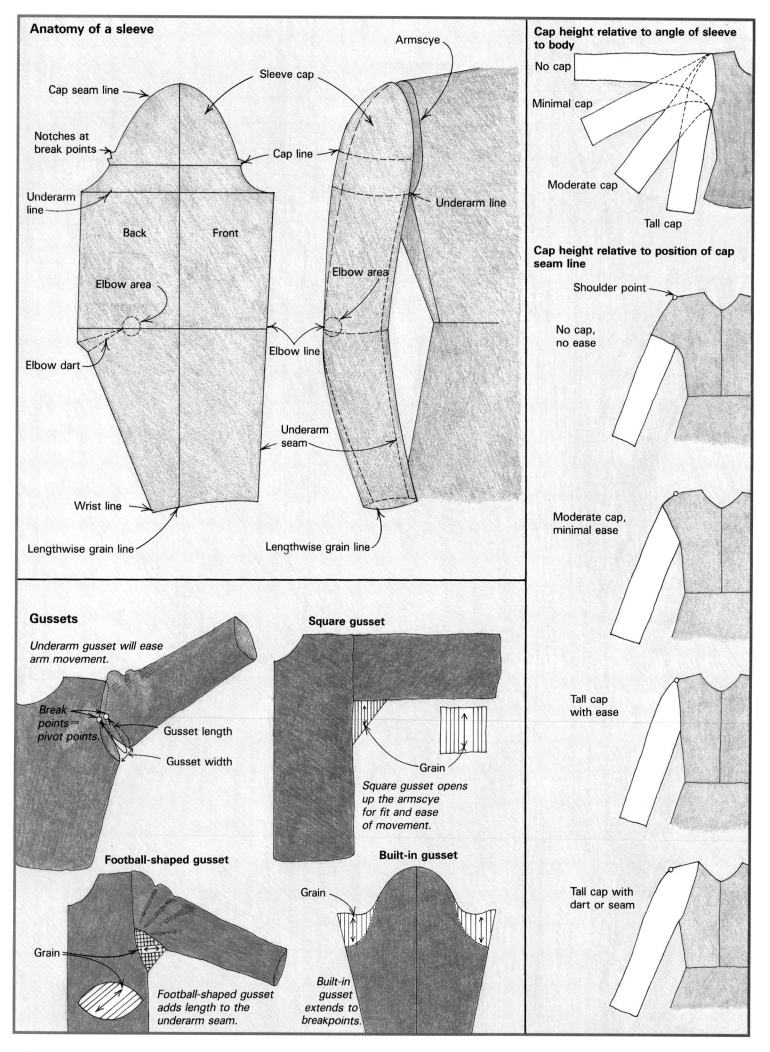

Anatomy of a sleeve

Cap seam line

Sleeve cap

Armscye

Notches at break points

Cap line

Underarm line

Underarm line

Back   Front

Elbow area

Elbow area

Elbow dart

Elbow line

Underarm seam

Wrist line

Lengthwise grain line

Lengthwise grain line

Gussets

Underarm gusset will ease arm movement.

Break points = pivot points.

Gusset length

Gusset width

Square gusset

Grain

Square gusset opens up the armscye for fit and ease of movement.

Football-shaped gusset

Grain

Football-shaped gusset adds length to the underarm seam.

Built-in gusset

Grain

Built-in gusset extends to breakpoints.

Cap height relative to angle of sleeve to body

No cap

Minimal cap

Moderate cap

Tall cap

Cap height relative to position of cap seam line

Shoulder point

No cap, no ease

Moderate cap, minimal ease

Tall cap with ease

Tall cap with dart or seam

Tape a rectangular piece of paper into a cylinder. Draw a line around the top, with the bottom of the ellipse at the taped edge, and cut along the line.

Open the cylinder, and you have a simple sleeve shape.

Sewing a set-in sleeve

Nothing gives away an amateur sewing job more quickly than a puckered, twisted, or lumpy sleeve. Common errors include poorly distributed ease at the cap, wobbly seam lines, notches and dots that are not matched, sleeves sewn in backward or even upside down, and seam allowances caught in the seams.

Before starting to stitch your sleeve, consider the fabric. Is it easy to handle? Or is it slippery? Loosely woven? Bulky? Velvet? Each fabric requires special handling. You'll need pins or basting stitches or both, especially with tricky fabrics. To check for fabric slippage as you machine-stitch, test-sew together two identically marked samples of your fabric. If the marks aren't aligned after stitching, you may have to pull the under fabric more than the upper or hand-baste.

On each sleeve, mark front and back, top and bottom, and all dots and notches. Put a safety pin in the middle of the sleeve cap on the inside to distinguish the right from the wrong side. For consistency, complete each step on both sleeves before going on to the next.

For a smooth cap with well-distributed ease, first sew a line of easestitching, using the longest machine stitch with slightly loosened tension on the top thread, as for gathers. Sew around the cap from notch to notch (break point to break point) just in the seam allowance, next to the seam line. If you sew too far from the seam line, you're liable to get puckers in the cap.

Pull the bottom thread to make the cap pull in to approximately the length of the armscye from notch to notch. Distribute the gathers gradually upward toward the shoulder peak from both sides. There must be a smooth transition from the lower armhole to the gathered cap, with most of the ease in the shoulder-peak area. The seam allowance will ripple, but the cap should be smooth. If it is not, you may have pulled too hard, so loosen the easing thread. Knot the threads, or wrap them around a pin to secure your carefully prepared easing. With a malleable fabric such as wool, you can put more ease in the cap and still maintain the cap's smoothness by pressing, steaming, and shaping over a dressmaker's ham. Generally it's a good idea to press the ease area before you sew in the sleeve.

Hand-baste the sleeve into the armscye, try on the garment, and check in the mirror before machine-sewing, especially on easily marred fabrics. It is cleaner and less frustrating to catch and correct errors before they take the wind out of your sails or send you jogging around the block. Never sew with tiny stitches; they're too hard to remove. Eight to 12 stitches per inch is small enough.

For beginners, sewing in the sleeve in two sections is easier than doing it in one step. First stitch the underarm area from notch to notch, making sure the underarm seam allowances of the bodice and sleeve are pressed open and not pulling. Stitch again for strength. Then sew from notch to notch over the shoulder. If you start and end a little below the notches, thus overlapping the underarm stitching, you won't have to backstitch.

More experienced sewers can sew the sleeve in one step. Starting at the front or back notches, stitch under the arm, then up to the shoulder and back around under the arm and up to the opposite notch so the underarm is reinforced with a double line of stitching. There's no need to backstitch.

I like to sew on the sleeve side, with the sleeve right side out and the body of the garment inside out, flipped back over the sleeve. This way, using a regular sewing machine, I sew on the inside (wrong side) of the sleeve and can readily see my ease stitches so I can make subtle adjustments as I sew and avoid puckers. But with a thick fabric, like a coat wool, I reverse this. I take advantage of the fabric's thickness to smoothly distribute the extra length of the sleeve-cap seam line around the shorter armscye seamline. A free-arm sewing machine comes in very handy here. If you always use a free-arm, you will no doubt sew on the body side, with the free arm inside the sleeve. Be sure you have the seam lines in the ease area well lined up.

When I'm too lazy to baste, I often sew over pins on a difficult sleeve. I put the pins perpendicular to the seam, pointing away from the seam allowance, about 1 in. apart, and pin on alternate sides to prevent a ridge. To avoid broken machine needles, stitch slowly and hand-turn the wheel as the pin approaches.

Trim, do not clip, the underarm section between the front and back notches. This reduces binding and distributes tension evenly. Clipping will weaken the seam. There is usually no need to clip or trim the shoulder area, unless a heavy fabric requires grading and/or V clips to reduce bulk. Never trim closer than ¼ in. from the seam line. Always overcast with a zigzag or serge stitch. Better yet, tape the seam edges with double-fold bias tape.　—*R.L.N.*

can be varied, though; the wider the gusset, the greater the freedom of movement.

Hang and the elbow dart—The elbow dart is probably the most mysterious part of the sleeve. It is hidden under the arm, and we know it adds finesse to the fit, but why? The elbow does not hit the underarm seam; it hits the middle of the back half of the sleeve, in what I call the elbow area.

If you bend your arm in an undarted tight sleeve, you'll feel constricted at the elbow. The elbow pushes against the sleeve back, and the sleeve pulls in the front. Because of this, the sleeve needs some extra fullness in the elbow area. We get it by elongating the back-underarm seam line and slanting the hemline at the cuff down at the back of the sleeve. We then add a dart to the back-underarm seam line, pointing toward the elbow area, to take up the extra length. The dart provides the needed shaping. Ease, instead of a dart, will achieve the same shaping. In Germany, the whole sleeve is made longer, and a fish-eye dart is sewn in the front of the sleeve at the elbow line. Not very discreet, but to the point.

When the arm is relaxed and hanging down naturally, it is bent slightly at the elbow and leans a little toward the front. The sleeves of well-fitted garments mimic this position so that wrinkles won't distract from their beauty and shaping.

If you place an unsewn, one-piece fitted sleeve flat on the table, you'll see that the front seam is cut more on grain than the back seam, which looks bent, like an elbow. It's bent so the sleeve will bend forward, not backward, once the dart is sewn. The result is a sleeve that follows the natural hang of the arm, has extra width at the elbow for ease of movement, and is slightly longer in back than in front. A line drawn on the straight grain from the shoulder to the wrist hits the wrist line toward the back, not in the center. A striped or plaid fabric demonstrates this clearly.

Even if you never design and pattern your sleeves, I hope you have a better understanding of them. They're not the formidable, mysterious things they sometimes seem to be. Redesigning a sleeve shape often requires no change to the armscye, even if you alter the sleeve cap. There's a lot of flexibility in sleeve shapes, and the design possibilities are virtually limitless. If you don't know where to begin, try the exercise in the drawing on page 57.

Sleeves never cease to amaze and inspire me. I love being in control of them—to feel that I have the freedom to envision and realize my own creations. I love it when sleeves transcend the mechanics and their magic takes over. Born of a pattern, with our help sleeves can speak a language of imagery. □

Rebecca Lanxner Nebesar is a clothing and costume designer who has worked in Boston and West Germany. She lives in Canaan, NY. Photos by Joseph Kugielsky.

Fitting the fitted sleeve

When you use a commercial pattern for a fitted sleeve, the finished sleeve often doesn't meet your expectations. Most people aren't standard sizes, but they know how to alter the length only. Aware of this, pattern companies make loose armscyes by lowering the underarm of both sleeve and armscye. The result is a fitted sleeve that doesn't fit. Here are some ways to avoid disappointment.

Measuring—Take body measurements and check them against the pattern before you cut. Measure for sleeve-cap width, upper-arm width, forearm width, back length over the elbow, elbow-to-wrist length, and wrist width, as shown in the drawing below.

When measuring, hold the arm slightly bent and away from the body. Flex the muscles. If you are right-handed, measure your right arm (it is bigger); vice versa for lefties. Bend your hand back at the wrist to measure the length. To find the proper spot to measure from the shoulder, put a forefinger on your shoulder where the arm joins the shoulder. Press to feel the joint, and raise your arm; if your finger moves in, you are not on the shoulder. To measure for cap width, first tuck your forefinger under your arm horizontally as high as you can, and clamp down. Where your finger sticks out in front and in back are the break points, or notches. Measure over the deltoid muscle from one break point to the other. Always hold the tape loosely to allow for some ease in fit; a skin-tight sleeve is usually too tight, unless you are sewing with a knit fabric. If your hand must fit through the cuff with no closure, measure the widest part of the hand instead of the wrist. Compare your measurements with the pattern measurements.

Alterations—Knowing that commercial patterns have loose armscyes, cut the

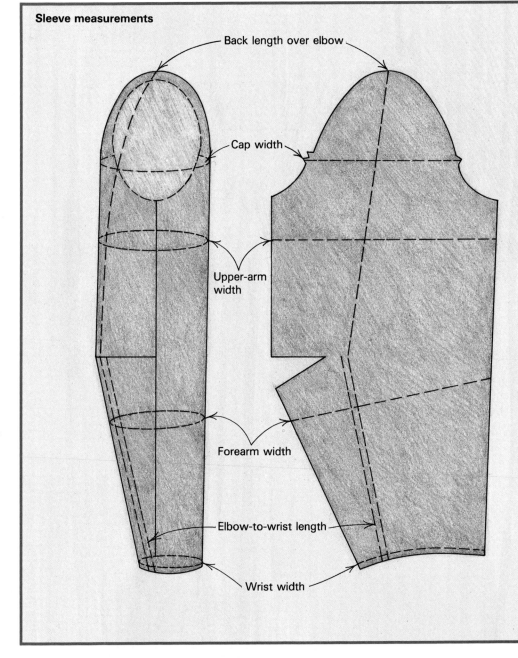

Sleeve measurements

Back length over elbow

Cap width

Upper-arm width

Forearm width

Elbow-to-wrist length

Wrist width

underarms of the sleeves and armscyes about 1 in. higher, as in the drawing at right. You can always lower them.

If the sleeve cuts you at the break point (usually the front), cut the sleeve a little wider there, and trim the curve of the body in that area. This is a common problem with athletes. If the sleeve pulls across the cap, widen the curve of the sleeve cap a little so that the curve is not so steep. You can also raise the cap slightly.

If the whole sleeve is too tight, slash the pattern lengthwise all the way down, centered on the lengthwise grain, and spread it apart. If the sleeve is too loose, overlap the pattern halves and increase the underarm seam allowance. Round out the curves in the cap where the pattern was spread or overlapped. You may need to cut the armscye larger or let out the side and shoulder seams (or do the reverse if you've made the sleeve narrower).
—*R.L.N.*

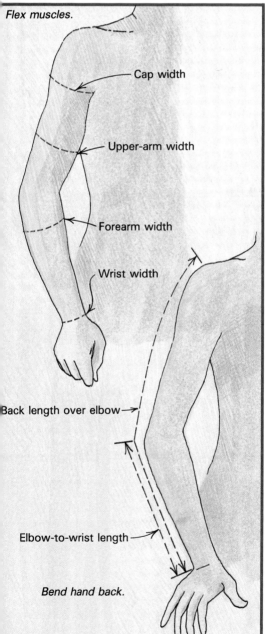

Flex muscles.

Cap width

Upper-arm width

Forearm width

Wrist width

Back length over elbow

Elbow-to-wrist length

Bend hand back.

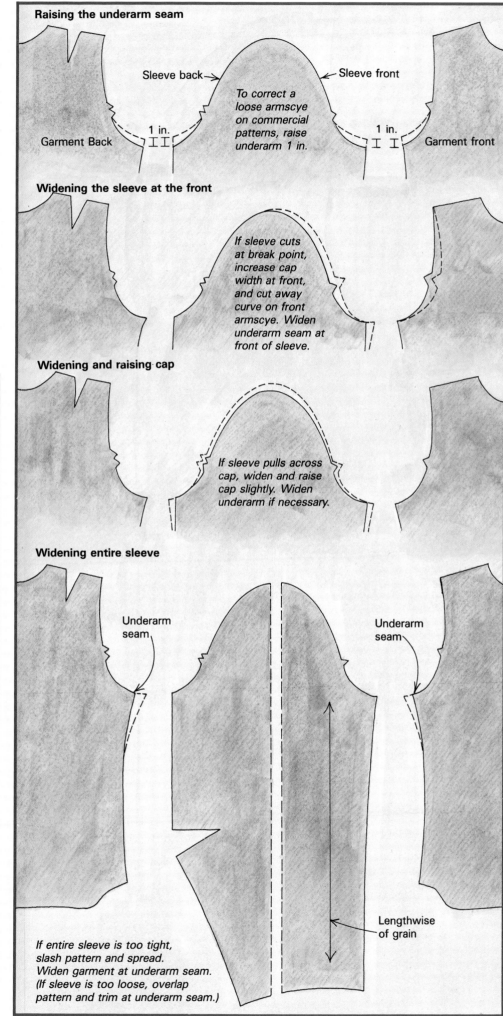

Raising the underarm seam

Sleeve back → ← Sleeve front

To correct a loose armscye on commercial patterns, raise underarm 1 in.

1 in.   1 in.

Garment Back   Garment front

Widening the sleeve at the front

If sleeve cuts at break point, increase cap width at front, and cut away curve on front armscye. Widen underarm seam at front of sleeve.

Widening and raising cap

If sleeve pulls across cap, widen and raise cap slightly. Widen underarm if necessary.

Widening entire sleeve

Underarm seam   Underarm seam

If entire sleeve is too tight, slash pattern and spread. Widen garment at underarm seam. (If sleeve is too loose, overlap pattern and trim at underarm seam.)

Lengthwise of grain

Understanding the Waistband

Fitting band to waist means more than just making ends meet

by Margaret Deck Komives

Considering how basic they are, waistbands can cause sewers lots of trouble. And considering how much the wearability and appearance of skirts, slacks, and shorts depend on well-fitted waistbands, it's a good idea to take a close look at them.

It makes sense to refer to the waistline as a line; you can usually establish its position with a piece of string. But where a band will rest in relation to this line depends on both the width of the band and the shape of the figure above and below the line. High-hipped figures, for example, will hold bands high against the waistline, and wide bands will almost always need to be longer than narrow ones to accommodate the figure's larger measurements on each side of the waistline, as you can see in the drawings below and on the facing page.

My students and I tested these ideas in class. For example, when we measured the waistline on my dress form with a tape measure, it measured 27¾ in. A length of 1¼-in.-wide stiff waistband interfacing pulled snugly over this same waistline measured 28¼ in., and 2-in.-wide interfacing measured 28⅝ in. The greater the difference between the waist and hips, the longer that wider bands will need to be. Straight figures will notice less or no difference as bands get wider.

At the same time, we noted where the bottom edge of these waistbands fell in relation to the waistline string—in other words, where the waist seam allowance of the garment should be. On the dress form, the edge of the 1¼-in. band was ⅜ in. below the string; the 2-in.-band fell ¾ in. below the string.

Getting it right—Pattern companies routinely add 1 in. to the given waistline measurement for waistband ease, but that may not suit your style or provide the comfort you want. In my class, we fit each student by analyzing a garment with a waistband that feels right to her. The first step is to examine the position of the side seams. Do they really fall at the side, or do they veer to the front or, less likely, to the back? Put a pin in the spot you choose for the side seam, on both sides. Make sure the pin is the same distance from the existing side seam on each side. Then, with the garment off, measure the band and note the length of the front and back waistbands. The centers should be halfway between the sides. Also note the width of the band.

In class we record all this information by transferring it to a length of ribbon or tape

Matching waistbands to waists

Each of these three waistlines measures the same size, but because each figure is shaped differently, an identical waistband will comfortably fit each waist in a different position. To adapt this principle to your own figure, fit each band you make to your waist before attaching it to the garment; then mark along the bottom of the band onto the fitted garment to establish the seamline.

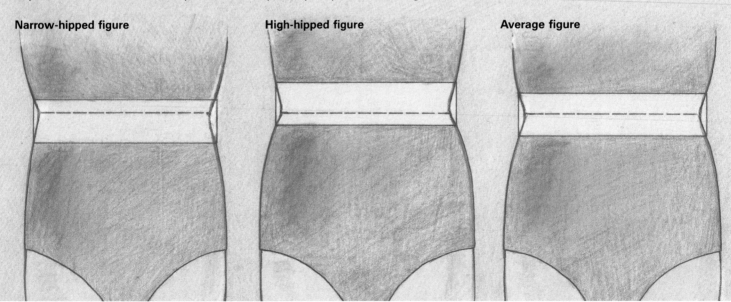

Narrow-hipped figure   **High-hipped figure**   **Average figure**

that doesn't stretch, which we refer to as a "waist-tape." Armed with a waist-tape every time you make the same width waistband, you can adjust it easily to match the tape. You will need to make minor adjustments for different weights of fabric, but until your waistline changes, you'll have a a permanent waistband pattern. If you want more than one width of band, make as many fitting bands as you'd like out of stiff fabric belting in your chosen widths, and mark each so it becomes a waist-tape.

When trying to determine the best position for the waistline seam on a new garment, most people automatically pull the unfinished garment up so that the specified seamline rests at the waistline. This creates a common fitting problem: After the band is attached and it settles naturally below the waistline, the garment will try to rest slightly lower on the figure, as well. If it has been closely fitted to the hips, it won't be able to, and the result will be crosswise ripples just below the band.

We've found that a best guess for the seamline during a first fitting is to position the seam allowance's cut edge at the actual waistline. Assuming you've cut out at ⅝ in., this puts the seam ⅝ in. below the waist. Variations from this are generally minimal.

A more precise approach, which we prefer, is to prepare the waistband first and chalk below it onto the garment during fitting. Prepare the waistband with the interfacing you prefer, using the dimensions from the same width waist-tape, and press it to its finished width. Mark the side and center points from the waist-tape, and pin the band to size over the garment with the marks in the proper place. Chalk a line below the band and put in tailor tacks along the markings. Then apply an ease thread to the chalk line in order to fit the gar-

ment to the band so that the marks align. If the waistline is much smaller than the hip area just below it, you may have to deepen tucks, darts, and side seams a little bit. With some fabrics you'll be able to steam out any puckers caused by easing.

You can fit garments with elasticized waists in a similar way. Try on the garment; then adjust the elastic over it until you're happy with the fit. Mark above the elastic for a fold line instead of a seamline.

Contoured waistbands—There are some figures for which waistlines are difficult to locate. One way to determine where the waistline should be is to have the wearer bend sideways. The body should bend at the waist, but often this area seems to lie between two alternate locations. The uppermost of these is usually smaller than the lower. Typically, a woman will prefer the smaller upper waistline because of the snug feeling and smaller size, even though the result is a short-waisted appearance. Men usually prefer the lower location.

One effective design for this type of figure is a contoured waistband, the top edge of which rests on the desired waistline area, and which continues the shaping of the darted hip area of the garment, as shown in the photo below. If your pattern comes with a contoured band, cut a muslin from a firm interfacing like stabilizer Pellon. If you need more length, add it at the center back and front, not at the sides as you normally would, so you don't alter the curve. Verify and adjust the side seams just as you would do with a straight band. Once fitted to your taste, the adjusted Pellon can serve as a contoured waist-tape.

To make your own contoured band, cut a strip of firm interfacing to the width you want and the length you need. Slash the

interfacing from the bottom edge up to about one quarter from the top edge at each quarter mark and at least twice again in each quarter. With the top edge against your preferred waistline, tape the band closed at a comfortable length, and tape each slash so the amount of spread each takes comfortably is preserved. Use as many slashes as seem appropriate. You may have to move the waistline seam up or down on the garment to suit the new band, but you won't need to alter the garment's waist contour.

Interfacings—Your choice of waistband interfacing will have a major impact on the comfort and appearance of the finished band. The softer the band, the more comfortable it will be, but the less it will hold its shape. You can use the following interfacings (listed from softest to firmest): Fold-a-Band (formerly Fuse-n-Fold) from Pellon and Waist-Shaper from Stacy are common options among fusibles. Shapewell, or some other firm woven fusible, fused to the entire waistband, is frequently used in ready-to-wear. Alternately, you could cut a strip of fusible Acro hair canvas the width of the finished band and then fuse it to the outer layer, excluding the seam allowances.

All the above methods can be attractive and appropriate, but none results in a waistband that won't roll. Only the stiffened interfacings sold as Ban-Rol and Armoflexxx really always spring back flat after you bend, and so they have become my favorites. (Ban-Rol is widely available from retail and mail-order fabric stores. Armoflexxx can be ordered from The House of Laird, Box 23778, Lexington, KY; 606-276-5258.) Ban-Rol does not shrink appreciably, and its edges are covered to keep it from piercing through the outer fabric and scratching. It is also available in elastic.

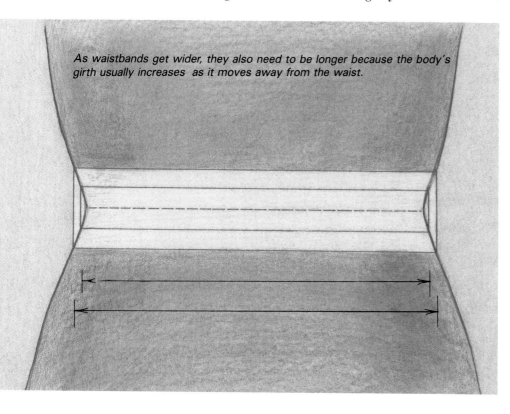

As waistbands get wider, they also need to be longer because the body's girth usually increases as it moves away from the waist.

Contoured waistbands stop at the waistline, not above it, and continue the shape of the skirt beyond the darts.

Armoflexxx does shrink considerably, and its edges are uncovered, but you can trim it to any width, and after you preshrink it, you can contour it with a hand iron. A yard of Armoflexxx shrank 1¼ in. after I tossed it into a permanent-press wash load. I regained ¼ in. by pressing it while it was still damp, and I discovered I could shape it to match the contour of my waistband. Before you put Armoflexxx in a waistband, you can singe the edges, fuse a strip of Easy-Knit over them, or coat them with Tacky Glue or Fray Check. If you plan to contour Armoflexxx, finish the edges later.

Applying waistbands—One way to fit the garment to the prepared waistband is to match the seam marks, with band and garment right sides together, easing as necessary. Pin or baste them together, and try the garment on before final stitching. Finish the ends as shown in the bottom-left drawing below, and then the inner edge. If the fabric is bulky, I trim away the inside seam allowance and serge or overcast it. Slipstitching the inner edge gives a softer, more flexible result, but stitching in the ditch or topstitching will save time.

It is also possible (and a time-honored menswear technique) to cut out the band so that you can use the selvage as a prefinished inside edge. This obviously requires that the band be cut on the lengthwise grain, but the lengthwise grain won't stretch as much as the cross or bias grain.

A simple method you can use to achieve excellent, though not nonroll, results is to cut the band with the selvage as the inner edge, fuse it to lightweight, firm interfacing, and then press under the outside seam allowance. Topstitch the band along the fold to the garment, matching the side and center marks and easing the garment as necessary. Then finish the ends and, finally, the inner edge, by any method you like.

Apply an Armoflexxx or Ban-Rol waistband by first machine-basting it to the seam allowance of the band with a straight or zigzag basting stitch, as shown in the top-left drawing below. Then apply the band to the garment, right sides together, stitching close to the edge of the interfacing, finishing the ends and inner edge as you like.

Here's how to apply a contoured band: First shape the band and the Armoflexxx to match. Then seam the band to its facing at the upper edge. Next, staystitch and clip the seam allowance of the garment, and join it to the lower edge of the band, right sides together. Press all layers toward the band, insert the Armoflexxx beneath the just-pressed seam allowance, and pin it close to the stitching. Carefully fold away the band so you can machine-baste the seam allowances to the interfacing. At this point we like to stabilize and cover the upper edge of the Armoflexxx by fusing a narrow strip of Easy-Knit over the edge, stretching as we press. Finally, tuck it all underneath the top-edge seam allowances, finish the edges, and slipstitch the inside edge by hand. See the drawing at right, below, for a detail of the process.

One style of waistband won't work for every garment, but I have it down to a few styles. For a summer garment, for which I like a narrow band for cool comfort, I use the topstitched method. If appearance and longevity are major factors and I know that the band will be worn exposed, I use the Armoflexxx technique. I've used it with all kinds of fabrics. And years after I've made them, I can still wear them with pride—firm, crisp waistbands without a wrinkle or a roll. And they fit! □

Margaret Deck Komives teaches all levels of sewing at the Mequon Campus of the Milwaukee Area Technical College. See her article on fitting pants on pp. 66-69.

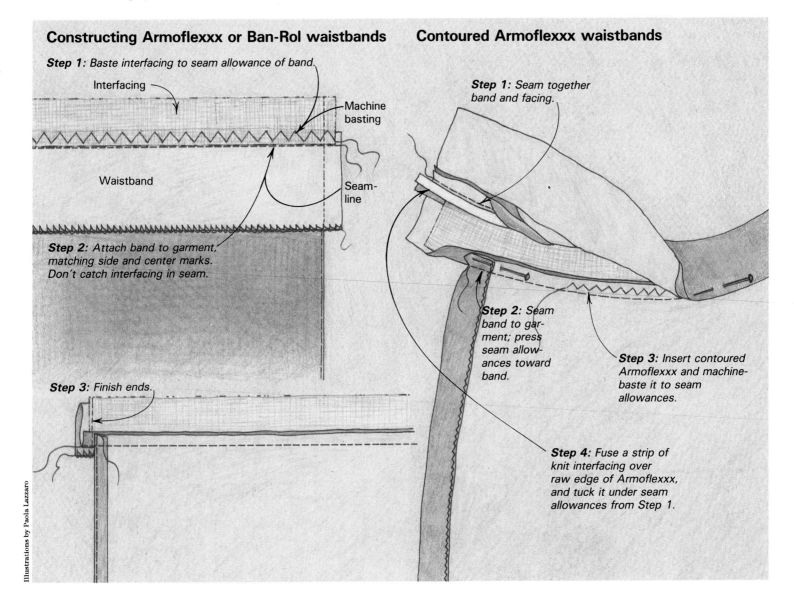

Constructing Armoflexxx or Ban-Rol waistbands

Step 1: Baste interfacing to seam allowance of band.

Interfacing

Machine basting

Waistband

Seam-line

Step 2: Attach band to garment, matching side and center marks. Don't catch interfacing in seam.

Step 3: Finish ends.

Contoured Armoflexxx waistbands

Step 1: Seam together band and facing.

Step 2: Seam band to garment; press seam allowances toward band.

Step 3: Insert contoured Armoflexxx and machine-baste it to seam allowances.

Step 4: Fuse a strip of knit interfacing over raw edge of Armoflexxx, and tuck it under seam allowances from Step 1.

Illustrations by Paola Lazzaro

Making Swirly Skirts

With gathers, gores, or tiers, the circle can be as full as you want

by Grace Callaway

Illustration by Jayne Ludlow

t he new look in skirts for spring is full and decidedly feminine. Billowing gathers, swirling tiers, and swinging circles are not difficult to sew, and with just a little bit of planning, any figure type can enjoy these new skirt styles.

If you're short or stocky, keep most of the fullness below the hipline. But too much fullness, even below the hips, will overwhelm a petite figure. Tall, slender bodies easily balance the extra fabric, and the ad-ditional fullness helps camouflage the an-gularity of some longer-limbed women.

Pay close attention to selecting the right fabrics. Heavy or crisp materials stand away from the body, creating an illusion of more bulk, while soft ones drape and cling for a narrower image. Small prints are kind to small, short, and wide figures; large prints, stripes, and plaids don't lend themselves to some full-skirted styles. They can be spectacular in circular skirts, though match-ing plaids and stripes is very tricky.

All the pattern companies offer full-skirted styles in their spring lines, but if you're fa-miliar with the basic cuts, you can adapt an existing pattern or quickly make your own. For many of us, our first garment in beginning sewing class was a plain *gath-ered skirt*. It requires only two or three straight seams, a waistband, and a hem.

The width of a gathered skirt needs to be one-and-one-half to four times the waist measurement, depending on the desired amount of fullness and the weight of the

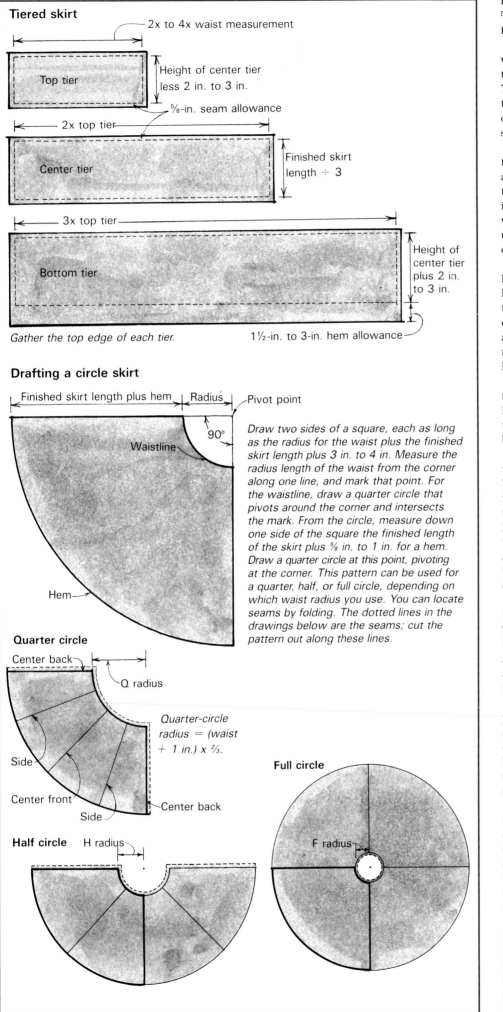

Tiered skirt

2x to 4x waist measurement

Top tier

Height of center tier less 2 in. to 3 in.

⅝-in. seam allowance

2x top tier

Center tier

Finished skirt length ÷ 3

3x top tier

Bottom tier

Height of center tier plus 2 in. to 3 in.

1½-in. to 3-in. hem allowance

Gather the top edge of each tier.

Drafting a circle skirt

Finished skirt length plus hem | Radius | Pivot point

90°

Waistline

Hem

Draw two sides of a square, each as long as the radius for the waist plus the finished skirt length plus 3 in. to 4 in. Measure the radius length of the waist from the corner along one line, and mark that point. For the waistline, draw a quarter circle that pivots around the corner and intersects the mark. From the circle, measure down one side of the square the finished length of the skirt plus ⅝ in. to 1 in. for a hem. Draw a quarter circle at this point, pivoting at the corner. This pattern can be used for a quarter, half, or full circle, depending on which waist radius you use. You can locate seams by folding. The dotted lines in the drawings below are the seams; cut the pattern out along these lines.

Quarter circle

Center back

Q radius

Quarter-circle radius = (waist + 1 in.) x ⅔.

Side

Center front

Side

Center back

Half circle H radius

Full circle

F radius

Cut out the front and back skirt panels, which should be of equal width, and stitch the side seams, leaving one seam open about 7 in. at the top for the placket. If you wish to add a zipper, insert it next, or if you're omitting the zipper, finish the placket edges so they won't ravel.

Although there are several ways to gather fabric, zigzagging over a cord is best. Place a piece of cord, such as gimp or perle cotton, along the seam line. Holding the cord in front of the presser foot, zigzag over it with a stitch of maximum width and medium length, being careful not to catch the cord with the needle.

Pin the cord at the center back and pull half the gathers from one direction and half from the other. Match the skirt edge to the waistband, adjusting fullness as needed, and baste the band in place. When you are sure no more adjustment is needed, remove the cord. Stitch the waistband and hem the bottom of the skirt.

A *tiered skirt* is also made from gathered rectangles—generally three—sewn together horizontally. Tiers are most attractive if they vary in height and if the second tier begins above the fullest part of the hips.

An easy way to determine dimensions is to divide the finished skirt length by three. Use the answer as the height of the center tier. Then subtract 2 in. or 3 in. from the top section and add it to the bottom tier. For example, if your finished length is 27 in., the center tier is 9 in. high, the top is 7 in., and the bottom is 11 in. Keeping the center tier one-third of the finished skirt length ensures pleasing proportions.

The width of the top tier should be from two to four times the waist measurement. The center section is twice as wide as the top one, and the bottom tier is three times as wide as the top. When you compute the amount of fabric you'll need, remember to figure in seam allowances and hems.

Begin sewing by joining the ends of the panels for each tier, leaving an opening for a placket in the top section. Gather the top edge of the first tier and sew it to the waistband. Gather and stitch the top edge of the second tier to the bottom edge of the first. Sew the third tier to the second, and hem.

Circular skirts include all of the styles with curved hemlines, whether or not there's enough fabric to spread out into an actual circle. They are more complicated than gathered skirts and take more time to make. You can make your own pattern or adapt an existing one, although you will save time by selecting a commercial pattern.

The simplest variations are parts of circles, like a half circle, quarter circle, or full circle, each divided into four wedges, or gores, by the seams at front, back, and sides, as shown in the drawing at left. You can create endless variations of these shapes by dividing, reshaping, or combining. With

fabric. To the desired finished length, add ⅝ in. for a waistline seam and 1½ in. to 3 in. for a hem at the bottom.

gored skirts there are no darts to slow down the sewing, the built-in flare adds ease without greatly widening the silhouette, and the seam lines add length and slenderness to the short or full figure. Skirt shapes based on circles are easy to design yourself and are all classic styles. The closer the skirt is to a full circle, the more width you'll have at the hipline.

If you decide to make your own circle-skirt pattern, you'll need to know the radius of the circle formed by your waist measurement plus 1 in. for seams. You can be mathematically correct about it, or you can approximate it by adding 1 in. to your waist measurement and dividing by 6. If your skirt is a full circle and your waist is 29 in., add 1 in. for seams and divide by 6: a circular opening with a 5-in. radius will fit your waist.

For skirts that are less than complete circles, you will have to refigure the radius of the waist circle. The waist radius of a half-circle skirt is one-third the waist measurement; that of a quarter-circle skirt is two-thirds the waist. Once you know the waist radius, you can make a pattern on paper, as shown in the drawing at left. Tie a string to a pencil to draw the waistline on the pattern. Then check the measurement by standing a tape measure on edge around the curve. Adjust the line until it's 2 in. longer than your waist (enough for a seam and ¾ in. of ease).

A commercial pattern will have grainline markings on the pieces, but you can change the placement to have the fullness fall on your body the way you wish. There is no way to prevent some sagging of the hemline when parts of a garment must be on the bias. Loose weaves sag more than firm weaves, and the crosswise grain sags more than the lengthwise grain.

If the sides of the skirt fall on the bias, while the center front and back of the skirt are on the straight grain, the sides will sag, and you will have an uneven hemline. In addition, placing all of the flare at the sides of the body creates a wider silhouette. If you cut the skirt so that the straight grain is at the sides, the sides will hang straight while the centers sag. This silhouette is straighter and more slenderizing, however. I would probably position the straight grain halfway between the center and the sides. This distributes the fullness evenly around the hemline.

You should start to control sag when you're stitching seams. Use the same technique as for seaming knits—stretch while you sew in order to put as much give into the seam as there is in the surrounding fabric. To further remove sag, allow circular skirts to hang for at least several hours before hemming. Some fabrics must hang for several days. Check the length of the bias sections. When they stop getting longer, the fabric has stopped sagging.

A quicker method of removing sag is to pull down on the bias seams as you press.

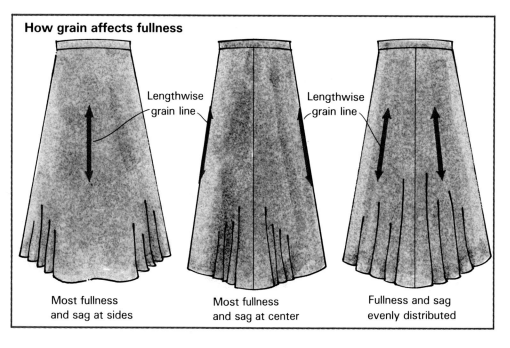

How grain affects fullness

Lengthwise grain line

Most fullness and sag at sides

Lengthwise grain line

Most fullness and sag at center

Lengthwise grain line

Fullness and sag evenly distributed

Since a seam can't stretch more than it will ultimately sag, you can remove most of the sag in this way, but you probably can't pull hard enough to prevent some sag from showing up later.

When it comes to preparing the top of the skirt for attaching the waistband, stay-stitch slightly more than ½ in. from the cut edge. To allow the curved edge to straighten, clip to the stitching at ½-in. to ¾-in. intervals all around the waistline.

On skirts with straight edges at the bottom, you can use any type of hem you want. With circular skirts, however, narrow hems look best and are least bulky. A neat finish that works well on all full skirts, straight or circular, requires only a ⅝-in. hem allowance. Turn up ¼ in. and stitch in place. Turn up again ⅜ in. and stitch ⅟₁₆ in. from each edge. If you prefer only one visible line of stitching, sew the final row ¼ in. from the bottom edge.

You can add extra fullness with overskirts, underskirts, and petticoats. Overskirts go on top of the skirt panels and are sewn together with the skirt at the waist. Underskirts go underneath the skirt sections and give the look of a petticoat peeking out. They may be plain, ruffled, or lace-edged.

Separate petticoats will add all the extra fullness you may want, but be careful not to spoil the outer silhouette with an undergarment that is too bulky in the wrong places. Keep petticoats close to the body until just below the fullest part of the hips, where most of the flare should begin.

The petticoat should conform to the shape of the skirt. Cut the petticoat for a circle skirt from the same pattern as the skirt. A gathered skirt can have a petticoat with the same fullness or less, but not more. A tiered petticoat or an A-line petticoat with a flounce at the bottom will reduce some of the fullness at the waist and hip. The A-line shape makes a good, basic petticoat foundation on which you may sew ruffles for extra fullness. One or more rows of horsehair or nylon braid stitched around the bottom of a petticoat will hold it out in a smooth circle, like a hoop. You can use feather boning in the same way. Just be sure the circle of the petticoat isn't too big around, or the braid won't support it.

Crinoline is a favorite petticoat fabric because it's crisp and light, so you get fullness without a lot of extra weight. Since crinoline ravels easily, finish all raw edges before assembling the petticoat. A serger is perfect for this task and will make quick work of gathered skirts also.

Organza is stiff and very thin, so it, too, is good for petticoats. It's made from cotton, silk, or polyester, in a wide range of colors. Sheer nylon tricot comes in both crisp and soft versions and is often used for square-dance petticoats. There is a new semicrisp version that doesn't fray, but it isn't widely available (you can order it from Fit For You, 781 S. Golden Prados Dr., Diamond Bar, CA 91765). Tulle, which you can find among bridal fabrics, also offers fullness without weight. One or two layers for the body of the petticoat can easily support multiple rows of ruffles.

There are two ways of obtaining superfull skirts by combining gathers with the circle-skirt style. The first way is to double or triple your waist measurement and use that number to figure the radius. Gather it to fit your waistband. This method takes a lot of fabric, and there is a good bit of waste, but the results are worth it. The second way is to cut twice as many pieces as you would for the basic style, seam them together, and gather the top to fit the waistband. Silks and silky blends will give you the most fullness with the least bulk. You'll see these methods used in many commercial patterns and ready-to-wear swinging skirts this spring. □

Grace Callaway, a frequent contributor to Threads *magazine, teaches clothing design and construction at Georgia College.*

A Fitting Pair of Pants

Adjusting the curve is the key

by Margaret Komives

Pants were not always part of a woman's everyday wardrobe. It wasn't until the early '40s, when Rosie the Riveter went to work in the arms plant that women began to wear what is now considered such an essential garment.

I remember the first pair of women's pants that I dealt with as a sewing teacher. They were extremely easy to fit because the length from waist to crotch was so long in those days (see top photo, p. 69) that all I had to do was fit the waist and the hips. If you could fit a skirt, you could just as easily fit a pair of pants. Nobody had crotch problems in my classes.

I still have a pattern from those "good old days." It was copyrighted in 1952, it cost 50¢, and it measures 12¾ in. from waist-line to crotch line. My most recent purchase, in the same size, measures 11½ in. (and cost $5.50). Little by little, as this more snug fit became fashionable, our problems in fitting increased.

In the early '70s I found myself waist deep in the problem of pants fitting. I was teaching in evening school and department stores, and more and more women wanted to wear pants. I'd read everything available and could come close to getting a good fit, yet I still didn't feel I had the answers.

One day, a student brought in a pair of good, ready-to-wear pants that fit so well she wanted help in copying them. They had a certain beautiful hang to them that ours lacked. A close examination revealed there was something very different about the crotch curve—it sloped downward from front to back.

In the wee hours of the following morning, I suddenly recalled a diagram from my college anatomy text that showed cross sections of the female and male pelvises. The text read: "The female pelvis tips from front to back." The light finally dawned! I could now see what had been the underlying problem with fitting women's pants. The crotch curves weren't shaped like a woman's pelvis. Correcting this curve (left-hand drawing, p. 68) so it would follow the female pelvic structure has become the basis of the fitting method I've applied to pants ever since. Let's go through it step by step.

What size pattern to buy?—More than likely the home sewer will opt for a commercial pattern, and the first question she'll ask is: "What size pattern should I buy?" In my classes, we've found it easier to fit a

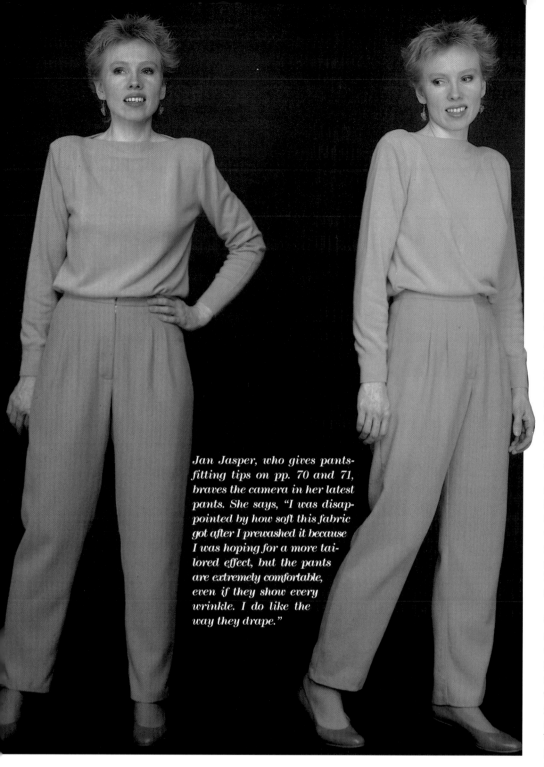

Jan Jasper, who gives pants-fitting tips on pp. 70 and 71, braves the camera in her latest pants. She says, "I was disappointed by how soft this fabric got after I prewashed it because I was hoping for a more tailored effect, but the pants are extremely comfortable, even if they show every wrinkle. I do like the way they drape."

A more accurate method is to measure the side-seam area of the figure from the base of the interfacing to the floor and from the inseam area at the base of the crotch, also to the floor. Or, preferably, if you have a pair of pants that fits, measure them the same way. Subtract the inseam measurement from the side seam, and the result will be the crotch length.

You'll need to add ease to body measurements. The rule of thumb is to add ½ in. for small sizes, ¾ in. for average sizes, and 1 in. for large sizes, but firmer fabrics may require more to be comfortable, and some people prefer more room. If you're measuring pants, and the top of the inseam looks crumpled, it's a sign that the pants were stretched, so add a bit of ease in this case too. But don't overdo it. The crotch curve can be lowered but not raised.

You can establish the crotch length when you're fitting the muslin if you add an inch or more above the presumed waistline seam as you're cutting out the muslin. Then, after you've fit the pants, trim away the excess. However you do it, it's a good idea to leave some room for experiment when you're cutting the waistline seam.

For the hip measurment, measure the fullest part of the hip, usually about 7 in. to 9 in. down from the waist. Also measure the high hip, which is 3 in. down from the waist. We've observed that as a figure matures, what used to be a full seat is often replaced by a fuller tummy and high hip. You can usually solve this problem by shortening, and sometimes curving, the darts.

The last measurement to take is the "depth-of-figure," or "waist-to-waist," measurement, which combines the crotch length with the distance through the figure, front to back. A figure can be wide from side to side but small from front to back, or vice versa. The hip measurement won't give any indication of depth-of-figure, and commercial patterns often pay no attention to it. We compared a size 12 pattern with a size 20 pattern made by the same company and found that the distance between center-back and center-front seams was actually smaller on the size 20! The size 12 pattern allowed 7¾ in., while the size 20 allowed only 6½ in.

You can find this distance by measuring the crotch seam of a comfortable pair of pants. Measure the front and back separately from the inseam. Another method is to use what is known in the trade as a crotch-ometer. You can make one by taping or stapling together two tape measures so the zeros meet and then hanging a weight by a string from the join. Measure from the base of the waistband in the front to the base of the band in the back, with the weight centered between the ankles, as shown in the bottom-right photo, p. 69. Write down the front and back measurements; then subtract 1 in. from the front and add it to the back, which seems to always improve the

muslin that's too small rather than one that's too large. If it's tight, you can usually see where it's tight, but if it's loose, it will probably appear loose all over, and you won't know where to start. We cut beyond the seamlines; copy carefully from the pattern at side seams, inseams, and waistline; pin the pants together on those lines; and let out only where it's necessary.

If you buy a conventional commercial fashion pattern and choose the size according to your hip measurement, you'll most likely get a pattern that's too full in the seat, especially if the pattern is described as loose-fitting. I'd buy one size smaller than the envelope suggests. Basic pants patterns, or those described as snug-fitting, generally have limited ease, and it would be wise to purchase that type of pattern by your hip measurement.

Taking measurements—We begin by taking a few basic measurements. As usual, it's important that the woman being measured wear the undergarments and shoes she'll wear with the finished pants. We put a length of nonroll waistband interfacing the width of the finished waistband around her waist and take all measurements from it.

First measure the waist. We've found that it's a good idea at the same time to estimate where the side seams should be and to mark them on the interfacing, as described in "Understanding the Waistband" (see the article on pp. 60-62). Next, measure the length of the figure from the base of the band to the crotch. One often-suggested technique is to measure the seated figure from the waistline to the chair. However, we've found this to be an unreliable method because you can't really tell where the crotch is.

hang of the pants. Finally, you can add ½ in. to 1 in. of ease, but I've often found that it isn't needed.

Correcting the pattern—After writing down your basic measurements, put them aside for a moment and take a good look at the pattern you've purchased. To see if it has a good crotch curve, we pin the inseams together, seam on top of seam, for about 4 in. below the crotch seam, as shown in the drawing at left, below, and check to see if it slopes downward from front to back. If it doesn't, sketch a new one as shown, being careful not to remove any of the pants width. Don't worry about the crotch measurements at this stage.

The next thing we do is shift the center-back seam. If the pattern shows only one back dart, we make two darts, with the second dart as wide as the amount we shifted the seam, and arrange them so that they divide the back more or less equally. You'll be amazed at how much flatter you'll look and how much more smoothly your pants will fit.

The secret behind the flatter appearance is this: A very angled center-back seam has the effect of one large dart right in the center of the back. The purpose of any dart is to provide fullness for a curve below. This fullness will fall right below the seat where it is probably undesirable. Jeans are cut this way, and it works—on some figures—because, with their snug-fitting thighs, this

is the only way to get any fullness in the seat. Dress pants should hang more smoothly, with no horizontal pulling, as shown in the right-hand photo on p. 71.

The same problem can exist in front if the center front is cut on an angle, as appears to be the current trend in patterns. The result is cupping at the base of the center-front seam, which seems to be inappropriate for women's pants.

Now, to use the measurements you've taken, correct the waistline overall by using the side-seam markings you established when you measured the waistband interfacing. If the tummy is full and some adjustment is needed, make it just below the waist in the form of ease, tucks, or very short darts beside the center front.

Once you've adjusted the darts to your liking, you can make a dart template by copying the entire top of the pattern onto a piece of cardboard. Cut around the seamlines and down into the darts, and trace it onto any skirt or pants pattern on which you want the same elegant effect.

At the hip you'll need at least 2 in. of basic wearing ease in addition to your hip measurement. Designer ease for front pleats or gathers will be added to this. You can expand the pattern at the side seams or, if side-seam details are in the way, expand it by slashing on the crease line down to the hem, tapering the slash so that the hemline is unchanged, if possible. The new grain line will be down the center of the

slash. If it looks as if the figure is full in the front but conforms to the pattern size in the back, only the front needs the addition, or vice versa.

The next adjustment to be made is for crotch length. Measure the front pattern from the waistline seam close to the side seam and parallel to the grain line, down to the crotch line. This line, running from the crotch point to the side seam, is usually shown on the back of the pattern. The adjustment will be more accurate if you measure the front, so draw a similar line, if there isn't one already, on the front pattern, perpendicular to the grain line, and through the crotch point. If you need to adjust, do both front and back equally, tucking or spreading above the crotch curve, but below the darts. It is very important to make this adjustment *before* you make the next one, for depth of figure, because you'll be changing the crotch-depth measure if you make the adjustment afterward.

Next, measure the front and back pattern pieces from the crotch point up to each waistline seam along the adjusted crotch curve, with the tape on edge. Compare this with your waist-to-waist measurement. At this point, you can make any adjustment, front or back, only by changing the respective inseams, pivoting from the knee line, as shown in the right-hand drawing below. Finally, recheck the curve for shape, and check the overall length; that should just about do it.

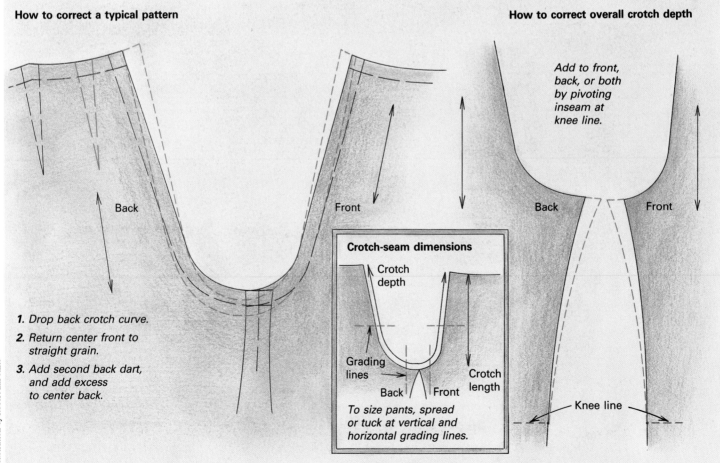

How to correct a typical pattern

Back

Front

1. *Drop back crotch curve.*
2. *Return center front to straight grain.*
3. *Add second back dart, and add excess to center back.*

Crotch-seam dimensions

Crotch depth

Grading lines

Back | Front

Crotch length

To size pants, spread or tuck at vertical and horizontal grading lines.

How to correct overall crotch depth

Add to front, back, or both by pivoting inseam at knee line.

Back

Front

Knee line

You probably already know if you have any other unique figure problems. Are your thighs heavier than average? Do you have a fuller-than-average tummy? Watch for these as you cut, and allow extra fabric or anticipate taking in a seam.

Making a muslin – It's important to cut your test pants from a fabric that's neither flimsy nor boardy, such as heavy muslin, poplin, kettle cloth, or twill. Then be sure to transfer all pattern markings, including seam allowances. When you've made the necessary corrections, you'll be able to transfer them accurately to your pattern.

One way to determine if the crotch curve you've drawn is right for you is to try on half the muslin. Clip and press away the seam allowances from the center-front and center-back seams of one leg of the muslin. Pin the inseam and side seam, and try the muslin on over a pair of panty hose. By lining up the center seams with those of the panty hose, you'll see how the pattern curve corresponds to your figure.

It's important that you follow a good procedure in assembling the test pants. The crotch won't hang properly if the inseams have been sewn as one continuous seam, up one leg and down the other. Sew the inseams, front to back, each set separately. Next, assemble the crotch seam and zipper. Then, fit the side seams, pinning right sides out and checking the darts, as described by Jann Jasper on pp. 70 and 71.

To remove excess fullness in the legs, pin out a tuck just beside the inseam, as shown in the bottom-left photo. This will correspond to the amount that you need to take out of the back inseam, tapering down to the knee line. If you take the excess out all the way to the hemline, you'll have to change the crease line so that it falls at the center of the leg.

Fabric affects fit – A perfectly fitting pair of pants from any pattern is often determined by the fabric you choose. One of my students achieved a truly lovely fit in a menswear suiting and then cut the very same pattern from a soft wool flannel; the flannel pants looked baggy. Gabardine and other hard finishes will look sharper and hold a crease better than softer fabrics. Bulky fabrics will result in a bulky appearance.

I suggest that you window-shop. What type of fabric do you think makes the best-looking pants? Take into consideration the total cost and the cost per wearing. A fine fabric will be a fine garment, and it won't stretch out of shape, wrinkle, or lose its crease. A well-fit pair of pants that is made from the right fabric will make your efforts completely worthwhile.

Margaret Komives teaches at the Mequon Campus of the Milwaukee Area Technical College. She is a frequent contributor to Threads *magazine.*

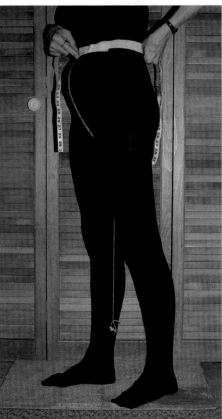

Katherine Hepburn (above) is blissfully unconcerned about the crotch length of her classic gabardines (The Bettman Archive, Inc.). Margaret Komives (below) adjusts the fullness of her student's pant leg by pinning out the excess close to the inseam. When she's satisfied, she'll remove an equivalent amount from the inseam, tapering to the knee. To use a crotchometer (right), center the weight between the legs and above the ankles. Measure to the center front and center back at the waistband. Add the measurements for the total crotch depth, and use each separately to adjust front- and back-crotch seamlines.

How to spot and correct three common pants-fitting problems

Wrinkles in the upper thigh and back crotch that point toward the front are probably the most common pants-fitting problem. They are the result of insufficient room in the back-crotch curve. You can correct them by adding to the back-crotch inseam.

Loose folds below the seat that don't fan out from the crotch often result from the center-back seam being cut too sharply off-grain. Fix this by returning the grain line (marked in pen on muslin) to a more vertical position and removing the excess in the dart, or darts.

by Jann Jasper

during the many years that I've worked as a professional patternmaker, I've identified what seem to me to be the most common pants-fitting problems, problems shared by manufacturers and home sewers. These also appear to be problems unsolved by most sewing texts and fitting methods. The method I prefer is to examine and correct pants right on the figure, by opening seams and letting the pants relax into a better fit.

The easiest way to begin is to study the best-fitting pants you've made. You won't destroy the pants when you release the seams. Instead, you'll discover how to correct the pattern from which you made the pants.

If you're not that far from a good fit, the photos and information on these pages may be enough to guide you to a solution without your having to open any seams. If you do go straight to the muslin-fitting stage, having adjusted your pattern from suggestions here and on p. 68, you can use the following analysis to fine-tune the muslin. The point is to learn what you can from an existing pair of pants before you cut another so the time you spend making adjustments will be as short as possible.

A sewing friend comes in handy of course, but you can do all the fitting and correcting I describe by yourself. Either way, your most important tools are two good mirrors. Place them opposite each other so you can see your backside without twisting around to look over your shoulder.

Mechanics of the crotch seam — To improve the fit of pants, the first thing you must understand is the distinction between crotch length and crotch depth and how they relate to the flat pattern. Total crotch depth is the measure you get by pulling the tape measure between the legs from center-front waist to center-back waist. Crotch length is the vertical measurement of your torso from your waist to the top of your thigh, as shown in the center drawing on p. 68.

The drawing also shows where patternmakers in the industry adjust these measurements to grade the pattern, or make it larger or smaller for different sizes. Adjusting the vertical measurement alone will change total length, but it won't deal with the thickness of the body front to back. This is why attempting to loosen a crotch that's too tight by merely altering at the "adjust-crotch-length-here" line shown on commercial patterns will help only if you're too short or tall for the pattern. Sewing the crotch seam lower at the inseam rarely works for the same reason and may aggravate the problem if the pant legs are tapered because then you'll also be tightening the top of the thigh. Unless your tight fit in the crotch results from your height alone, the solution is usually to widen the crotch hook, as explained below.

Problem 1: The back inseam — For a custom fit in pants, not only must the overall crotch measurements correspond to your individual figure, but the front and back crotch seams also must be the correct length and shape. To accommodate the buttocks and upper thigh, the back crotch hook must be longer than the front crotch hook. However, if you have a large stomach, the front crotch hook may need widening too. As womens' figures vary greatly here, the amount needed will vary, but fitting problems for many women are caused by the back crotch hook not being long enough. Especially if you have heavy thighs or a large buttocks, you should try the following experiment first to see if this is the problem. It can clarify and sometimes eliminate other problems.

A typical symptom of this are wrinkles fanning out downward from the back crotch, as shown in the left-hand photo above. Try releasing the upper inseam down to the knee. If the back crotch hook merely needs to be lengthened, the wrinkles will disappear. You can baste in a wedge of fabric to see the exact amount needed, or make a note to add fabric to the muslin. This single experiment may solve your biggest fitting problem.

Problem 2: The center-back seam — If your pants have a sharply angled (relative to the grain) center-back seam, you may still have wrinkles and folds below the buttocks, like those in the right-hand photo above, or the pants may still be cupping under the buttocks, but the wrinkles won't seem to pull into the crotch like the wrinkles from the first problem. Patterns designed this way are appropriate when you want a very tight fit in the seat and thighs. Often there is no dart on patterns of this type. For a fit that drapes smoothly down from the widest part of the hip, rather than cups in, the pattern must be widened at the center-back seam, starting from nothing at the hip level and increasing to an inch or more at the waist. Unsew the center-back seam from the waist seam to the hip level. You don't have to cut the waistband; it will help hold the loosened pants in place. Just unsew the waistband seam from center back to about halfway to the side seams. Again, you can add a wedge of scrap fabric, pinning it in the gap until the hang of the pants below the buttocks is smooth. The extra room you gain is needed across the derrière. At the high hip and waist, where it isn't needed, you add a dart or widen the existing one.

Problem 3: Back darts — If the hip circumference is adequate, but the darts look strained or have bubbles at the points, they may be the wrong width or length. A mistake commonly made by sewers is to try to fix this by lengthening the darts (see left-hand photo, facing page). What is usually required is to shorten or narrow them or do

From *Threads* magazine (August 1988) 18:36-37

When dart points extend beyond the widest part of the hips, unpin and shorten them. If the dart releases too much fabric over the hips, it's usually not because the dart is too short. Remove the excess from the side seam. This generally results in a narrower dart.

both. If you've made corrections to the center-back seam, the darts may also be in the wrong place. In either case, you must unsew them. Then put the pants back on and pin them in smoothly. If you have a full, rounded figure just below your waist, you may have to cut the pants waist a little looser and ease the extra fabric into your waistband in addition to using darts.

If there's a lot of adjusting to do above the hip, cut the back pattern of your muslin with extra seam allowances at the center back, waist, and side seams, and make the corrections as you fit the muslin.

Working with the muslin—When you've incorporated the desired changes into your pattern (or have allowed extra in the right places) and are ready to cut a muslin, use 1-in. seam allowances, except in the curved areas of the crotch seams, where you'll use the regular ⅝-in. seam allowance. You must also clip the crotch curve; otherwise, it will seriously distort all your efforts. Once you've clipped it, however, it's virtually impossible to retrace your steps, so clip carefully. Mark the darts, but don't sew them shut. Baste all seams together, but don't apply a waistband—fitting will be easier with the waistband off. If you can work with a friend for any part of this project, do so when you'll be fitting the back, but, as I've already said, you can do it alone. Try on your pants muslin, wearing a leotard underneath to provide a pinning surface, or tie a piece of elastic around your waist to hold the muslin up. Adjust the waist, hip, and crotch fit by again releasing the seams and letting out where tight or smoothing any excess into the side seams and darts where loose.

The important thing to remember is to let the fabric go where it wants to go. Don't distort it. For example, if the whole seat and crotch area isn't smooth, undo the center-back and side seams from the hip level, smooth the fabric upward so it's flat

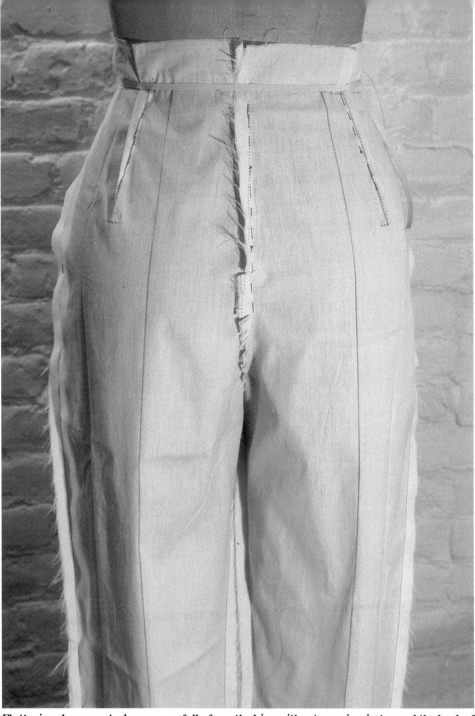

Flattering dress pants drape gracefully from the hips without cupping in toward the back of the thighs, and the inseams don't pull toward the front. The crease line, which is also the grain line, bends softly toward the center back but remains vertical.

over the buttocks and crotch, pin it at the waist, smooth it across the fullest part of the hips over to the center, and pin. Then smooth over the hips again toward the side and pin. Continue smoothing and pinning up to the waist.

The wrinkles at the waist should easily fall into a fold, which forms your dart. Pin in the dart and mark its end point. You can make minor dart adjustments when you try the muslin on with the waistband attached, but if the dart area seems really distorted, you may need to unpin and readjust the center or sides or do both. If the problem extends into the thigh, undo the seams that far, and follow the same procedure. Keep the grain straight up and down in the area between the side seam and dart.

When you're satisfied, take off the muslin and mark all the corrected seams and the inseams and outseams with notches. Then take the muslin entirely apart and smooth the pieces flat (don't iron them; it's too easy to distort the grain). Carefully pin the muslin pattern pieces to the corresponding paper pattern pieces. Transfer all markings and corrections. Then cut the corrected pattern out again in muslin, this time sewing on a waistband, and try it on. Don't be discouraged if you need to make further adjustments. It's normal to go through a few muslins before you get things perfect. Once you do, it will be well worth it. You'll never again have to waste your time and patience with sewing, or buying, pants that don't fit! □

———————
Jan Jasper of New York City is a professional patternmaker and artist whose media are fabric and clothing.

Sewing with Knits

State-of-the-art techniques for zigzag machines and sergers

by Jan Saunders

When polyester double knits burst upon the scene in the '60s, they indelibly changed the home-sewing world. The demand for sewing tools to handle knits gave us the ballpoint and "universal" needles and the reverse-action stretch stitch. It made the zigzag machine a necessity. The serger owes much of its appeal to its "knitworthiness." But the memory of those sagging, shapeless, unbreathing garments has tarnished the very word *knit* in many a sewer's mind. Fortunately, knit fabrics have developed alongside these improvements, and so have our ideas for making attractive, comfortable knitwear.

As I've explored these fabrics on the modern machines, I've collected a number of techniques that home sewers can use to get predictably good results with knits. With a little ingenuity we can usually mimic the best effects of ready-to-wear clothes and can often improve on them, with or without a serger. If you have a serger, it's even easier, but you can sew beautifully on knits with just a zigzag machine.

Knit types and characteristics—The most significant change in knit fabrics has been blended fibers. Today's knits almost always have natural fibers blended into the yarn so the fabric breathes. My favorite for cooler climes is wool or wool-and-polyester jersey. For summer, I like cotton-and-polyester-blend interlocks. You'll also find fleece, sweater knits, tricot, stretch terry cloth, velour, and a host of others.

Despite this variety, most knits are either single or double knits. Knit fabrics stretch varying amounts, but single knits usually stretch more and are less stable than double knits. You'll have to judge each fabric on an individual basis, but the stability will determine how you should sew the seams, whether or not you have to face a neckline, and what type of hemming technique you should use.

Single knits are knit on machines with a *single set of needles,* all knitting in the same direction. If you look closely, you'll usually see the knit front and purl back of ordinary handknit stockinette fabric. Its most distinguishable characteristic is that it curls to the right side of the fabric, particularly when stretched across the grain. Jersey, nylon tricot, stretch terry, velour, some sweat-shirt fleeces, and sweater knits are examples of single knits.

Double knits are knit on machines with *two sets of needles,* working face to face. Because of this, they don't curl, and because they are generally more stable than single knits, they can at times be sewn with more conventional construction methods. You can usually distinguish a double knit because both sides look the same. Cotton/poly interlock is a double knit used to make T-shirts and active sportswear. A jacquard double knit is heavier, is textured, and has two or more colors knit into it. The right and wrong sides don't have the same pattern, so you can use the wrong side of the fabric to create contrasting details.

Ribbing is a type of double knit. Its super-elasticity makes it ideal for bands, just like its handknit counterpart, but it's sometimes impossible to find an exact color match for your garment fabric. I've used jersey and the wrong side of velour and stretch terry successfully in place of ribbing. I cut crew or turtleneck bands across the grain two-thirds the length of the opening, and all other bands three-quarters the length. If the band stretches to fit the opening, the fabric is stretchy enough.

Stitches for stretch—Back in the days before most sewing machines could zigzag, there was much talk about stretching knit fabrics as you sewed them so that when the garment stretched, the straight-stitched seams wouldn't pop. If you can't zigzag on your machine, you'll still have to do this when you're sewing with knits, but it's a pretty risky idea because it's very easy to deflect the needle. At best, this could break the needle; at worst, it could drive the needle into the hook or needle plate, creating a burr only a mechanic could remove. There are many knit construction techniques that call for some stretching, often of one short layer against a longer one, so you must get used to the idea, but I prefer to let the feed dogs do all the fabric handling if possible.

Jan Saunders made her knit dress entirely by machine. Only the buttons were sewn on by hand.

From *Threads* magazine (October 1988) 19:60-65

A more basic problem with stretching as you sew is that it can easily result in a wavy, rippled seam that never quite returns to its original shape because the sewn stitches don't relax. When I'm sewing with knits, I'm invariably using some sort of zigzag or reverse-action stretch stitch (the feed dogs move the fabric forward, then backward, while the needle moves from side to side). I've found that I can control stretch with whatever stitch I'm using by adjusting the stitch length. If the fabric waves out of shape, which commonly happens on cross-grained seams, there's too much thread in the seam. To eliminate thread from the stitch, lengthen it. If the fabric puckers, there isn't enough thread in the seam, so shorten the stitch length.

In the chart at right are some stretch stitches found on almost all modern machines, with my recommendations for their use. I developed the chart by testing each stitch on one and two layers of a variety of knit fabrics and noting the effects I liked. It might make a good starting place for your own explorations with the stitches on your machine and with the fabrics you prefer.

On my serger, the stitches I use most for knit sewing are the 3-thread overlock, the 3/4-thread overlock, and the 3-thread flatlock, also shown in the chart. Apart from using my serger to make seams with the 3/4-thread overlock, I mainly use it to mimic ready-to-wear stitches. I still use my regular machine for almost all the basic construction of knit garments.

Layout, cutting, and marking—Unless you're using two-way-stretch swimwear fabric (see the article on pp. 78-83 for more on swimsuits), lay out your pattern so the most stretch (usually along the crosswise grain) is around the body. That means fronts, backs, ribbing, bands...everything. This way, the fabric creates the comfortable, eased fit that makes knits so popular.

The simplest way I've found to cut a knit is to use a rotary cutter and an appropriate board to cut on. Rather than pin pattern pieces to the fabric, I use pattern weights. Any flat, weighted object—a kitchen knife, scissors, or a ruler—will work just as well.

Most patterns still call for ⅝-in. seam allowances. Whether you use overlock stitches from a serger or a sewing machine, for the most part you'll be using ¼-in. seam allowances on your knit projects. I think it makes sense to skip a trimming step by cutting your pattern out with ¼-in. seam allowances to begin with, as long as you're sure the pattern really fits. Don't cut around the notches; after you've cut out the pattern, go back and snip ⅛-in. notches into the seam allowance. A snipped notch is more precise and saves a lot of cutting time.

On light-colored fabrics, instead of marking with tailor tacks, I use a disappearing or water-soluble fabric marker. To mark both layers at once with an accurate, visi-

Stretch stitches for knits

Tiny zigzag stitch
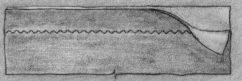
Set at your machine's narrowest zigzag width (not 0!) and at a length equal to width. This stitch is perfect for plain, unfinished seams that need to stretch.

Straight stretch stitch

This stitch will stretch a bit, while firmly reinforcing stressed seams at underarm, crotch, and pockets. Almost impossible to rip out, use only after fitting garment.

Stretch blind hemstitch
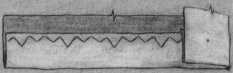
Because of flexible zigzag stitches between wider hemming stitches, this stitch creates an elastic blind hem. Use half-width setting.

Multiple zigzag stitch
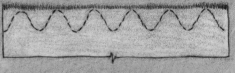
This stitch is ideal for overcasting raw edges and understitching facings. Unlike plain zigzag, it won't tunnel fabric under stitch.

Interlock, or overedge, stitch

For very lightweight knits and wovens, like Qiana, tricot, batiste, and organza, this stitch will stitch and finish a ¼-in. seam in one step. Seam allowances won't tunnel.

Overlock stitch

Designed to simulate a serged stitch, this stitch will stitch and finish a ¼-in. seam in one step, but it's too dense for many lightweight to medium-weight fabrics.

Double-overlock stitch

Because there's a straight stitch at each side of this stitch, it tunnels narrow seam allowances less. It is often the ideal one-step seam finish for ¼-in. seams.

Superstretch stitch

For very stretchy fabrics, like swimwear Lycra and sweater knits, this is least dense of ¼-in. overcasting stitches and has best recovery.

Picot stitch
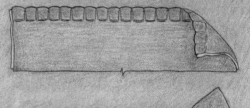
Designed to duplicate a delicate handsewing stitch with same name, this stitch can seam very fine knit and woven fabrics without puckering or tunneling.

3-thread overlock flatlock stitch
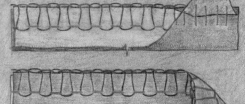
Flatlocking is a way to topstitch seams without disengaging or removing serger's knife blade. Try loosening tensions if seams won't pull open easily.

3-thread overlock stitch
For narrow seams and seam finishes on lightweight knits and wovens, use a narrow-width setting and short stitch length. The lower looper can be tightened for a rolled hem.

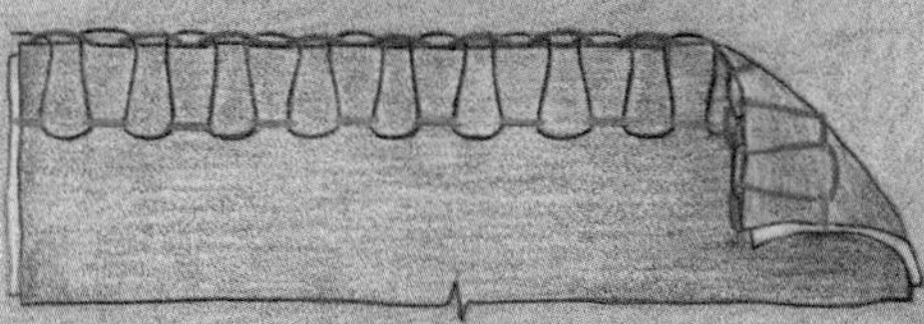

3/4-thread overlock stitch
This stitch is used for ¼-in. seams on knit or woven fabric. The safety stitch created by right needle prevents narrow stressed seams from popping open.

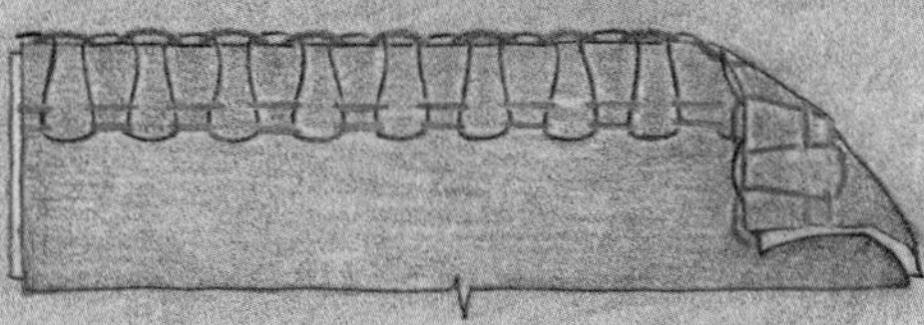

Machine-made finishes for knit garments

Piped armhole/sleeve seams *use contrasting knit yardage for emphasis and strength.*

Bound hems *can be made to match piped seams.*

Flatlocked serger seams *mimic ready-to-wear seam finishes. For strength, a line of straight stitches can be added down the center.*

Mock double-track seams *look like their manufactured counterparts but are made without the factory's elaborate equipment.*

Twin-needle hems *combine topstitching with stretch and durability.*

---

ble mark, I put the tip of the marker on the pattern tissue on top of the dot I want to transfer and leave it there a few seconds. The ink from the marker bleeds through the tissue, through the first layer of fabric, and onto the second layer. On darker fabrics, I use a chalk wheel, which makes a very accurate line. An alternative on washable fabrics is a bar of pure soap that's become too thin to wash with; its sharp edge makes a great and safe marker. Soaps with moisturizers can leave a mark on the fabric when it's pressed.

It's often tricky to draw a straight line on wobbly knit fabric. I use the long edge of Scotch tape as a stitching guide or template for topstitching a zipper, marking buttonhole placement and length, or marking a dart. Be sure to test the tape on a scrap first. You don't want to pull off the nap.

Interfacing and pressing — I interface knits sparingly, frequently only the neckline facing and crisp details, like belts or patch pockets. I prefer a stretch buttonhole (described on p. 77) to interfaced buttonhole bands. If the pattern calls for knit bands, and you want to use ribbing instead, don't interface the ribbing. If you do, you'll defeat its purpose.

When I do interface, I use an all-bias fusible, like Pellon's Sof-Shape, or a fusible knit, like Stacy's Easy-Knit. Easy-Knit also comes in a fusible ¾-in.-wide strip in a straight cut as well as a bias cut. You can use the straight cut to stabilize shoulder seams, under buttonholes if you like, and to add body to straight, narrow hems. Use the bias cut to stabilize shoulder seams where you want more stretch, to stabilize bias seams, and to add body to curved hems.

You can cut the strips narrower, and you don't have to fuse them to use them.

In knit ready-to-wear, fusible nonwovens seem to be the most common interfacings. However, I've seen sew-in nonwovens used to stabilize seams and pocket-mouth curves; nylon broadcloth used in tailored, topstitched collars and stands; and even very thin foam rubber used to interface the back facing of a halter top to help it stay put and to add emphasis to the topstitching. You can use almost anything to interface knits if it gives you the effect you're after.

It's critical that you avoid any ironing motions and actually press knits with your iron. I use a mini-press when I'm working on knits to eliminate the risk of distorting the fabric. I press seams flat as sewn first to set the stitches. Then I press them open or to the side, depending on their type. I al-

Zippers that look hand-picked can be inserted with no hand-stitching.

Stretch buttonholes, made with an overlock stitch instead of a zigzag satin stitch, won't stretch out of shape.

Pressed-open ⅝-in. seams look just like straight-stitched seams but will stretch because they're sewn with a tiny zigzag.

Knit button loops can be made without turning because of a single knit's tendency to curl.

Machine-finished ¼-in. seams are very durable but won't press flat.

---

ways press overlocked side seams to the front so the slight ridge that forms faces to the back and the seam doesn't show.

Needles and thread—When starting a project, use a fresh needle. I use a universal size 70 (American size 9) for interlocks and jersey and a size 80 (American size 11) for sweater knits, stretch terry, and velour. If your machine is skipping stitches, you can use a stretch needle, available in two sizes—a 75 for fine knits and a 90 for heavy knits. Also, remove the lint from under the feed dogs regularly and oil your machine when necessary. Both cotton-covered polyester and polyester threads are appropriate for knits. They have enough stretch to support the natural flex of knit garments, but if you're using stretch stitches, you can even get away with using 100% cotton thread.

Pattern selection—Which comes first, the fabric or the pattern? Judging from my own stockpile, it's the fabric. When I'm looking for a pattern to pair with my current knit choice, I look for something simple. The stretchier the fabric, the less I'll have to worry about fit and shaping, so I can choose a style without a lot of darts, gathering, and complex seaming.

Once I've settled on a pattern, I check to see if I can simplify it further without compromising the style or the fit. I've noticed that many patterns call for a back-neck zipper even when there is plenty of room or stretch at the neckline to pull the garment over the head. Ready-to-wear never bothers with such unnecessary details, and back-neck zippers are tricky to put in, so I eliminate the zipper, and often the entire seam down the back.

Seams—In the following directions, notice particularly the recommended sewing-machine feet; they often make the difference between success and failure. The embroidery foot, for example, has a channel underneath to accommodate the increased bulk of the many stretch stitches.

No matter what type of knit you're working with, you must stitch and finish side seams to ensure durability and prevent bulk. Refer to the chart on p. 73 for a zigzag, stretch, or serger stitch that suits your fabric. If you choose a zigzag stitch, you'll need to complete the seam in two steps.

Two-step ¼-in. seam allowance: Pin the fabric pieces, right sides together. With a tiny zigzag stitch (1mm to 2mm long) or the fine setting (15 stitches/in.) and 1mm wide, sew the seam at the ¼-in. or ⅝-in.

seamline, using a zigzag foot or an embroidery foot. Always pull the pins out before you get to them. The zigzag stitch stretches with the garment, so you don't have to stretch the fabric as you sew.

Reset your machine for the multiple, or three-step, zigzag stitch, and set the stitch length to 1mm, or the fine setting, and the stitch width to 4mm. Place the seam under the foot so the needle stitches next to, and to the left of, the first row of stitching. The multiple zigzag stitch stretches with the seam and flattens the seam allowance. Trim away the excess seam allowance if necessary, and if this is a side seam, press it toward the garment front.

One-step ¼-in. seam allowance: If you can use the overlock, superstretch, or double-overlock stitch or your 3/4-thread overlock, you can complete the seam in one step, as I did in the dress on p. 75. From the front it looks just like a two-step seam.

Test-sew on a fabric scrap to choose the stitch most compatible with your fabric. Then pin the fabric pieces right sides together. If you've trimmed the seam allowance to ¼ in., guide the seam allowance so the needle bites into the fabric on the left and swings off the raw edge on the right. If you have a ⅝-in. seam allowance, sew at the ⅝-in. seamline; then trim up to the stitch. If you use a serger, the seam allowance will be trimmed off automatically. Press the finished seam allowance to one side.

Pressed-open ⅝-in. seam: This type of seam is usually the flattest and least conspicuous, and with a tiny zigzag stitch (1.5mm long by 1mm wide) it will be very elastic. I like to use it for the center-front or center-back seam, as in the dress on p. 75. Pin right sides together, and stitch at the ⅝-in. seamline, using an embroidery foot. Because knits don't ravel, you don't have to finish the raw edges. Seam allowances that are less than ⅝ in. are too narrow to easily press open and stay flat.

Flatlocked serger seam: I mimic the manufacturer's 4-thread flatlock stitch in two steps: first with the serger, then with the conventional sewing machine; you can see the results on the blue top on p. 74.

Thread the left needle and loopers with matching thread. Use the widest needle plate to test your serger for appropriate flatlock tensions. Set the left-needle tension very loose, the upper-looper tension loose, and the lower-looper tension tight to very tight.

Place wrong sides together. Align the raw edges along the edge of the needle plate so that the blades don't cut the fabric. I achieve the flattest results if I keep the fabric edges approximately ⅛ in. from the blades. Serge the seam, using a 3-thread flatlock with a stitch length of 2mm to 3mm and a stitch width of 4mm to 5mm. Then pull the fabric apart to see the exposed seam, and press the seam flat.

Thread your conventional machine with matching thread and set it for a 2mm straight stitch. With the right side up, and using an embroidery foot, stitch down the center of the flatlocked seam. An all-polyester thread will stretch considerably. For more stretch, use the straight-stretch stitch; for less, stabilize underneath with tape.

Mock double-track seam: You can make a narrow version of this popular sportswear effect by stitching the seam with a tiny zigzag, right sides together, and then pressing the seam open. From the top, center the seam under a 4mm-wide, double-needle topstitch, and then trim the allowances underneath. See "Twin-needle hemming" on the facing page for more on using a double needle; the finished seam is shown on the blue top on p. 74.

Piped armhole/sleeve seam: The attractive ready-to-wear technique used on the dress on p. 74 employs a contrast color of the garment knit fabric as both a piping and a hem finish. Sometimes manufacturers use a bias-cut strip, but a cross-grain cut is just as flexible in a knit and saves fabric. Trim the seam allowances to ½ in. on the bodice, and ¼ in. on the sleeve. Cut the contrasting knit fabric across the grain, double the finished width plus ¾ in. I usually cut one long strip and later cut it into the appropriate lengths for specific areas. Cut the bands positioned at the sleeve seams the same

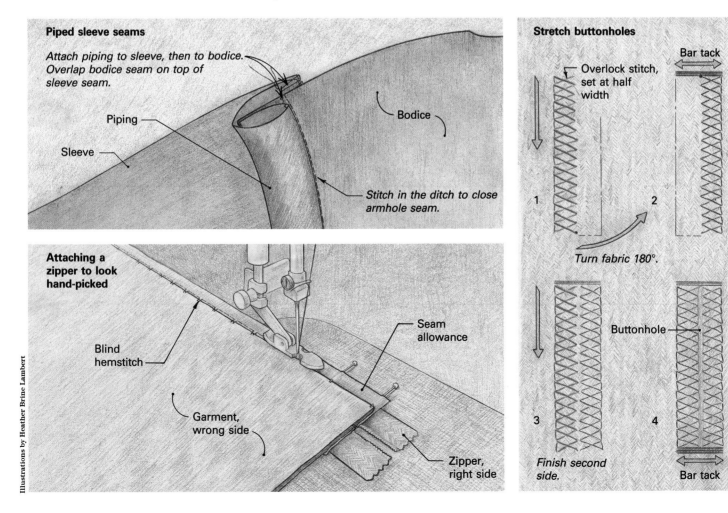

Piped sleeve seams

Attach piping to sleeve, then to bodice. Overlap bodice seam on top of sleeve seam.

Piping

Sleeve

Bodice

Stitch in the ditch to close armhole seam.

Attaching a zipper to look hand-picked

Blind hemstitch

Garment, wrong side

Seam allowance

Zipper, right side

Stretch buttonholes

Bar tack

Overlock stitch, set at half width

1

2

Turn fabric 180°.

Buttonhole

3

4

Finish second side.

Bar tack

Illustrations by Heather Brine Lambert

length as the sleeve opening plus 1¼ in. for seam allowances.

Seam the contrasting bands into a circle. Seam the dress side seams and sleeve underarm seams. With a tiny zigzag stitch, and with right sides together, sew one edge of the band to the bodice piece with a ½-in. seam. Stitch the other edge to the armhole but with any one-step ¼-in. seam.

Press the garment seam allowances toward the inside of the band. Pin the trim to ½ in. wide so the band doubles over the seam allowance around the dress armhole, while the sleeve seam allowance lies flat on the inside (top-left drawing, facing page).

Set your machine for a 3mm straight stitch (or 9 stitches/in.), and use a blind hem foot. Positioning the blade or the inside of the right toe of the blind hem foot in the seamline as a guide, stitch in the ditch around the armhole where the band meets the sleeve seam.

Hem finishes—Because knits don't ravel unless the yarns are very slick, hem treatments can be minimal. In fact, for tops that will always be tucked in, whose hems you want to be as flat as possible, you can even get away with no hem. Just make a single line of straight stitches trimmed to about ⅛ in., but I prefer a more finished look. For the neck edge of my single-knit turtleneck dress, I turned down the raw edge ¼ in. and topstitched with a zigzag stitch that was 2mm long and 1mm wide. Then I trimmed the excess fabric to the stitch. For a regular hem on a heavier, stable knit, I usually machine-stitch a stretch blind hem. For a lightweight, stretchy knit, which may get a lot of stress on the hem (T-shirts, sweaters, sleeves), I prefer hemming with twin needles.

Twin-needle hemming: For a twin-needle hem like the one on p. 74, use a 2.0-4.0 twin needle (front- or top-loading-bobbin sewing machine only) and set your machine for a 2mm- or 3mm-long straight stitch (or 10-12 stitches/in.) and a 0 stitch width. Use an embroidery foot. For a flatter hem finish, loosen the upper tension a bit.

Thread the twin needles with the same thread color as the fashion fabric. As the two spools sit on the spool pins, be sure one thread pulls off the back of the spool, and the other off the front of the spool. This way, they won't tangle. Pin the hem up the desired amount and press. Place the fabric under the foot, right side up, so the foot is resting on a double layer of fabric.

Topstitch the hem in place. Then press it and trim the excess fabric up to the line of stitching. Because there are two threads on top and one bobbin thread, the bobbin thread must share itself between the two top threads, creating a zigzag stitch on the wrong side of the fabric. The zigzagged bobbin thread enables this hem treatment to stretch and withstand lots of wear and tear.

Bound hems: For a hem or neckline that matches the piped sleeve seam described above, use the same cross-grain strips of contrast fabric. For the neckline, cut the trim the length of the neckline opening; then seam it into a circle with a ⅝-in. seam allowance. This way, the band will be 1¼ in. smaller than the neckline opening so that the band hugs the neckline. Press and shape it after stitching it on. Cut bands for hems the desired finished length plus 1¼ in.

For the neckline, divide the band and the neckline into quarters. Place right sides together, matching quarter marks. With the band side up and your machine set for a tiny zigzag stitch and fitted with an embroidery foot, stitch with a ¼-in. seam allowance, stretching the neckline band slightly. Don't stretch the hem bands. Press the seam allowance up into the band; then fold the band over the seam allowance so that it is ½ in. wide. Pin the binding so the raw edge extends beyond the seamline about ¼ in., and press.

Reset your machine for a 3mm-long straight stitch (or 9 stitches/in.) and put on the blind-hem foot. Then, using the blade or toe of the blind hem foot as a guide, stitch in the ditch around the neckline or hem. Press and shape the binding with steam. Trim away excess seam allowance from the band.

Garment details—Perfectly executed details are the hallmark of sewing craftsmanship, but the stretch of knit fabric can make it difficult for the sewer to control the fabric during the involved construction that details usually require. Here are a few of my favorite, virtually foolproof, techniques.

Hand-picked zipper by machine: A center-back zipper that looks hand-inserted is much easier to install than it looks. Buy a zipper longer than the pattern calls for. This way, the pull won't interfere with the presser foot while you're sewing.

Stitch the center-back seam, basting where the zipper is to be sewn. Place the closed zipper face down and centered over the seamline. The pull must be on the extra length of tape, out of the way above the planned opening. With extra-long quilting pins, pin the zipper from the wrong side so the pin enters the zipper tape and seam allowances ¼ in. from the teeth.

Set your machine for a regular blind hemstitch, about 2mm long (or 10 stitches/in.) by 2mm to 2.5mm wide. If your blind-hem foot has a narrow toe on the left, use it. Otherwise, use your zipper foot. With the garment face up, fold back one side to expose the seam allowance up to where the pins enter the fabric (drawing at bottom left, facing page). The straight stitches sew into the seam allowance and zipper tape; the zigzag stitches bite into the fold of the fabric, creating the "pick." Repeat for the other side of the zipper. Remove the basting stitches, lower the slide, and cut off the excess zipper. Bar-tack over the teeth by hand (but don't go through the garment) so the zipper won't pull off track. I put the zippers into the dress on p. 75 this way.

Button loops: Rather than sew a long, skinny tube that you have to turn, you can use the curling feature of a single knit to your advantage to make button loops like the ones on the turtleneck of my beige dress on p. 75. Cut a strip of single knit ¾ in. wide across the grain, and stretch it so the edges turn in, forming a long tube. Put the tube under the pressure foot, stretching it with one hand in front of, and one hand in back of, the foot so it stays rolled.

With your machine set for its widest zigzag and a stitch length of about 3mm to 4mm (or 6-10 stitches/in.), put on the embroidery foot and begin sewing so the stitch clears the fabric on both sides of the tube. If the needle hits the fabric and skips a stitch, cut a narrower strip and try again.

Stretch buttonholes: A buttonhole made with a reverse-action overlock stitch instead of a zigzag stitch will keep its shape on knit fabric no matter how much it is used. For a little extra security on single knits and on the cross grain, you can add a cord to this buttonhole just as you would to an ordinary buttonhole. On heavier fabrics, try topstitching thread for a hand-worked look.

Set your machine for a normal-length but half-width (2mm on most machines) overlock stitch, and use your buttonhole foot. Mark the buttonholes. I use Scotch tape to establish the ends and the distance from the edge. Following the right-hand drawing on the facing page, stitch down the left-hand edge of the buttonhole, with the straight-stitch side of the stitch away from the center of the buttonhole.

At the bottom, stop with the needle down and in the right side of the stitch, lift the foot, and pivot a full 180° so that the stitches that you just made are on the right of the buttonhole. Lower the foot, and raise the needle. Then reset the machine for a stitch length of 0 and a 4mm width, and bar-tack the end of the buttonhole with a few stitches.

Return the machine setting to the 2mm overlock stitch and sew down the remaining side of the buttonhole. Again, reset the machine so you can bar-tack the end; then cut the threads and pull them through the back and tie them off. □

Jan Saunders is the European-trained author of Speed Sewing *(1985), which offers additional techniques for sewing both wovens and knits. She is currently working on* Know Your Viking *for Chilton's Creative Machine Arts Series.* Speed Sewing *is available from her at 3939 W. Henderson Rd., Columbus, OH 43220.*

Sewing Swimsuits
How to get perfect fit

by Grace Callaway

These swimsuits were made by Grace Callaway and several of her students.

Sewing your own swimwear is easier than you may think, and there are advantages too. You get better quality at a lower price, the style and color you want, perfect fit, and a chance to be creative. Making a swimsuit takes very little time and will provide you with a feeling of satisfaction and accomplishment.

Materials—Swimsuit fabrics have improved dramatically over the past few years. Materials available for home sewing are as good as those used in ready-to-wear suits. Wool used to be the preferred swimwear fabric because of its natural stretch and warmth. But wool absorbs moisture, which makes it both heavy to wear and slow-drying.

Man-made fabrics do not absorb water, so they feel lighter than wool and dry faster. A blend of nylon and spandex is the most widely used for swimsuits. Nylon has a natural luster that resembles silk, and its ability to take dyes makes possible brilliantly colored fabrics. Spandex, a man-made fiber

similar to nylon, provides the elasticity necessary for the figure-hugging smoothness and comfort needed in a swimsuit. It weighs less than the old-fashioned Latex (made by wrapping a rubber core with another fiber, usually rayon) and has more resiliency. It also wears longer than other elastic yarns used today. Man-made fabrics' lack of absorbency, however, may make them too hot for sunbathing and active sports other than swimming.

In the past couple of years spandex has been combined with polyester and cotton for active wear. The cotton reduces the luster and increases drying time, but the fabric is cooler and more absorbent and still has the stretch of spandex. This fabric, which is simply called poly/cotton spandex, is used primarily for leotards, bodysuits, and dance costumes, but it's turning up more often in swimwear.

Patterns for swimsuits, once extremely difficult to find, are now widely available in a broad range of sizes and styles from

the major pattern companies, as well as from several companies that specialize in multisized patterns: Sew Lovely, Kwik-Sew, and Stretch & Sew. A multisized master pattern is the best choice for a swimsuit because it's easy to alter.

The pattern must be compatible with the amount of stretch in the fabric. Suitable fabrics and the amount of stretch required are given in a chart on the pattern envelope. Directions for determining the amount of stretch of a particular fabric generally are included as well.

Special swimsuit elastic, which is resistant to deterioration from sun, oil, chlorine, and salt water, usually can be obtained from the same sources as swimwear fabrics. The width required for most suits is ⅜ in., though some styles call for ¼-in., ½-in., or ¾-in. widths.

Bra cups are optional and may be purchased or custom-made along with the suit. You might prefer to make your own, since many ready-made bra cups are molded of

From *Threads* magazine (June 1986) 5:24-29

firm polyester and lack the soft, natural look currently in vogue. Instructions are included with most swimsuit patterns.

Lining is another option. Thin fabrics and light colors may be transparent when wet, so you may want a full or partial lining. Lining for swimwear is the most difficult material to locate. Fabric stores that sell nylon/spandex seldom stock suitable lining materials, so you may have no choice but mail order. (See "Sources," p. 82.)

The lining must have two-way stretch and a greater degree of stretch than the swimwear fabric so that the swimwear fabric doesn't lose any of its elasticity. Banlon, lightweight girdle spandex, stretch-knit bra fabric, and other two-way stretch fabrics are all appropriate linings. The swimsuit fabric itself may be used if it is lightweight, or a lightweight swimsuit fabric may be used to line a suit of heavier fabric. If you use swimwear fabric as lining, however, you must increase the width of your pattern a small amount in order to compensate for the slight loss of stretch that will occur.

Strong thread is essential for swimwear—100% nylon is the best. Not only does it have great tensile strength, but it also has some natural stretch, so the danger of popping seams is reduced. All-nylon thread is difficult to find, though shops that carry lingerie fabrics usually stock a limited number of colors. White or beige may be used on all but the darkest fabrics. Nylon thread is slightly transparent and so fine that it tends to get buried in the surface of the fabric. The strength and thinness of this thread allow it to cut through other fibers, however, so it should be used only on fabrics composed mostly of nylon.

There is a new nylon thread for sergers (overlock machines) that has recently been made available to home sewers. Called "woolly yarn" or "woolly nylon" because of its texture, it is even stretchier than regular nylon thread and is just as strong. Its fluffy texture also makes it more comfortable next to the skin, and it covers the raw edges of fabric better.

After nylon, the next best thread is longstaple polyester, available in most fabric shops under various brand names. Always buy new thread, since old thread can dry out and become brittle, causing tangling and breaking. Sale threads are often old and all right for basting, but they're not strong enough for swimwear.

Swimsuit fabrics are tough, so always use a new needle when starting a suit to reduce the chances of a blunt or rough tip damaging your fabric. Use a size 14 ballpoint or universal-point needle for heavy fabric and a size 11 for lightweight fabric.

Fitting—One-piece swimsuits are the most difficult to fit, but they take the least amount of time to complete. Accurate measuring is the key to perfect fit, and the most important measurement for a swimsuit is the overall body length. To take this measurement, place one end of a tape mea-

Altering length

Marking alteration lines
Mark alteration lines on pattern front and back halfway between bust and waist and between waist and hip. For a low-back suit no alteration line is needed at upper back.

Lengthening
Slash pattern at alteration lines and spread pieces by the measurement you got when you divided by 3 or 4. For a low-back style, do not slash and spread at upper-back alteration line.

Shortening
Slash pattern pieces and overlap by the measurement you got when you divided by 3 or 4. No alteration is made at upper back for a low-back style.

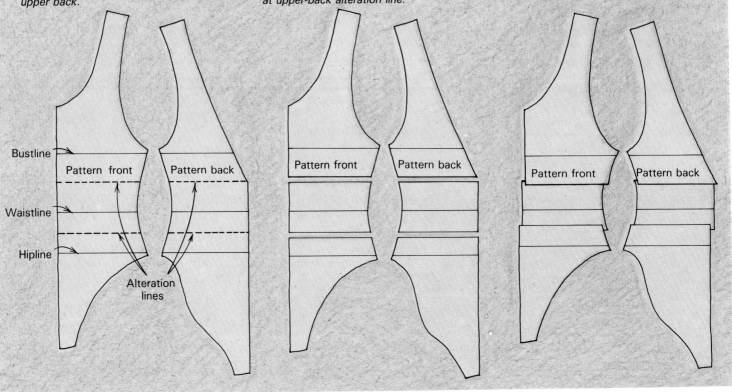

sure in the center of the hollow at the base of the throat, and then carry it down through the crotch and up the center of the back to the most prominent bone at the nape of the neck. This measurement is used to adjust the suit length to fit the trunk length of the body.

The pattern you use should correspond to your bust measurement. If you fall between sizes, use the next larger one if you're more than a size 36; otherwise, use the next smaller size. This eliminates bust alterations, which are the most difficult to make, especially if there are darts. Waist and hip adjustments are easy to make and can even be done as you trace the pattern.

Most swimsuit patterns include a chart comparing standard body-length measurements with bust sizes. If your pattern doesn't have a chart, you can easily determine what the standard should be for your size. The standard body length is 55 in. for a size 34 bust. The body length increases or decreases 1 in. for every bust size 2 in. larger or smaller than size 34. Thus, for example, the standard body length would be 57 in. for a size 38 and 54 in. for a size 32. The amount your overall body length varies from the standard is the amount you need to add to, or subtract from, your pattern length so the suit will stay in place comfortably.

Since most swimsuit patterns are designed for knit nylon/spandex fabrics with 100% lengthwise and 50% crosswise stretch, the pattern pieces may be smaller than you ex-

pect. Synthetic fabrics lose a great deal of stretch when wet; hence, patterns must be small so that even a wet suit maintains a sleek fit.

You probably are accustomed to comparing body measurements with pattern measurements to determine the fit of a garment; you can check the fit of a swimsuit pattern the same way. Measure across the front and back pattern pieces at waist and hip, from seam line to seam line, and double the measurement if the pattern pieces are of only half the suit. The sum of the back and front measurements should be 3 in. smaller than your body measurements for a lined suit and 4 in. smaller for an unlined suit.

When elastic fabrics are stretched crosswise, they contract lengthwise. A suit that's too tight will stretch to go around the body, but it will also pull down from the top and up from the bottom. Length alterations are made first so that changes in width will be made at the right spot on the body. Length adjustments are made at three or four of the alteration lines shown in the drawing above. Compare your overall body length with the standard length for your bust size. Divide the difference between the measurements by 4 if the swimsuit is higher than the waistline in the back, and by 3 if the suit ends at the waist or below in the back, and use the result to lengthen or shorten your pattern pieces, as shown in the drawing above. For example, if your overall body length is 3 in. shorter than the standard body length, you'll shorten your pattern by 1 in. at all but the upper-back alteration line for a low-back style (3 in. divided by 3) or by ¾ in. at each alteration line for a high-back style (3 in. divided by 4).

All suits to be lined need lengthening by 1 in. to compensate for the slight loss of stretch that occurs when two pieces of fabric are placed together as one. This is true even if your overall body length is the same as the standard body length for your size, providing the pattern is for an unlined suit that you wish to line. Never make a suit shorter than your measurements indicate, or it won't fit.

To alter width, divide the number of inches you need to alter by the number of vertical seam edges, and add or subtract this amount at each seam edge. For example, if you need to add 2 in. to the hips, you would divide 2 in. by 4 (since each side seam has two seam edges), resulting in ½ in. to be added to each seam edge at the hipline, as in the left-hand drawing on the facing page.

Construction—You must pretreat the swimsuit fabric to remove excess dye and sizing and to allow it to shrink before you cut out the suit. Hand-wash, or machine-wash on the gentle cycle, using a mild detergent, and line-dry out of the sun. Follow this same procedure after each wearing to remove suntan lotion, salt water, and chlo-

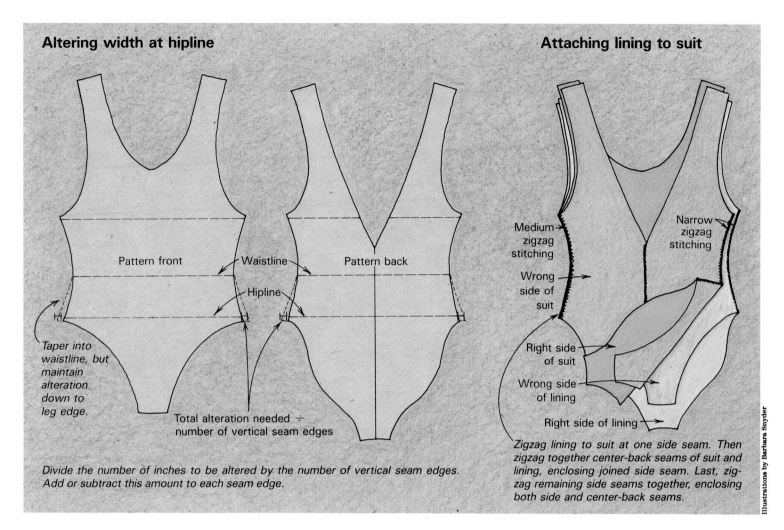

Altering width at hipline

Pattern front

Waistline

Hipline

Pattern back

Taper into waistline, but maintain alteration down to leg edge.

Total alteration needed ÷ number of vertical seam edges

Divide the number of inches to be altered by the number of vertical seam edges. Add or subtract this amount to each seam edge.

Attaching lining to suit

Medium zigzag stitching

Narrow zigzag stitching

Wrong side of suit

Right side of suit

Wrong side of lining

Right side of lining

Zigzag lining to suit at one side seam. Then zigzag together center-back seams of suit and lining, enclosing joined side seam. Last, zigzag remaining side seams together, enclosing both side and center-back seams.

Illustrations by Barbara Snyder

rine, which can damage swimsuit fabrics. Don't preshrink elastic, as it loses some stretch during construction, and a small amount of shrinkage will restore it.

After the fabric has dried, you must determine and mark the right side. The right side is usually the more lustrous side, but occasionally you may have trouble telling the difference. Once you've made the choice, though, be consistent, since differences may be more apparent once the suit is made and worn. The pink paper tape used for setting hair is the best for marking. Its adhesive is less likely than that of other tapes to leave a residue on the fabric.

Now you're ready to cut out the suit. Place your pattern so the fabric's maximum stretch goes around the body. Cut out the suit and lining, and mark the right side of each piece with the hair-setting tape. Mark darts and other construction symbols.

Prepare your sewing machine by cleaning it thoroughly and inserting a new needle. Stitch the seams with an overlock stitch if possible, using either an overlock machine or the overedge stitch on your sewing machine. Set the stitch length slightly shorter than you use on nonstretchy fabrics, or 15 stitches per inch. A three-thread overlock stitch is the stretchiest. You can also stitch seams with two rows of narrow zigzag stitching, stretching the fabric slightly as you sew. If you must stitch straight, stretch firmly as you sew. Stitch first on the stitching line, and then sew another

seam just inside the seam allowance. For straight or zigzag stitching, lockstitch all seams at each end by making three or four stitches in the same place. To secure the beginning of a serged seam, make one or two stitches in the fabric. Then bring the loose thread chain around the left side of the needle, lay it along the edge of the fabric, and stitch over it.

At the end of a serged seam, stop stitching about two stitches off the fabric edge. Pull about ½ in. of slack on the needle thread so you can slide the chain off the stitch finger of the presser foot. Raise the presser foot, turn the fabric over, and position the seam in front of the needle again. Lower the presser foot and stitch back over the finished edge for about 1 in., keeping the edge of the fabric away from the knife. Stitch off the edge and cut the threads.

Most swimsuit pattern instructions are well written and easy to follow. If no lining instructions are given, the general procedure explained here will work.

Stitch the front, back, and side seams of both the suit and the lining, right sides together. Then place one side seam of the suit on top of the corresponding side seam of the lining, with edges even and wrong sides together. Using a medium-width and medium-length stitch, zigzag or overlock the seam allowances together (see drawing, above right), sewing through all of the four seam allowances. Do not allow the zigzag stitching to extend over the seam

line, or it will show on the right side when the suit is worn.

Place the next two seams—usually the center-front or center-back seams—together, and zigzag them in the same way. Continue around the suit until all lining seams are secured to corresponding suit seams. Turn the suit right side out. Zigzag-baste the leg, armhole, and neck edges of the suit to the lining. Straight-stitch a ⅝-in. crotch seam. Then turn all the seam edges to the back of the suit and topstitch ⅜ in. from the seam line. Trim close to the stitching.

Before cutting elastic for the leg openings, measure the length suggested and try it around your leg for comfort. Then cut the elastic and stitch the ends together to form a circle. Along the raw edge, on the wrong side of the suit, align the elastic's seam line with the center of the crotch area.

With a wide, long zigzag stitch, sew elastic to the edge of the leg opening on the wrong side of the fabric. Starting at the elastic's seam line, and with edges even, stitch elastic to the leg front first, stretching the elastic only slightly. Stop at the side seam. Divide the remaining elastic in half and mark the midpoint. Find the center of the back edge of the leg, and pin elastic to this spot. Continue zigzagging, stretching the elastic to fit the leg opening.

Stitch along the edge with one zigzag stitch catching the elastic and the next falling off the outside edge, as in the top photo on page 82. Most of the stretch is at

Elastic is zigzagged to the leg edge so that one stitch catches the elastic and the next falls off the outside edge.

The elastic is turned toward the wrong side of the suit and topstitched with a multiple zigzag stitch.

Color blocking

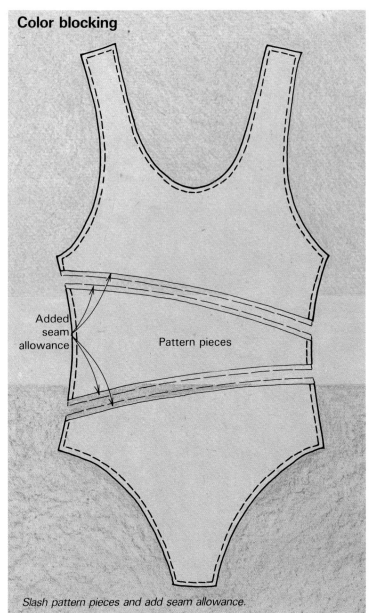

Added seam allowance

Pattern pieces

Slash pattern pieces and add seam allowance.

the back of the leg opening to ensure a smooth fit over the seat and reduce the tendency of the suit to pull up.

You can also serge elastic to the suit with a two-thread or three-thread overlock machine set for a medium-width and long-length stitch. Tack the midpoints together instead of pinning. Serge the elastic to the wrong side of the suit edges, with the elastic on top. Keep the elastic and the fabric edges away from the knives.

Cut the elastic for the armholes 1 in. smaller than the armhole opening, and evenly distribute the stretch by quartering both the elastic and the armhole edge and matching these points. Neckline elastic is cut according to the pattern instructions. Attach the elastic to the neck and armholes just as for the leg openings, by zigzagging with one stitch on and one stitch off the elastic.

To finish the edges, turn the elastic to the wrong side, making sure the fabric covering the elastic is smooth. Topstitch ¼ in. from the turned edge, using a regular or multiple zigzag stitch, as in the bottom photo above, stretching the elastic just enough to fit the fabric.

Straps and hooks are completed according to the pattern specifications, and that's it! Your suit is ready for a trip to the beach.

Plain suits can be more interesting with decorative accents, such as lace medallions, ruffles, appliqués, decorative zippers, portholes, self-fabric ties, waistline tucks, and lacing. Color blocking is a favorite of the younger set. To achieve this effect, slash your pattern pieces in whatever design you choose. The back may be left whole, and only the front of the suit needs to be blocked. Add seam allowances to the cut edges, as in the drawing above, and cut each section from a different color or print fabric. Stitch the color blocks together again, and then stitch the side seams.

Once you've made at least one swimsuit, it will be difficult for ready-to-wear suits to please you. With little time and money, you can duplicate the expensive designer suits in your favorite colors and have a perfect fit every time. □

Grace Callaway, an associate professor at Georgia College in Milledgeville, GA, teaches advanced clothing construction.

Sources

Kieffers Lingerie Fabrics and Supplies
1625 Hennepin Ave.
Minneapolis, MN 55403
Linings, fabrics, elastics, threads, Sew Lovely and Kwik-Sew swimwear patterns, hooks, bra cups. Catalog available.

Stretch & Sew
P.O. Box 185
Eugene, OR 97440
Patterns, fabrics, elastics, bra cups, instruction book. Catalog available.

Nancy's Notions
P.O. Box 683
Beaver Dam, WI 53916
Threads, children's swimwear patterns.

Newark Dressmaker Supply
P.O. Box 2448
Lehigh Valley, PA 18001
Threads, elastics.

Home Sew
Box TH
Bethlehem, PA 18018
Serger thread, swimwear elastic.

Kwik-Sew Pattern Co.
3000 Washington Ave.
North Minneapolis, MN 55411
Multisized patterns for whole family.

Sewing men's swimsuits

Swimsuits for men have a sleek new look because they're being made from the same fabrics used for women's swimwear. Designs range from a boxer look, minus the bulky gathers, to bikinis. A kaleidoscope of colors has replaced the traditional black, brown, and navy blue. Hot pink, silvery blue, and fluorescent orange appear with increasing regularity at beaches and pools. Very little fabric is needed to make a man's swimsuit, usually only ½ yd. to ¾ yd. Since no fly or zipper is necessary when stretch fabrics are used, construction is fast and easy.

The same companies that sell swimwear patterns for women have them for men and boys. Patterns for tennis shorts or other fitted pants are easily adapted, so a special pattern isn't needed.

If you're using a shorts pattern, select one that's a size smaller than is normally worn, and trim away all of the vertical seam allowances. When you sew, use ¼-in. seam allowances, and the suit will fit just snugly enough. It should be 3 in. to 4 in. narrower than the measurement around the body to fit properly.

Shorten the legs of the pattern to the length you want, and add ½ in. for a hem. Mark the new length on one side seam; then mark the inseam the same distance from the bottom edge. Connect the marks with a French curve for the new cutting line, as in the left-hand drawing below. There should be a slight curve up to the side seam for more comfort in wearing. You may want to taper the leg seams of a shorts pattern so that the circumference at the leg edge is the same as the leg measurement. This gives the suit a neat appearance.

For a hip-hugger suit, lower the waistline edge 2 in. to 3 in. For a bikini, lower the waistline edge 4 in. to 6 in. and shorten the leg. Men's suit silhouettes are shown in the middle drawing below.

Cut out the suit with the greatest amount of stretch going around the body. For the lining, cut the same pieces again from lining fabric, lowering the waistline edge 1 in. to prevent bulk. Mark the right sides of the suit and lining pieces with hair-setting tape.

For extra support in the crotch, you can cut a second set of back and front pieces from the lining fabric, making them 1 in. shorter at the waist than the lining pieces. This inner lining will have a shorter crotch depth than the suit and lining pieces. Shorten the legs of the inner lining as for the bikini.

To join seams, use the same stitching techniques that are used in women's swimwear. Stitch the crotch seams of the suit and the lining(s) separately. With suit and lining pieces wrong sides out, stitch the lining seams to the swimsuit seams as described for a woman's suit. The top of the lining will be 1 in. lower than the top edge of the suit.

Turn the suit right side out. Zigzag-baste the leg-opening edges together. Stretch-baste the top edge of the lining in place 1 in. below the top edge of the suit, beginning at one side seam. To stretch-baste, handsew for short lengths, cutting the thread in between, as in the right-hand drawing below. Use a small needle and the finest thread it will take to avoid leaving marks in the fabric. This method of basting will hold the lining in place while allowing the two fabrics to stretch as needed. The threads are easily removed without damage to the fabric after the waistline is completed. Zigzag basting on this edge could damage the fibers when the basting is removed and would leave needle holes showing on the right side of the suit.

If you're using an inner lining, place it inside the suit with the wrong side against the right side of the lining and the upper edges of the two linings even. Stretch-baste both layers to the swimsuit fabric.

Cut 1-in.-wide swimsuit elastic 1 in. to 2 in. shorter than the circumference of the body at the suit's "waistline" (which differs for trunks, hip-huggers, and bikinis). Overlap the ends of the elastic ½ in. and join securely. Quarter the elastic and mark each quarter point, with the seam at the center back. Mark the waistline edge of the suit at the center front and back.

Halfway between the center front and the left side seam, place a ½-in.-wide by 1-in.-long strip of lightweight interfacing on the wrong side of the suit, ¼ in. below the waistline edge. Make a ½-in.-long vertical buttonhole for the drawstring down the center of the strip, ½ in. below the top edge of the suit. This may be either hand- or machine-worked, but a machine buttonhole is usually stronger, especially if stitched twice.

Match markings and pin waistline elastic to the inside suit edge at each point, with the elastic's seam at center back and the top edges even. Zigzag the elastic to the fabric edge, using the same technique as for a woman's suit: one stitch on the elastic and one off. When you have sewn all the way around, overlap the stitching at the beginning 1 in.

Fold the elastic to the inside of the suit, with the top edge of the suit snug against the edge of the elastic. Matching the quarter marks again, zigzag-topstitch along the same edge of the elastic that was just stitched. Begin at a side seam and end by overlapping the stitching 1 in. Remove the stretch-basting threads.

For the longer-leg style, cut ⅜-in.-wide elastic the exact measurement of the leg opening, plus ½ in. For the shorter, shaped leg, cut elastic 1 in. shorter than the measurement. Elastic is applied to the longer legs in the same manner as at the waistline, but without stretching. To attach elastic on the shorter-leg style, follow the technique described for the woman's suit, positioning all the stretch at the back of the opening. Finish the leg opening of the inner lining, if included, with ⅜-in. or ¼-in. elastic. For the longer-leg style, you can omit the elastic at the bottom edge entirely. Just turn under a ½-in. hem and use a stretch stitch, such as the multiple zigzag stitch, in order to hold the raw edge in place.

To finish the suit, cut a thin cord of ¼-in.-wide twill tape 18 in. longer than the body measurement. Use the buttonhole on the inside left front to insert the drawstring in the casing. If ¼-in. twill tape is not available, fold ½-in. tape down the center, and stitch the edges together. —*Grace Callaway*

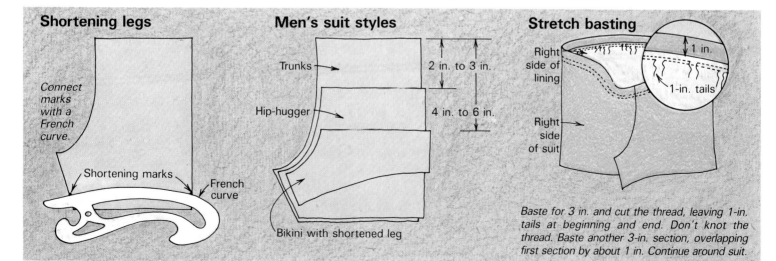

Shortening legs

Connect marks with a French curve.

Shortening marks

French curve

Men's suit styles

Trunks

Hip-hugger

2 in. to 3 in.

4 in. to 6 in.

Bikini with shortened leg

Stretch basting

Right side of lining

Right side of suit

1 in.

1-in. tails

Baste for 3 in. and cut the thread, leaving 1-in. tails at beginning and end. Don't knot the thread. Baste another 3-in. section, overlapping first section by about 1 in. Continue around suit.

Sewing for Stretch

How to handle spandex fabrics

Nylon/spandex garments have revolutionized the sportswear industry, not only because they're ideal for strenuous activity, but because they're easy to sew, fit, and manufacture. Arlene Haislip's Lite Speed line gets a workout. (Photo by Clarke)

by Arlene Haislip

many sewers think that if knits are challenging to sew, *elasticized* knits must be murder. The fact is that while knits, and particularly those made with spandex, were revolutionizing the actionwear industry, they were also simplifying almost every aspect of sewing, from stitching seams to pattern drafting and fitting. Sewing spandex knits on the machine without stretching them and making the seams sturdy and attractive takes some testing, but the photos of test seams at right should prove helpful. Once you've mastered this, you can begin to explore the simplified patterns and comfortable, uncritical fit that spandex fabrics provide.

My experience as a spandex-fabric retailer, and lately as a manufacturer of spandex actionwear, hasn't been in the realm of high fashion, where spandex is starting to appear, but the same sewing information will apply if that's where you want to go. After all, it's the characteristics that make spandex fabrics ideal for action that have attracted fashion designers to them: easy care, easy fit, easy manufacture.

Types of spandex fabrics—Spandex is a generic term used in the U.S. for an elastic fiber around which various other fibers are spun, creating what the industry calls a core-spun yarn. The resulting yarn has the characteristics of the outer spun fiber, but it will stretch and recover. Lycra is the trade name for spandex made by Dupont.

Most actionwear stretch fabric is made of spandex and nylon and is knit, but spandex has been blended with all the natural fibers and has been woven into crepes, denims, and corduroys (photo, p. 86) Nylon/spandex fabrics remain the most common, but even they vary in weight, in

From *Threads* magazine (June 1989) 23:62-65

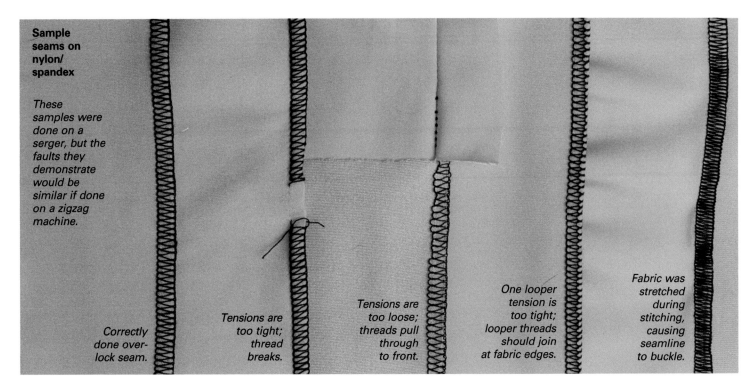

Sample seams on nylon/ spandex

These samples were done on a serger, but the faults they demonstrate would be similar if done on a zigzag machine.

Correctly done over- lock seam.

Tensions are too tight; thread breaks.

Tensions are too loose; threads pull through to front.

One looper tension is too tight; looper threads should join at fabric edges.

Fabric was stretched during stitching, causing seamline to buckle.

percentage of spandex used, and in the way they're knit. Each of these factors affects how the fabric performs. The variations in weight are easy to identify by touch, and the directions of greatest stretch make it easy to determine how the fabric was knit. As the fabric gets heavier, it loses some of its stretch, and the added weight makes the garment less comfortable. So, when choosing your fabric, you'll need to decide how you want the end garment to perform. If comfort and ease of movement are more important than durability, then choose a lighter-weight fabric.

For our Lite Speed line of active sportswear (see photo at left), we chose a 5-oz. to 6-oz. fabric. This is heavy enough to be durable and opaque, yet light enough to retain maximum stretch. For a cross-country ski suit, I'd choose a 5.5-oz to 8-oz. fabric, perhaps cut one size larger to fit over insulated underwear, as comfort and ease of movement are the primary requirements for this type of garment. However, for stretch downhill ski pants, I'd use a 12-oz. to 14-oz. fabric because it's more durable and warmer. This same fabric would make excellent pants for everyday horseback riding, while for show riding I might choose specialty fabrics like those in the photo on p. 86. These heavier fabrics will still be comfortable for pants, but they won't have nearly the stretch nor the body-conforming qualities of lighter-weight fabrics. At the other end of the scale, the very lightweight (under 5 oz.) nylon/spandex fabrics would be excellent choices for lingerie.

One- and two-way stretch—Knit spandex fabric is available in raschel and tricot. Both are complex warp-knit structures, but for the home sewer the main distinction is that tricot stretches equally lengthwise and

crosswise (two-way stretch), while raschel stretches far more lengthwise than crosswise (one-way stretch). In a raschel-knit fabric, the spandex-containing yarns are laid down in parallel, lengthwise rows, and nonstretch fibers are knit around them, so they have great lengthwise stretch but no more crosswise stretch than ordinary knits. They usually contain 10% or less spandex.

Tricot knit spandex fabrics are knit entirely with yarns containing spandex, so they stretch in both directions and have a higher percentage of spandex—usually about 17% to 20%. They're especially good for active-sportswear garments.

Woven spandex fabrics can have either one- or two-way stretch, depending on which yarns—warp, weft, or both—contain the spandex. Whether you're using knits or wovens, if you have a one-way stretch, the rule is to cut so that the maximum stretch goes around the body, not lengthwise.

When you're shopping for spandex, you'll find that price is a good measure of quality, but only on plain, solid-color fabrics. With fabrics that are more elaborately decorated, it's harder to tell what you're paying for. Besides checking the feel and drape for your project, stretch the fabric hard near both edges, checking for good recovery.

Choosing a pattern—Patterns designed for nylon/spandex knits are usually reduced in size by 10% to 25%, depending on the design. If the garment is a close-fitting one designed for tricot knit spandex fabric, the sizing will be reduced in length and circumference, and you must use a tricot knit spandex fabric for these patterns if you want the finished garment to fit well and to stretch with the body. For example, Green Pepper pattern #409, a bicycle-racing-shorts pattern that's designed for tricot knit span-

dex fabric, has been reduced in circumference by 25%, and the crotch depth has been reduced by 20%. The crotch depth is reduced less because the shorts are supposed to come up higher on the waist than regular shorts. On the other hand, our racing-suit pattern #408 is reduced in circumference by only 15% because this garment is to be worn over insulated underwear. The crotch depth hasn't been reduced much, because its long front zipper prevents the garment from stretching in length. Our shorts pattern #404 has been reduced in size even less, and hardly at all in length, because we intended it for the more widely available, less flexible, raschel knits. Swimwear patterns generally are designed for raschel knit fabrics because they need more stretch around than lengthwise.

The point of all this is that it's important to find out what kind of fabric your pattern was designed around and what its end use is expected to be. Read the envelope, and use the stretch guides on it. Because these fabrics vary a lot in stretch as the weight of the fabric changes, there's no better way to ensure that your fabric will work.

The reduced stretch of the heavier-weight and woven spandex fabrics is less of a factor in garment sizing. Usually you can treat these fabrics like knit fabrics that don't have spandex, so take out any excess ease in the pattern, but don't make the garment smaller than your body measurements.

Needle, thread, marking, and cutting—I use a small size (9 to 11) ballpoint needle for nylon/spandex fabrics. These fabrics are densely woven, and the ballpoint needle separates the fibers without damaging them.

A good-quality, all-purpose size 50 polyester thread is my choice. It's stronger than a comparable weight cotton or cotton-covered

Spandex fabrics come in a bewildering range, from bulletproof corduroys to see-through lace. Clockwise from top: A gauzy, wool crepe; a woven silk jacquard; cotton lace, with an interwoven grid of spandex threads; two cotton-textured knits; two wool wovens for riding breeches.

Spandex fabrics

Most fashion-fabric stores carry spandex fabrics in their swimwear departments. They can also be ordered from the following places:

Britex-By-Mail
146 Geary St.
San Francisco, CA 94108
(415) 392-2910
Good collection of fashion fabrics with spandex; also some nylon/spandex.

Equi-Breeches
Box 1242
Southern Pines, NC 28387
(919) 692-3786
Elizabeth Guffey imports a few superb heavyweight two-way-stretch spandex fabrics from Europe for her custom-riding-breeches business; sold by the yard.

The Green Pepper, Inc.
941 Olive St.
Eugene, OR 97401
(503) 345-6665
Regularly stocks nylon/spandex tricot and raschel fabrics, Teflon press cloths, and 100% polyester thread. Catalog, $2.

G Street Fabrics
11854 Rockville Pike
Rockville, MD 20852
(800) 333-9191; (301) 231-8998
Good collection of fashion fabrics with spandex; also some nylon/spandex.

Nylon/spandex patterns

The Green Pepper, Inc. (see address above)

Kwik-Sew Patterns Co., Inc.
3000 Washington Ave. No.
Minneapolis, MN 55411
(800) 328-3953

Prime Moves
Box 8022
Portland, OR 97207
(503) 235-0678

Stretch & Sew
Box 185
Eugene, OR 97440
(503) 726-9000

polyester thread, and there's also some stretch to it, so it's less likely to break under the extremes of tension that these garments undergo. Many people recommend a popular serger thread called woolly nylon for spandex actionwear, but after a thorough test in which the seams split on all our manufactured samples, we've concluded that it isn't strong enough, and it makes tension adjustments a nightmare.

All spandex knits, and most wovens, need to be laid out "with nap" for cutting, since the knit stitches are directional, and colors will appear to change if you aren't consistent. I prefer not to prewash nylon/spandex because it often seems to cut a little more easily before the manufacturer's finishing sizing is washed away. Unfortunately, this sizing can sometimes cause slipped stitches, so you must be willing to test a swatch first. Otherwise, go ahead and prewash. With sharp scissors, you should have no trouble.

Sewing spandex on the machine—All of the nylon/spandex fabrics are particularly well-suited for sewing with an *overlock machine* because overlocked seams stretch so well. The settings of the machine may need to be adjusted to accommodate the stretch of different fabrics, but once set, almost all the construction can be done with the overlock. The stitch width should be set as close to ¼ in. as possible. The stitch length should be set at the closest setting, allowing no more than ¹⁄₁₆ in. between stitches. This will give the stitches more stretch and will make a smoother stitching line on the outside of the garment. The tension may also need to be loosened slightly. Do a test seam at least 12 in. long; then stretch the seam lengthwise as hard as possible. The stitches shouldn't break if the machine is properly adjusted. Next, hold the fabric on each side of the seamline and pull it crosswise. The stitches shouldn't

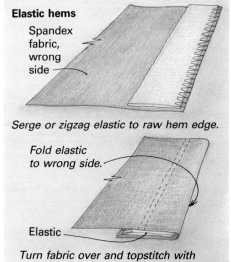

Elastic hems

Spandex fabric, wrong side

Serge or zigzag elastic to raw hem edge.

Fold elastic to wrong side.

Elastic

Turn fabric over and topstitch with a double needle, checking tensions to see that zigzag underneath isn't pulled flat when hem is stretched.

Illustration by Staff

Do-it-yourself spandex?

by David Page Coffin

Among the most intriguing fabrics to cross my desk in preparation for this article were several that weren't actually made of spandex but that had been given some of spandex's wonderful flexibility in clever ways that could be duplicated at home. The idea isn't new, but considering how attractive the fabrics are (and how expensive—one of the silk prints is $195/yd.), it seems to take on new meaning.

The silk prints at right were sewn down flat, in a continuous, meandering allover pattern, to a lightweight piece of one-way-stretch spandex knit, while the spandex was stretched. As a result, when the spandex relaxes, the silk crinkles up in an apparently random way and thus has the same one-way stretch that the knit underlayer has.

Another approach that I saw in a red rayon velvet (a mere $90/yd.) is to stitch the fabric in the same meandering pattern, but not onto anything. Instead, elastic thread is used in the bobbin, which relaxes to create a texture in the velvet like a Shar-pei's coat, complete with two-way stretch.

These are variations on an idea I first saw in my sewing machine's decorative-stitch manual. But I never tried it, perhaps because the manual called it smocking, and I knew it wasn't really smocking. The idea is to thread your bobbin with elastic thread, under no tension, and then to stitch straight lines across fabric, holding it taut until you're done. When

you relax the fabric, it compresses into a variety of amazingly regular patterns, if you've been careful, and depending on which decorative stitch you've used. I thought it was hokey.

Consulting with sewing-machine magician Jan Saunders (see her article on state-of-the-art techniques for sewing with knits on pp. 72-77), I learned that the kind of elastic you use makes all the difference. A Swiss elastic called Gold-zack, distributed by Viking dealers, is a polyester core-spun thread that won't disintegrate in your bobbin. You have to hand-feed the thread onto the winding bobbin without stretching it, but then you put it in the case under the normal tension spring, like ordinary thread (most dealers suggest buying a special case for this). Instead of holding the cloth you're sewing under constant tension, Saunders suggests that under the fabric you use a strip of adding-machine tape or computer paper for wide areas. This will hold the whole thing more or less flat until you tear the paper away, a bit of a chore, but Saunders has tried easier-to-remove tear- or wash-away underlayers—they don't work. I stitched the rayon velvet at right with the feed dogs down and a darning foot and made a variety of big, regular zigzags. Does anyone else have ideas? We hope someone will take up the challenge.

David Page Coffin is an associate editor of Threads.

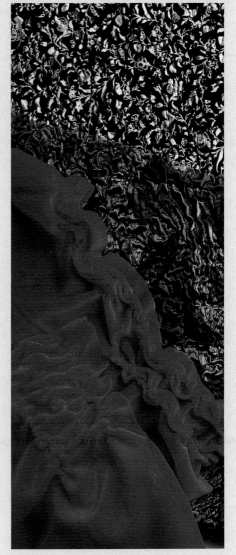

These lightweight woven fabrics have been given all the stretch of spandex by being overstitched, either directly onto a layer of spandex (prints) at the factory, or with an elastic bobbin thread (red velvet) at home.

come to the outside of the fabric. If they do, then your tension is too loose.

In order to achieve sergerlike results with spandex fabrics on a *zigzag machine,* you'll need to set the stitch length at 16 to 18 stitches per inch, and the width at approximately ¼ in. Without allowing the right-hand stitches to fall off the raw edge of the fabric, sew a sample seamline; test it by pulling both lengthwise and crosswise. If the stitches break, loosen both the top and bottom tensions slightly. When properly adjusted, the seamline threads won't break, and they won't pull to the outside of the fabric.

Whether you sew with a serger or a zigzag sewing machine, hold the fabric taut—not stretched—as it goes through the machine. The dense stitches of either machine, properly adjusted, will distort the fabric if it's allowed to stretch, and it simply isn't necessary.

If you have only a *straight-stitch sewing machine,* you can ignore these directions and stretch each seam as hard as you can as you sew it. There's no other way to build in stretch with straight stitches, but you'll never achieve the flexible seams that can be produced by the serger or zigzag machine. Test all your straight-stitch seams, and overstitch any that have popped stitches, restretching as you go.

Finishing techniques—You can turn hems up and finish them by using a zigzag stitch. However, a much more professional way to finish hems is to use a double needle and stitch from the right side of the fabric, catching the raw edge with both needles, including elastic in the fold if you like, as is shown in the drawing on the facing page. The stitch length should be set at 8 to 10 stitches per inch. First do a test seamline and stretch it. If the threads break, loosen

the tensions, especially the bobbin tension, slightly.

Most sportswear manufacturers use either elastic or zippers in nylon/spandex garments. It's easier to apply a zipper if you use a narrow strip of iron-on interfacing under the zipper to keep the fabric from stretching while you sew in the zipper. I use a Teflon press cloth when I apply the interfacing to ensure that the iron doesn't melt the nylon fibers. If you want to use buttons and buttonholes, or snaps, stabilize the fabric with iron-on interfacing underneath the fastener. For years I managed without interfacing, but since I've tried it, I'd never apply fasteners without it. □

Arlene Haislip is president of The Green Pepper, for which she designs Green Pepper patterns and the bicycle and aerobics clothing The Green Pepper manufactures under the trade name Lite Speed.

A New Fit from the Old World

How to give your clothes a European look

by Sandra Betzina

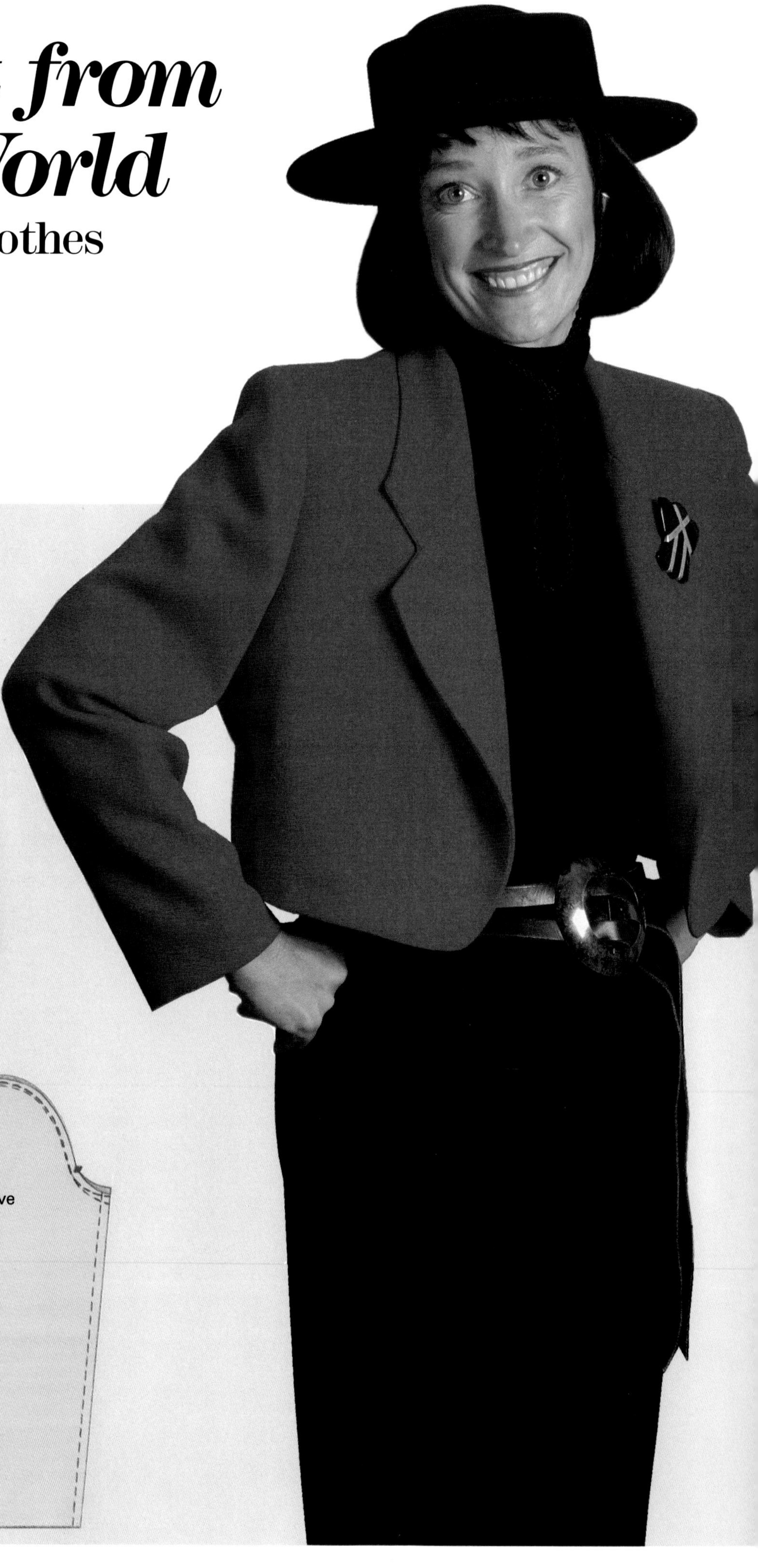

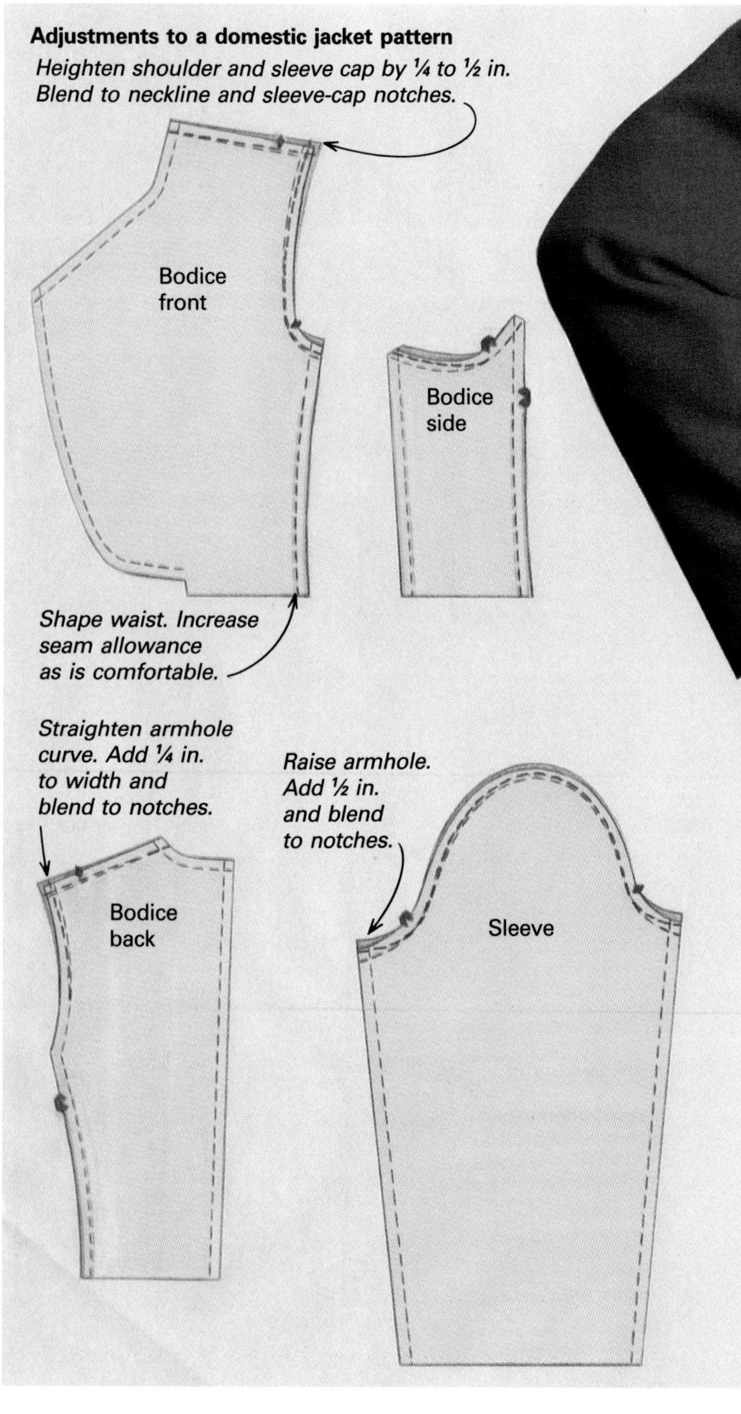

Adjustments to a domestic jacket pattern
Heighten shoulder and sleeve cap by ¼ to ½ in. Blend to neckline and sleeve-cap notches.
Bodice front
Bodice side
Shape waist. Increase seam allowance as is comfortable.
Straighten armhole curve. Add ¼ in. to width and blend to notches.
Raise armhole. Add ½ in. and blend to notches.
Bodice back
Sleeve

From *Threads* magazine (June 1989) 23:58-61

*t*o Europeans, great style and great fit are of equal importance. Clothes must be proportional to the body whether they're bought as ready-to-wear or made from a pattern. Europeans expect a good cut in all price ranges and will have clothes modified to fit. They approach patterns the same way; they expect to adjust patterns for a custom fit.

Few Americans subscribe to these standards. Our clothes and patterns are usually cut fuller to fit a broader range of body types. Only in expensive garments do we expect that great cut that makes us look and feel terrific. Even an unsophisticated American buyer knows that expensive garments fit differently and are more flattering.

What we really mean by *cut* is the sloper used by the designer. A sloper is a basic pattern to which styling details and wearing ease are added. American and European patterns are produced from slopers that have some basic differences. Most of the differences show up clearly in a comparison of a jacket, pants, and a skirt.

A basic European jacket or shirt has broader and squarer shoulders with higher armholes than an American one, and the bodice and sleeves are shaped to mirror the body's curves. The squarer shoulders and a fitted bust and waist make the hips appear narrower. The wearer looks slimmer, more in proportion, and less boxy.

The philosophy of a close, yet comfortable, fit extends to European pants and skirts as well. The close fit in the pants seat gives more freedom for movement, and the pants don't wrinkle at the crotch when the wearer sits. The skirt hangs closer to the legs because it is pegged (cut narrower at the bottom) for a slender silhouette.

Having used both American and European patterns, I'll give you some guidelines for modifying American patterns for a European fit (see photo at left). You can make these changes along with your basic fitting adjustments. Another way to get a European fit is to try a European pattern. Once you get the hang of using multisize patterns without seam allowances, you'll find them a pleasure to work with.

A snappier jacket—If you took apart a basic European jacket and compared it or a European pattern with its domestic counterpart, you'd find that the shoulder is about ¼ in. higher and wider in the bodice front and back and in the sleeve cap. The armholes would be about ½ in. higher, and the side seams would be curved inward to fit closer around the waist. A higher armhole

Starting with an American-cut pattern, Sandra Betzina gave her bolero jacket, facing page, a European fit. The armholes are higher, and the shoulders are more boxy than in the original pattern. (Pattern changes are shown to the left of the photo.)

is flattering because it creates a longer line between armhole and waist. It's also comfortable, since the bodice doesn't pull up from the waistline when the arm is lifted. The combination of a high armhole, a fitted bodice, and a squarer shoulder prevents a problem that's common to American-cut jackets: a fold at the hollow of the shoulder (see photos below).

You can straighten the armhole line by adding ¼ in. in width at the shoulders, tapering to nothing at the notches of the armhole pattern (drawing, facing page). If you have narrow shoulders, you can subtract ¼ in. instead. To complete the square-shoulder look, add ¼ in. in height to the shoulder seam (front and back), tapering to nothing at the neckline. The sleeve will need adjustments to match those in the shoulders; add ¼ in. at the top of the sleeve cap to accompany the increase in shoulder height, blending to nothing by the sleeve-cap notches. To set the sleeve in the slightly smaller armhole, run an ease line of machine basting all around the sleeve instead of just over the cap between the notches.

To raise the armhole, add ½ in. to the underarm seam on the front and back bodices and to the sleeve. You can raise them higher; just be sure to make the corresponding adjustments to the sleeve. Taper the addition to nothing at the side seam and sleeve-cap notches. Raising the armhole usually requires a better fit in the bust area, so you may want to make a muslin of the jacket first.

Slenderizing pants and skirts—On a pattern for European pants, the front-crotch depth is about ¼ in. shorter than on a pattern for domestic pants (photo, p. 90). A shorter front crotch brings the inner leg

seam more toward the front and eliminates excess fabric above the front crotch, which tends to wrinkle when you sit. To modify a domestic pants pattern, subtract ¼ in., tapering to nothing about 7 in. below the crotch (drawing at top left, p. 90).

European pants are about ⅞ in. wider at the upper center front, which places the seam more on grain and makes the pants roomier across the tummy. The extra ⅞ in. tapers to nothing at the beginning of the front-crotch curve.

The lower front leg is narrower by about ¾ in. on the inner and outer leg seams, tapering to nothing at about 7 in. below the crotch seam on the inner leg, and to the hipline on the outer leg. The amount of tapering varies from one pair of pants to the next, depending on style. Unless you're very tall, a pants leg wider than 16 in. is unflattering. A pants leg narrower than 14 in. is difficult to get over the foot. Always measure the pants-pattern width to determine the ideal amount of tapering.

The differences between European and domestic pants are obvious on the pants back. The European back-crotch curve is about ½ in. deeper, which adds room in the seat and prevents the pants from pulling down from the waist when the wearer sits. In addition, the back-crotch depth on European pants is about ¾ in. longer, tapering to nothing at 8 to 9 in. down the inner leg seam at the back. A longer back-crotch curve allows the crotch to fit snugly around and under the seat, eliminating the need for extra length from waist to seat for movement. The European crotch length is about ¾ in. shorter than its domestic counterpart. Few Americans like such a close-fitting crotch, so if you're using a European pattern rather than modifying a domestic

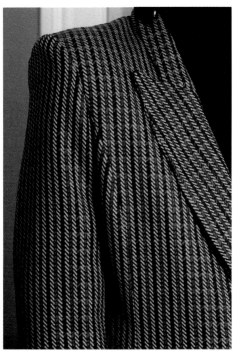

Squared shoulders and armholes set higher in the bodice are typical of a European-cut jacket.

Bagginess, visible in the shoulder of this jacket, is common in American-cut clothes.

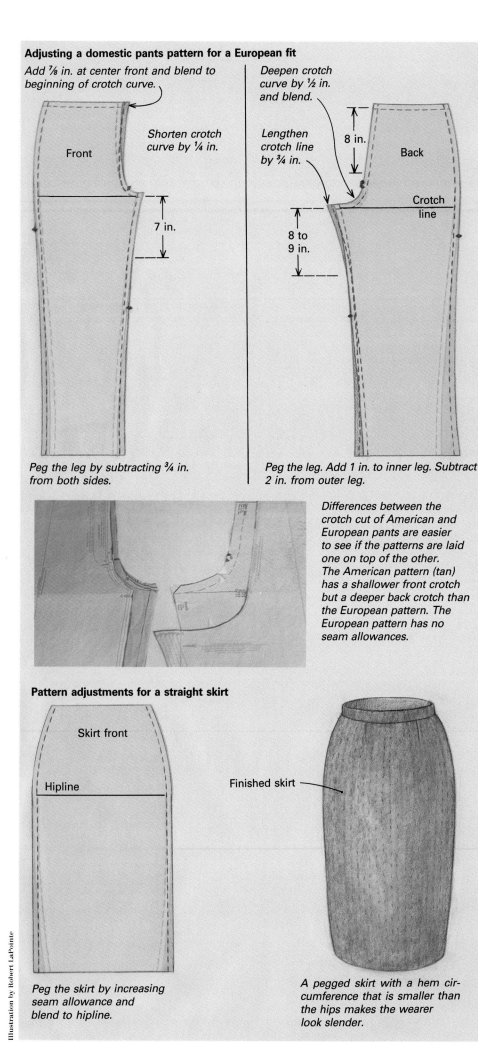

Adjusting a domestic pants pattern for a European fit

Add ⅞ in. at center front and blend to beginning of crotch curve.

Front

Shorten crotch curve by ¼ in.

7 in.

Peg the leg by subtracting ¾ in. from both sides.

Deepen crotch curve by ½ in. and blend.

Lengthen crotch line by ¾ in.

8 in.

Back

Crotch line

8 to 9 in.

Peg the leg. Add 1 in. to inner leg. Subtract 2 in. from outer leg.

Differences between the crotch cut of American and European pants are easier to see if the patterns are laid one on top of the other. The American pattern (tan) has a shallower front crotch but a deeper back crotch than the European pattern. The European pattern has no seam allowances.

Pattern adjustments for a straight skirt

Skirt front

Hipline

Peg the skirt by increasing seam allowance and blend to hipline.

Finished skirt

A pegged skirt with a hem circumference that is smaller than the hips makes the wearer look slender.

one, you might want to add ½ to ¾ in. to the length of both the front and back patterns to reach a comfortable compromise.

The ¾-in.-longer back-crotch curve of European pants fits around and under the seat, resulting in an inseam that hangs more to the pants front and pants that hang on grain even after they fit over the curve of the fanny. To adjust a domestic pants pattern, to complement this change in drape (drawing at top right), narrow the outside of the back leg by 2 in., tapering to nothing at the hipline. Extend the inner lower leg by about 1 in., tapering to nothing at 8 to 9 in. below the crotch. Most people find it easier to start with a European pants pattern than to adjust a domestic one, and they get better results.

Pegging a straight skirt (bottom drawings) is simpler than pegging pants legs. Just redraw the seamline at the skirt bottom at least ½ in. inside; taper the wider seam allowance back to the traditional seam allowance at the hipline.

Trying a European pattern—Besides reflecting a different sloper in fit, a European pattern differs from a domestic one in the absence of seam and hem allowances. Using a pattern without seam allowances has several advantages. The tissue can be taped together at the shoulder and side seams and tried on, giving an accurate placement of neckline, shoulder seam, armscye, darts, and styling details without the encumbrance of seam allowances, which are added after alterations are made. A more realistic picture of the proportions of the finished garment is possible, plaids can be more accurately placed during layout, and since fusible interfacings are less bulky when not included in seams and hems, cutting exact replicas of patterns without seam allowances for interfacing is faster and more accurate.

Only Burda, a West German company, offers individually packaged European patterns in the U.S. Burda's patterns have multilingual instructions, including English. Each pattern includes five to seven sizes. What at first glance seems to be an obstacle becomes an advantage in achieving a perfect fit. Multisize patterns, European or domestic, are ideal for the figure that's one size on top and another on the bottom or for the figure that's a size larger in the front or back. Clearly marked multisize lines enable the sewer to use different sizes for different parts of the body. While most home sewers are knowledgeable enough to add at the side seams, few can successfully grade a pattern up or down a size in all areas. Multisize patterns eliminate the possibility of grading errors. Pattern sizes can be changed many times throughout the garment, but you must remember to use the same size where pattern pieces are joined; e.g., at the shoulder, sleeve cap, and armscye.

The real key to perfect fit with a European pattern lies in a complete set of accurate body measurements. You'll need measurements of the full bust, waist, full hip, front-waist length, back-waist length, shoulder, sleeve length, upper-arm width, back width, bust point, and neck. Work with a friend knowledgeable in taking accurate body measurements. If you don't have such a friend, consider hiring a dressmaker to take your measurements. Burda Patterns has put out an excellent 90-minute video, *Secret of the European Fit.* This video is a good primer for working with European patterns; it has a segment on exactly how and where to take all body measurements.

European patterns list European sizes (34 to 54) with corresponding American sizes printed underneath. The European size is not a body measurement, just as a domestic size is not a body measurement. All pattern companies add ease to their patterns, but the ease isn't uniform from company to company. A domestic pattern has greater ease than a European pattern and often fits a larger figure than the pattern measurement indicates. If you usually buy a size smaller than indicated for your full-bust measurement or a different size for a loose-fitting garment, rethink before deciding on a European pattern size. When working with a European pattern, use the guidelines that match your measurements.

Before you begin to adjust the pattern pieces in a multisize pattern, compare your body measurements with the pattern measurements. Circle the pattern size corresponding to each measurement. For example, your measurements may correspond to a size 10 in the shoulder, a size 12 in the bust, and a size 14 in the waist and the hip. Using a felt-tip or highlighter pen, trace over the seamline on the pattern corresponding to your size for that section of the garment, indicated by your measurements (see photo at top right). Crossing over from one size to the next is very easy on a multi-size pattern; it can be done freehand or with a curved ruler. Don't add seam allowances or hem allowances at this stage. Cut away excess tissue from seamlines that you have highlighted.

You may add seamlines and hems by using a tape measure or a seam gauge, but there are two notions designed expressly for this purpose. A rotary cutter with an adjustable seam-allowance arm measures the seam allowance and cuts the fabric simultaneously. If you prefer scissors, try the double tracing wheel with a chalk marker, available from Burda. Run the tracing wheel along the edge of the pattern. The chalk marker will leave a streak of chalk to indicate the cutting line. Since the Burda chalk marker leaves a fatter line than is desirable, mark the fabric with a line at spaced intervals. Use whatever seam-allowance width you're most comfortable with, perhaps narrower at the neck and armholes and wider at the waist and hips. Don't forget to add a hem allowance.

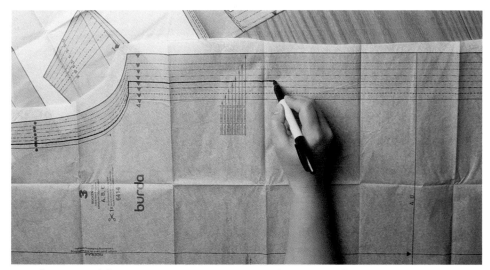

To adjust a multisize European pattern, follow the lines for the size that matches your measurements. This shirt-back pattern is traced along lines for size 38 at the neck, shoulder, and armhole, but for size 42 at the side seam.

Betzina outlines the pattern pieces she needs on the master sheet out of a European pattern magazine with a heavy felt-tip pen. She locates the patterns on the sheet by the reference numbers and by the type of line—solid, dotted, broken, etc.—that defines the pattern pieces.

Other sources of European patterns are *Neue Mode* and *burda MODEN* pattern magazines, which offer 20 to 100 patterns in every monthly issue. There is an instruction supplement in English, and patterns in one or two popular sizes are printed on sheets of paper that resemble road maps (bottom photo, above). Numbers next to the photo of the garment indicate the size and pattern number. The pattern instructions give the color and type of line (solid, dotted, broken, etc.) that defines the pattern pieces on the "maps." Numbers on the sheet margins make the search easier. (If you don't fall into the popular size, you must grade the pattern up or down or make a muslin.) After you locate a pattern piece on the sheet, trace over the lines with a felt-tip or highlighter pen. To obtain each pattern without cutting up the sheet, trace

over highlighted pattern lines with a tracing wheel and waxed paper. Sample copies of these magazines are available for $5 each plus $2 shipping and handling from GLP International, 560 Sylvan Ave., Englewood Cliffs, NJ 07632; (212) 736-7455 or (201) 871-1010. Yearly subscription rates are $54 for *burda MODEN* and $60 for *Neue Mode.* □

Sandra Betzina, syndicated sewing columnist, teaches at The Sewing Workshop in San Francisco, CA. She is the author of Power Sewing: New Ways to Make Fine Clothes Fast *(1985, $20) and has produced two videos,* Power Sewing: Designer Details Made Easy *(1987, $34) and* Pants That Fit *(1988, $19.95), available from Power Sewing, World Trade Center, Suite 275H, San Francisco, CA 94111.*

Bridal Dressmaking
Design and construction of a custom-made wedding gown

by Janice Steinhagen

*l*ike generations of little girls, I dreamed of my wedding and the magical, beautiful gown that would transform me into a storybook princess. By the time I'd grown up, I'd decided to design and make my own wedding dress. I knew I'd never find my ideal in a store, at least not within my budget.

My approach was to buy a simple commercial pattern and alter it beyond recognition to fit my sketched idea. It worked beautifully, and the dress fit like a dream. But I've since been curious to see how a professional dressmaker goes about designing these fantasy-steeped garments.

So I visited Sposa Bella (Beautiful Bride), a shop in New London, CT, that specializes in bridal design and dressmaking. Maria Pavani, who owns the shop, has spent the last seven years preparing gowns for women of all shapes and sizes, while often simultaneously playing amateur psychologist as her clients' minds and measurements waver in the weeks before the wedding.

Pavani's clients, most of whom arrive as a result of recommendations from friends or relatives, are usually looking for something distinctive and are not frightened by the $500 or higher price tag of a custom gown. They often have a clear idea of what they want and occasionally come armed with magazine photos. Sometimes a client's dream dress may not look dreamy on her, and Pavani may tactfully dissuade her from a potential problem feature. For example, "A short bride may have dreamed of a long, long train ever since she was a little girl, but she would look a lot shorter and appear lost," says Pavani. If a woman has no ideas about what she wants, Pavani will use the bride's body type and build, facial shape, and even personality to design a flattering style.

Pavani has learned from experience that compromise, at least in dress design and construction, is seldom satisfying. As a result, she will not approach a project when

Maria Pavani checks the bustle shape and bodice length of the wedding gown she designed and constructed at her custom-wedding-gown shop, Sposa Bella.

the bride is adamant about an awkward design element or insists on using cheap fabric. Pavani favors superb silks and laces imported from Italy, France, and Switzerland; crisp taffetas, shimmery charmeuse, laces adorned with embroidery of seed pearls, and filmy organzas. She frequently travels to New York City's 40th St. fabric houses, seeking fabrics to enhance specific designs. The prices of these sumptuous textiles may range from $10 or $15/yd. all the way up to $100 or $150/yd. for delicate silk laces. Harder to find than the right primary fabric is lining. The right lining, Pavani claims, makes the wearer more comfortable and adds an extra measure of body and richness to the style.

Quality construction is as important as the fabric. "How long you wear the gown is not important, after all, but why," says Pavani. A dress for a ceremony at which the wearer pledges to love "till death do us part" should reflect the ceremony's dignity and integrity and certainly should not part at the seams.

Design considerations—When I expressed an interest in her design and construction process, Pavani made arrangements with a cooperative client for me to follow the progress of a gown from sketch to completion. Client Ann Walsh has admired the simple yet elegant wedding gown worn by Caroline Kennedy and wants something similar. Questions ensue: "When is the wedding?" "June, late in the afternoon." "Will the ceremony be in a church?" "Yes." "What is the budget?" The design Pavani sketches includes a lined, fitted, lace bodice with a dropped waist to complement Walsh's long torso. A jewel neckline and padded shoulders add a bit of width without overpowering her tall frame. Short, cool sleeves made of transparent lace will be high and puffed at the shoulders. The skirt, a sweep of a stunning but simple fabric, will fall from gathers just below the waist to a moderate train, adding drama during the ceremony.

Before the consultation ends, Pavani takes measurements and gives Walsh some fabric swatches to consider. Because of the simple style, the choice of fabrics will be

crucial, particularly the lace. The Kennedy gown was sprinkled with brocade shamrocks. Walsh wanted bows, "but I saw little flowers," says Pavani. On her next trip to New York City she finds a 22-in.-wide Italian lace of organza embroidered with individually finished appliquéd tulips and leaves for $65/yd. Fortunately, a little of this lace will go a long way to enhance the crisp silk taffeta of the skirt. The pearly and light taffeta will nonetheless hold its shape without going limp in the heat. A lightweight satin will be used to line the skirt and bodice, while the sleeves will be underlined with two layers of organza to add body without disturbing the lace's transparency.

Pattern adjustments—Once Walsh has approved the design and the fabrics arrive, the real work begins. Pavani reaches for two sets of her basic pattern pieces: a fitted bodice with a jewel neckline and natural waistline and a full, short sleeve. Her pattern collection consists of only these two shapes, plus a long, fitted sleeve, repeated in standard dress sizes. All changes are made to these patterns. Walsh is closest to a size 10, but her torso is a bit longer than average, and she has a slight swayback. Although Pavani takes measurements, she can often predict them, a skill that came in handy once when she lost the measurements of a bride who lived some distance

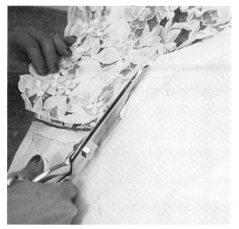

Pavani cuts lace for the bodice, using the bodice lining and the pattern as guides. (Photo by author)

From *Threads* magazine (June 1988) 17:52-56

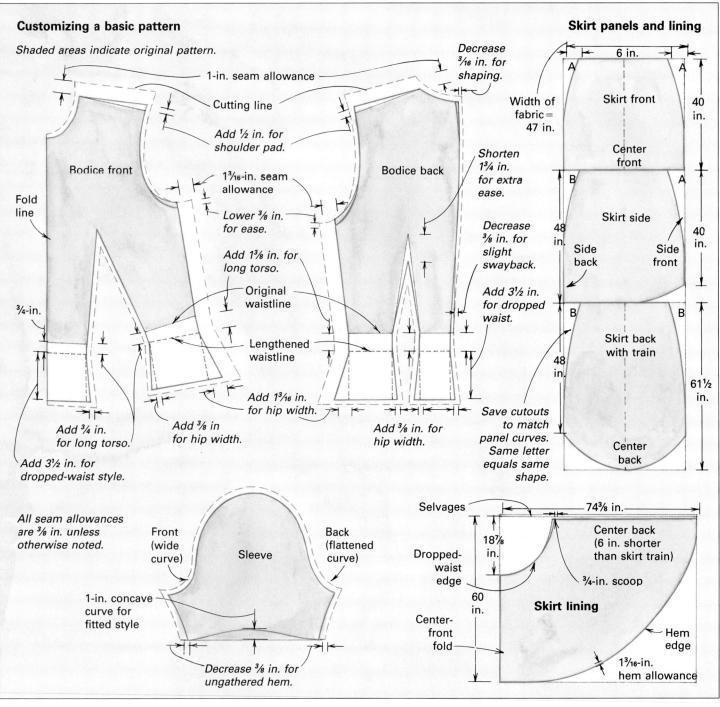

Customizing a basic pattern

Shaded areas indicate original pattern.

1-in. seam allowance

Cutting line

Add ½ in. for shoulder pad.

Decrease ³⁄₁₆ in. for shaping.

Bodice front

Fold line

1³⁄₁₆-in. seam allowance

Lower ³⁄₈ in. for ease.

Add 1³⁄₈ in. for long torso.

Bodice back

Shorten 1¾ in. for extra ease.

Decrease ³⁄₈ in. for slight swayback.

Add 3½ in. for dropped waist.

Original waistline

Lengthened waistline

³⁄₄-in.

Add ¾ in. for long torso.

Add ³⁄₈ in for hip width.

Add 1³⁄₁₆ in. for hip width.

Add ³⁄₈ in. for hip width.

Add 3½ in. for dropped-waist style.

Save cutouts to match panel curves. Same letter equals same shape.

All seam allowances are ³⁄₈ in. unless otherwise noted.

Front (wide curve)

Sleeve

Back (flattened curve)

1-in. concave curve for fitted style

Decrease ³⁄₈ in. for ungathered hem.

Skirt panels and lining

Width of fabric = 47 in.

6 in.

A | A

Skirt front

Center front

40 in.

B | A

Skirt side

Side back | Side front

48 in.

40 in.

B | B

Skirt back with train

Center back

48 in.

61½ in.

Selvages

74³⁄₈ in.

Dropped-waist edge

18⁷⁄₈ in.

Center back (6 in. shorter than skirt train)

¾-in. scoop

60 in.

Center-front fold

Skirt lining

Hem edge

1³⁄₁₆-in. hem allowance

Illustrations by Mark Kara

away. Embarrassed to call and admit the loss, she made a perfectly fitting gown from the measurements in her visual memory.

With a clear idea of the finished style of the dress, Pavani alters the pattern pieces shown above. She lengthens the bodice front at the waistline to fit Walsh's torso and adds several inches to the bodice bottom for the dropped-waist design. She adds width at the side and at the lower dart edges to adjust for upper-hip width. To allow for ½-in.-thick shoulder pads, she adds to the height of the shoulder, then lowers the armhole edge for ease.

Pavani alters the back-bodice pattern to correspond to the front, with a bit of shaping for Walsh's swayback. She narrows the top center back to add the fit that a shoulder dart would provide without an extra seamline to interrupt the lace pattern. For

the same reason, as well as to give extra ease across the shoulders and back, she shortens the back dart.

The sleeve pattern needs only minor changes because the sleeve is already tall and full. Pavani narrows the sleeve and draws a concave curve across the bottom edge. The sleeve should fit close to the arm, and the bottom curve should flatten to a straight line on the body.

Cutting—After the new patterns without seam allowances are traced and cut out (no patterns are used for the skirt panels and lining), the dress fabrics are unrolled across the cutting table. Pavani cuts the lining with seam allowances for the bodice and sleeves. Allowances vary in width according to the stress the seams will receive and the amount of alterations they may need.

Centering the lace motif on the pattern piece, Pavani pins the bodice tissue and lining pieces to the lace and cuts the lace. She'll save the lace scraps. Individual motifs will be carefully snipped apart and hand-stitched over the neckline, sleeve, and bodice's lower edges. This will finish the edges neatly and give a more natural-looking, less severe appearance than a straight-cut or hemmed" edge. Even for a designer who handles very expensive lace as a matter of course, the first snip of the shears is still vaguely traumatic.

The lace sleeves are to be underlined with two layers of sheer organza. To avoid sleeve hems, Pavani forgoes the curved sleeve hems and cuts the organza with the fold at the hems. Organza and lace are cut together.

The skirt and its lining are cut without a pattern (see drawings above), based on the intended finished length of the skirt from dropped-waist seam to the floor. Using four panels rather than two eliminates an awkward center-front or center-back seam. Each panel is cut to the full width of the silk taffeta, but the seam edges curve in slightly near the waist to decrease uncomfortable and ungainly bulk at the hipline. Curving also creates a slight bias at the seams and adds a bit to the skirt's length.

The curve of the skirt's hemline and train is carefully plotted; the hemline must be slightly above the floor in the front for walking ease, should skim the floor at the sides, and should sweep smoothly into the full length of the train. Pavani marks the measurements on the front panel with pins at the fabric's selvages and cuts it out. She saves the triangular side scraps to duplicate the curve on the side panels. She cuts the rounded bottom edges of the side and back pieces, judging the curve by eye.

To reduce bulk at the hip seam, Pavani decides to cut a semicircular skirt lining from 60-in.-wide satin. The lining will then fall smoothly yet sparsely from the seam (bottom-left photo) over the hips without sacrificing the generous fullness desired at the hemline.

The semicircular waistline opening is scooped out deeper at the center back to give a bit of extra fullness over the buttocks. Cutting a wider opening creates a longer waistline edge for the skirt; the extra fullness is taken in at the waistline seam by gathering. A smaller opening would make the skirt fit more closely at the waist and hips with fewer gathers.

Construction—The flat pieces take shape under the careful hands of one of Pavani's seamstresses. The seamstress treats the lace and lining of the bodice and each sleeve as one layer to give body to the construction and facilitate last-minute alterations. Seam-allowance edges are zigzag-finished, and the lace is released from the bodice side seams just above the skirt edge so it can lie over the hipline seam. The lace is trimmed around the motif edges, and the edge is covered with additional motifs (top photo).

A small ruff of organdy is stitched to the top of the sleeve-bodice seam on the inside to keep the sleeve cap tall and crisp (bottom-right photo). Pavani decides to allow the back-bodice lace to stand uninterrupted and unadorned. She chooses a zipper (rather than covered buttons), which will be streamlined and unobtrusive, especially when it is hand-stitched.

The skirt and its lining are kept separate. Gathers at the hip seam are arranged after basting to provide slightly more fullness at the back and sides; the front should be a bit smoother for a neat appearance. The skirt fabric is turned back at the hemline and zigzagged at the fold. The excess is trimmed off to allow the silk taffeta to float airily with no hemline weight.

Edge finishes for sleeve and skirt hems are important in a custom gown. The taffeta skirt (above) has narrow zigzag stitches sewn right on the folded hemline. Lace motifs overhang the edge of the organza sleeve lining. A hand-sewn zipper (left) is unobtrusive in the back bodice. Because the skirt lining is semicircular, it is less bulky than the main-skirt material. Below, an organza ruff maintains the tall, puffed sleeve cap, while a shoulder pad grabs the shoulder when the gown is worn.

First fitting—The bride-to-be arrives for the first fitting two weeks after the fabric is cut. Although the dress is fully assembled, it is unfinished. Now Walsh and Pavani make final decisions about design details and fine-tune the fit. The gown should be ready to take home after the second fitting in two weeks, barring drastic weight changes.

When Walsh emerges from the dressing room clad in the gown, Pavani sees minor details that aren't quite right. With the shoulder pads inserted, the shoulders seem a bit snug, so she decides to release ½ in. from the shoulder seam. She also lowers the underarm seam for extra comfort.

Attention moves to the hip seam. Walsh wears a crinoline half-slip to give the skirt fullness, but its bulk creates a lumpy mass of wrinkles across her abdomen. They decide to forgo the crinoline because the lin-

ing itself will give enough support and will keep Walsh cooler.

The seamline flower appliqué on the left hip is slightly lower than that on the right, and the asymmetry is disturbing. Pavani measures the position of the lower appliqué to duplicate it on the other side.

Now for the train. The lining, though shorter than the skirt shell, drags awkwardly and persists in peeking out, especially when the train is bustled up. Pavani recommends that the lining be trimmed to just above floor level all around. Since the dress fabric is opaque, lining for the train is not strictly necessary. To shape the bustle, Pavani picks up the skirt midway between the waist and floor and secures it with three pins at the hip seam. The taffeta holds its shape gallantly as a fine-quality fabric should, and the train hem just skims

Three pairs of hooks and eyes support the bustle's shape. Lace motifs at the bottom edge of the bodice hide the hooks; the white thread eyes are invisible on the skirt.

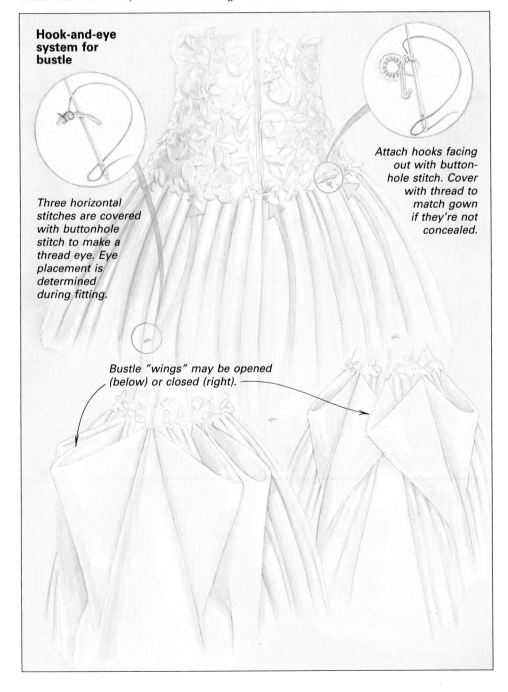

Hook-and-eye system for bustle

Three horizontal stitches are covered with buttonhole stitch to make a thread eye. Eye placement is determined during fitting.

Attach hooks facing out with buttonhole stitch. Cover with thread to match gown if they're not concealed.

Bustle "wings" may be opened (below) or closed (right).

the floor in the back. The pins will be replaced with hooks hidden under the petals of lace at the hip seam and nearly invisible white thread eyes on the skirt, shown in the drawing and photo at left. For extra insurance, a wrist loop concealed on the underside of the train can be used to lift the train should the hook-and-eye system fall prey to an overzealous dancing shoe.

The bride will wear pearl earrings. Could a sprinkling of seed pearls at the neckline or over the bodice tie the whole look together? Pavani hesitates. "The lace is like a beautiful picture," she observes finally. "You can't put it in an elaborate frame without detracting from its own beauty." The lace bodice will stand unadorned. How about some trim at the hemline? This idea is pondered but is ultimately rejected; both designer and bride agree that it would look too "average."

Final adjustments—With the wedding a month away and other dresses in the works, Pavani has her work cut out for her. The gown will leave the shop after a second fitting, by which time a host of details must be completed to everyone's satisfaction.

Commercially made shoulder pads are covered with lining fabric, gathered with long basting stitches at the armhole edges to help them "grab" the shoulders (bottom-right photo, p. 95), and stitched invisibly to the seam allowances.

Not least of all is the last detail—pressing. With masses of satin and silk taffeta engulfing her, Pavani manages to accomplish the task on a standard ironing board. She drapes the iron's cord over a folding room divider to prevent it from dragging over the dress and destroying her efforts.

This is the time to check for any spots that may have appeared on the dress. Pavani generally uses a cloth dipped in a solution of Ivory Snow and water. Starting at the center, she "smudges" a spot, blotting it with a dry cloth from the back and gently blending the wet area outward to prevent a harsh water stain. She usually tests a scrap of fabric first to determine whether this method will work safely.

The gown goes home—Two weeks to the day before her wedding, Walsh returns. The dress is completed and waiting, encased in a long, white garment bag. At this fitting everything is perfect. Walsh beams into the mirror as Pavani tugs lightly at this and that, nudging the gown into its final shape for a sneak preview of its debut down the aisle. Perhaps this garment will be worn for only a few all-too-brief hours, but what glorious hours they'll be! □

Janice Steinhagen is a weaver, seamstress, writer, and art teacher who lives in Voluntown, CT. She has written articles on Chinese drawloom weaving and double-sided embroidery.

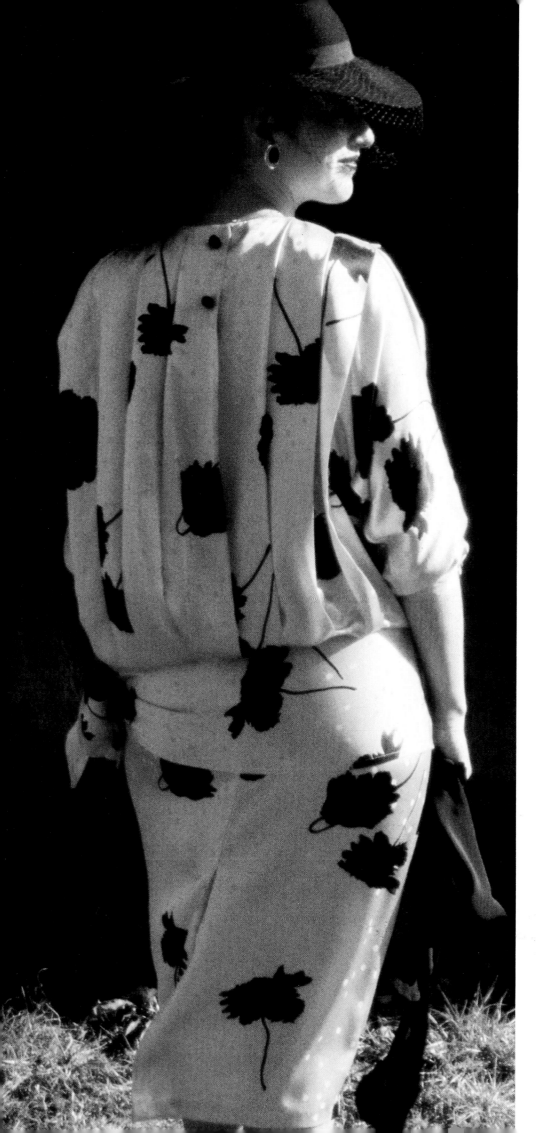

Sewing with Silk

This fiber deserves care, but don't be afraid to wash it

by Janet Stoyer

What is stronger than some kinds of steel, more resilient than elastic, made by worms, and known as the queen of fibers? Silk, of course. Silk appears delicate, yet is the strongest of all natural fibers. It can be stretched and later returned to its original shape. It is highly absorbent and therefore comfortable to wear in both summer and winter. Dyed silk cloth has a deeper, richer appearance than most other dyed fabrics, and it has a gorgeous luster and drape.

How does one get into the 5000-year-old silk business? In my case it was love at first sight. One experience with this natural fabric led to another, which in turn led me to start a business designing, sewing, and selling silk clothing.

Buying silk

The adventure starts when I buy the silk. I usually purchase it wholesale from New York or California, either on buying trips or by mail order. This is a difficult job for me because, when I see samples of all the types and colors, I want them all. To get a wholesale price, I have to buy in quantity, and so I must make careful choices. I am constantly looking for new wholesalers to obtain a wider variety of silks.

When buying silk, I consider both the source of the silk and the weave of the fabric, as both will affect the texture and drape of the garment. There are basically two types of silk: cultivated and wild.

Cultivated silk is spun by silkworms that are raised on silk farms and feed only on mulberry trees. Most silk produced and available today is cultivated silk. Silk crepe de chine, which is closely woven of fine cultivated silk threads, is one of the most popu-

Stoyer models one of her silk outfits.

lar silks with my customers. It has a beautiful drape, it gathers around the waist without adding extra fullness, and it enhances most figure types. I use it for dresses, blouses, and even skirts.

Wild silk, on the other hand (also called tussah silk), comes from wild silkworms that feed chiefly on oak leaves. Produced mostly in China and India, wild silk is difficult to bleach because it is naturally tan or brown. It is coarser and less shiny than cultivated silk and is suitable for skirts and unconstructed jackets.

Raw or noil silk is made from yarn that is tightly spun of short silk fibers. Dupioni is a raw silk that is popular with my customers. It is woven of nubby silk strands thicker than those of crepe de chine. It appears to be stiff and prickly, but is not at all uncomfortable to wear. It has a nice sheen and makes an interesting and eye-catching garment. This fabric is generally good for unlined, baggy, loose-fitting styles.

Another popular silk is a suit-weight raw silk. It has good body and therefore looks nice when worn, yet is soft against the skin. Raw silk is good for unlined jackets. Most of these silks retail for $20/yd. to $35/yd.

Lightweight silk is best suited to styles that fit loosely. If the fit is tight, undo strain is placed on seams, causing wrinkles. Because of the way lightweight silk drapes, fewer seams, darts, and fitting lines are required.

Preparing the silk

I prewash silk whenever possible, in plain water, to remove the chemical finish called sizing and to shrink the fabric before sewing the garment. Water does not harm silk fabric, but actually refreshes the fibers. It is used throughout the silk-making process both to loosen the fiber from the cocoon and to remove the sericin, a gummy, protective substance that surrounds the silk in the cocoon.

All fabrics are treated with sizing to keep them looking fresh and to keep them on the bolts evenly. But it's the sizing that causes the fabric to spot if water is splashed on it, because the sizing evaporates when wet. Prewashing usually eliminates the problem and makes sewing easier as well. Sizing, if left on the fabric, builds up on the sewing machine needle, slowing the machine and causing skipped stitches.

I also prewash to shrink the fabric before sewing the garment so that the garment won't shrink later. Although I sometimes lose a lot of fabrics like crepe de chine when I prewash, I still think prewashing is worthwhile because the garment can be hand-washed instead of dry-cleaned.

Before prewashing the whole length of fabric, I test a piece to see what changes occur and to decide whether the changes are acceptable. Has the color suffered? Dye runoff changes the color somewhat. If more than one color is to be used in the same garment, will the colors bleed into each other? Has the texture changed? If so, will the fabric be too stiff or too soft? Has the surface lost too much sheen? How much has the fabric shrunk? After prewashing a suit-weight raw silk I found that there was no shrinkage or color change, but the fabric had lost its stiffness and was no longer appropriate for the suit I'd planned to make. If your test suggests that you should not prewash, steam the silk with an iron before cutting it. This preshrinks the fabric so that dry-cleaning presses won't shrink the garment later on.

To prewash a length of fabric, I soak it for five or ten minutes in a tub of lukewarm water. Soap isn't necessary to remove the sizing or shrink the fabric. I sometimes wash up to 26 yd. at a time in the bathtub. I squeeze out as much water as I can, and I roll the yardage between sheets and towels on my living room floor. I then put the fabric over a drying rack to let it dry somewhat.

While the silk is still damp, I iron it dry on the wrong side, using a medium heat setting. For ironing, I use my dining room table layered with blankets because it provides a larger surface than an ironing board. After ironing, I return the silk to the drying rack to be sure all the moisture is out before I roll the silk back onto the bolt. Whenever possible, and especially with dark-colored fabrics, iron silk on the wrong side to avoid glazing the fabric. If you must iron it on the right side, for finishing touches, for example, either gently touch the iron to the silk, or use a press cloth between the silk and the iron. The iron should be just hot enough to get steam.

Constructing the garment

The quality of a finished garment is proportionate to the care you invest in its construction. Handsewing, finishing the seams, and making test samples all take time but add to the value of the garment. I use weights rather than pins to hold the pattern pieces on the fabric when cutting out a garment, as they're safer and faster. If you prefer pins, however, use very fine sharp pins, and test them on the silk to be sure they don't leave holes or pulls. It's also a good idea to pin in the seam allowance, which is usually ⅝ in. I cut just one garment at a time because most of my garments are one of a kind. Cutting only one or two layers at a time also minimizes the chance of the silk slipping and causing an off-grain cut.

Always test the needle on the fabric before sewing. Fine silk usually requires a size 9 or 10 needle, while heavyweight silk may require a size 14 or 16. It's best to put a new needle in the machine for each new garment. This helps eliminate skipped stitches. It's not necessary to use silk thread on silk fabric; a poly/cotton thread works fine. I often use imported long-staple polyester threads, which are more expensive but sew very evenly.

Interfacings—To protect areas of wear, such as collars, cuffs, and facings, and thereby extend the life of the garment, you should interface them. Interfacings also give garment pieces a nice crisp look. Like the fabric, interfacing should be preshrunk before it is cut; otherwise, it may pucker when the garment is washed.

There are no rules about what interfacing to use, and for each garment I must decide which will look best. I often test several before deciding. For example, on a very lightweight silk dress I made for my daughter, I felt that even the sheerest interfacing was not sheer enough, so I used an extra layer of the same fabric in the collar to give it the needed body.

On my crepe-de-chine garments I use a very lightweight interfacing, sometimes a sew-in one and sometimes a fusible one. Fusible interfacing tends to make the facing stiffer. On heavier-weight silks I use a woven fusible interfacing called Armo Weft (60% polyester, 40% rayon), and I've been very satisfied with it. It also comes in a lighter weight, called Whisper Weft. Another fusible interfacing I've used is Stacy's Easy-Knit, which is a 100% nylon knit suitable for lightweight fabrics.

If I don't like the look of fusible interfacing on the outer fabric, I sometimes apply it to the facing instead. It isn't visible there, but it still provides firmness and extra support. To keep facings from turning out, I understitch the seam, as in the photo below. Stitch on the right side of the facing, close to the seam, through all seam allowances. Then press the seam allowance toward the facing.

Seams—Seam finishes affect the total look of a garment, and finished seams add value to it. I use ⅝-in. seam allowances unless I'm putting in a narrow neck band or sleeve bands. Then I sew ⅜-in. seams. Pressing the seams is important to the finished appearance. Press gently, applying steam. I use a variety of seam finishes, depending on the garment and the fabric.

After sewing the seams right sides together and pressing them open, I some-

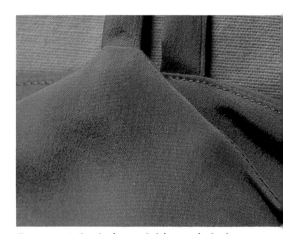

To prevent the facings of this camisole from turning out, Stoyer understitches the facing to all seam allowances, close to the seam line.

times overlock the edges with my overlock machine (a commercial Merrow machine). If you don't have an overlock machine, you can zigzag the edges with a sewing machine. Or, for a neater finish on lightweight silk, I turn under the raw edges ⅛ in. and straight-stitch.

I often use Seams Great, which is a narrow bias strip of soft, sheer fabric that comes in many colors and is available in fabric stores. Simply wrap it around the raw edge and straight-stitch. I use it on even the sheerest silk, as it is not at all bulky. In the photo directly below I've used Seams Great to finish the seam of a crepe-de-chine top. On lightweight silk I sometimes prefer to simply sew the raw edges together, then trim the seam to ⅜ in. I use this seam finish on crepe-de-chine slacks for a smoother look and on the side and underarm seams of dolman-sleeve blouses.

On camisoles I sew French seams so that the raw edges are locked into the seams. For a French seam, sew a ¼-in. seam with the wrong sides of the fabric together. Then turn the garment right sides together and stitch a ⅜-in. seam.

Bulky areas—Collars, cuffs, and plackets can be bulky areas. Grading seams (trimming them at different widths), notching out some fabric, and trimming corners close to the stitching all help to reduce bulk. Before trimming, reinforce the seam with an extra row of fine stitches to help prevent fraying. I sometimes apply a liquid plastic called Fray Check (available in most fabric stores) to corners where a close trim is necessary. Fray Check locks the threads together. It forms a stiff spot, though, so it should not be used where it would rub against the skin.

Pockets—Pockets are always popular. I usually finish the top of the pocket and then turn in and press the seam allowances at the sides and bottom. For pressing I insert a metal plate between the seam allowances and the pocket to prevent the seam allowances from making an indentation on the pocket. After the pocket has been formed, I position it carefully on the garment. If it is not lined up properly, it can ruin the look of the garment.

At times I sew on pockets by hand to give them a softer look. This takes time because I must make many small stitches to handle the strain on a pocket, and each stitch must be hidden.

Zippers—When I put in a zipper by machine, I baste the seam closed, then stitch each side of the zipper to the seam allowances only, aligning the teeth with the seam and stitching each side from bottom to top. Then I topstitch from the right side of the garment. This way, I can make sure the stitching lines are straight and evenly spaced from the seam. It's difficult to put a zipper in sheer fabric, such as crepe de chine, because the silk has a tendency to slip as you sew. Therefore, when I have an expensive garment and the zipper must look right, I hand-prick the zipper.

Buttons and buttonholes—Machine-made buttonholes are widely used on all garments. But I always test them on scrap fabric before making them in the garment. If I see that the feed dog is marking the fabric, I put tissue paper between the feed dog and the fabric to sew the buttonhole. I pull the tissue paper off when I'm finished. Sometimes I make bound buttonholes in jackets.

For a special effect I handsew buttonholes. After reinforcing the area with fine machine stitches and cutting the hole, I often apply Fray Check to the raw edges. I then sew around the buttonhole with a worked buttonhole stitch, as in the photo directly below, and sew a bar tack at the end. A hand-worked buttonhole helps to prevent pulled threads because the hand stitching locks in all the threads. I usually cover buttons with the garment fabric to give the garment an elegant touch.

Hems—The width of the hem and the hem finish depend on the garment style and the weight of the fabric. To finish the raw edge of the hem I zigzag the edge, enclose it in Seams Great, or turn the raw edge in once. The first two treatments are more suitable for heavier fabrics, where a turned-in edge would create unwanted bulk. I then hand-stitch or machine-topstitch the hem in place. On a straight-cut crepe-de-chine dress or skirt, I usually put in a 1½-in. finished hem, turn in the raw edge, and then hand-stitch it, as in the photo directly below. But on a full skirt or dress in lightweight fabric I put in a narrow ¼-in. hem, turn in the raw edge, and hand-stitch or machine-topstitch. On the heavier-weight silks I put in a 1½-in. to 3-in. hem because it makes a crisper finished edge. If the hem in a full skirt is not going in smoothly, steam the hem when you are finished sewing, without pressing hard, and much of the fullness will ease in.

Caring for silk

The most important thing to remember when caring for silk is that it should be cleaned often. If you preshrank the fabric when you started your project, you can also hand-wash the finished garment. Always use a mild detergent and lukewarm water. Then iron it on the wrong side while it is still damp. Frequent washing allows silk garments to come clean without the use of concentrated detergents or prolonged soakings. In addition, moths won't attack clean silk.

If you didn't preshrink your fabric, or if it's a suit-weight fabric or heavily constructed garment unsuitable for hand washing, have the garment dry-cleaned often. Make sure the dry cleaner knows it is silk, and point out any stains or marks.

Be careful what chemicals may come in contact with your silk fabrics and garments. The chemicals in both deodorants and perfumes, for example, will weaken the silk's protein fibers. You can use Static Guard, however, if you find it necessary to do so, but be sure to apply it to the wrong side of the garment. □

Janet Stoyer designs, sews, and sells silk clothing at Sensual Silk, her business in Schuylkill Haven, PA.

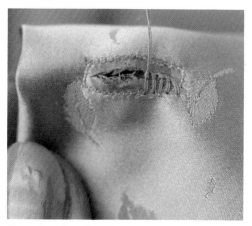

To make a hand-worked buttonhole, Stoyer outlines the area with a fine machine stitch, then hand-stitches with a buttonhole stitch.

At the hem of this silk crepe-de-chine skirt, Stoyer has turned the raw edge in and hand-stitched the hem in place with a catchstitch.

To make a quick seam finish for lightweight or heavyweight silks, Stoyer often encloses the raw edges in Seams Great, a narrow bias tape.

Lamé

These razzmatazz fabrics can add glamour to any garment, but first you need to know how to keep them from fraying

by Ann Boyce

When I see a piece of fabric, I want to attack it with my Ginghers, cut it up into shapes and strips, combine it with other fabrics, and sew it back together. I work with fabrics as a painter works with pigments. Strong colors and shapes when sewn together can be transformed into a unique fabric.

I spent several years making quilts, and now I create wearable-art clothing with patchwork or appliqué surfaces. When I was asked to design a wearable-art garment for the Fairfield/Concord Fashion Show, I chose solid-color cottons. After many years of working with printed fabrics in the quilts I made for clients, I felt it would be a welcome challenge to create a garment in solid colors, as an artist would use paint straight from the tube, with no shading of colors. As I began my surface design for the garment, a close friend said, "You need a little glitz on that to make it show on the runway." I realized the advice was right on target. The Fairfield show travels around the country as a modeled runway show, and the garments that catch your eye have some kind of glitter—either through the embellishments or fabrics.

I decided on lamé, that eye-catching metallic fabric. To give the cottons in "Saw Grass Fire" (see photo on page 103) some spark, I added two types of silver lamé between the appliqué sections in the Seminole patchwork and as a border for the entire garment. I even studded some of the silver patchwork with clear rhinestones so that they'd catch the lights on the runway and sparkle as the wearer moved. The inside of the garment is entirely patchwork and appliqué in black cotton and three types of silver lamé. I later appliquéd a silver lamé moon onto the outside of the shoulder with silver thread.

Lamé fabrics contain metals, such as aluminum, copper, gold, and silver, or stainless steel. Some of them are coated with plastic to prevent their oxidizing and darkening. Nylon, the generic term for polyamide, makes up 12% to 27% of the lamés

mentioned in this article, except for tricot lamé, which contains 82% nylon. Unlike natural fibers, nylon is impervious to the elements (although it will melt), is very strong, and doesn't tear easily.

I work with five types of lamé: tricot lamé, tissue lamé, soft-backed lamé, brocade lamé, and pleated lamé. I live near Boston and New York City, where I can easily purchase different colors and types of lamés, but an excellent selection is also available by mail from Jehlor Fantasy Fabrics (see "Sources," page 103).

Tricot lamé is the easiest lamé to work with. It handles and sews beautifully with all other fabrics, so I often use it for patchwork. It doesn't ravel like the other lamés, it's soft and pliable, it drapes well in a garment, and it doesn't shrink or become dull after being machine-washed. Tricot lamé consists of a metallic surface bonded onto a tricot (or knit) backing of nylon. Because of the backing, the lamé is opaque and needs no lining. When pinned to a pattern piece with sharp, fine pins, it is easily cut with a scissors, or a rotary cutter, which is fast and accurate. It can be cut out in any direction without regard to straight of grain. Free-form shapes can be clipped and turned easily. This lamé is the most economical, as every scrap can be used.

Tricot lamé is available in 11 colors and in a 54-in. width, so it's a good value. Like all lamés, this fabric cannot withstand direct contact with a hot iron; the metallic surface will stick to the iron, and the fabric will dull. Always use a press cloth. (With the VaporSimac iron, which has constant steam, you can iron all other lamés directly without dulling or damaging them.)

Tissu is the French word for *fabric,* and the English word, *tissue,* has come to mean a lightweight woven fabric. Tissue lamé is closely woven, usually available in 40-in. to 45-in. widths, with a 73% metal content and a 27% nylon content. It can be hand-washed and should be air-dried. Tissue lamé is rather translucent, and so I back it with another fabric in a complementary color. Fourteen solid colors are available from

Jehlor Fantasy Fabrics. I recently strip-pieced turquoise tissue lamé on top of turquoise 100% cotton fabric. Strip-piecing is a technique of sewing one strip at a time onto a backing fabric that's been cut to the exact size of the pattern piece or the quilt or appliqué shape. Gold and silver pleated lamés are permanently pleated versions of the solid-color tissue lamés.

Tissue lamé can also be cut into bias strips with the rotary cutter. The fabric ravels less when cut on the bias. The strips are pulled through a bias tapemaker (available through Imports by Clotilde—see "Sources," page 103). The tapemaker turns under both raw edges ¼ in. as they pass through it. I iron the turned-under edges, roll them onto a cardboard tube or plastic soft-drink bottle, and secure them with masking tape to get them flat and smooth.

For a more textured look in the same weight of fabric, I use one of the brocade tissue lamés. Brocade lamé is woven so that the pattern has a shiny, raised effect. Brocade feather tissue lamé is woven with black nonmetallic threads. The right side has just a touch of black pattern showing through, but the wrong side, which you could also use, has about a 50/50 proportion of color to black. Brocade lamé woven with all the same color metallic threads is heavier and much more textured.

There is a soft-backed lamé that consists of shiny acrylic, polyester, and nylon threads bonded onto a very soft, woven fabric. This fabric must be dry-cleaned. The colored metallic fibers are loosely woven, and the fabric has the brightest sheen of all the lamés, which is why I am partial to it, although it is the least durable. When this lamé is machine-stitched, the loosely woven threads can snap and poke out of the fabric. They can be trimmed off with scissors, but there's still a risk of their raveling.

After my "Saw Grass Fire" garment was ready to be shipped, I noticed the threads had popped out in the areas with soft-backed lamé. I spread Dritz Fray Check, a clear, runny fluid that prevents raveling, over the entire surface of these threads.

From *Threads* magazine (December 1986) 8:32-35

Brocade feather tissue lamé is woven with nonmetallic black threads. The front side (left) has just a touch of black pattern showing through, but the reverse side (right) has about a 50/50 proportion of color to black. Brocade lamés woven entirely with metallic threads are heavier and more textured.

The coat's interior batting prevented the Fray Check from bleeding through onto the lining. Fray Check will slightly darken the color of the lamé, but when applied evenly over the entire surface, it dries with even coverage. If you apply Fray Check to only part of the lamé, you'll see a line between the treated and untreated areas. (Fray Check does stain non-lamé fabrics, so it cannot be used on a colored silk or cotton that will be visible in the garment.) I recently used Fray Check on a blue soft-backed lamé before I sewed it. I spread the lamé out on wax paper and painted it liberally with Fray Check, then let it thoroughly air-dry. The fabric was stiff, but much more stable than usual. It handled well for machine appliqué, and the threads did not snap as they were sewn, as before. I love the brilliance of this particular fabric, and pretreating the fabric has given it the stability it needs for the wear it will get. The 15 colors make it an attractive alternative to the thinner tissue lamés.

Preventing raveling—No special laundering or preshrinking is needed before lamés are sewn, but all of them (except tricot lamé) ravel. I've learned the hard way that even if you leave a large seam allowance, the lamé will ravel and pull loose from the seam—a nightmare in a completed garment.

There are many solutions to the problem. The quickest is to fuse the lamé to a 100% cotton, woven fusible interfacing before you cut it to give it stability and keep it from raveling. Fusing is especially good for appliqué pieces, which need to be firm.

Steam-press and fuse the interfacing to the lamé by covering both pieces with a damp press cloth. On an ironing board, layer the fusible interfacing, glue side up (you can see and feel the dots of glue); the lamé, right side up; and the press cloth (I use a linen kitchen towel). The press cloth keeps the fusing substance from gumming up the iron's surface. (If some does get on the iron, put a handful of table salt on newspaper, and iron the newspaper until the iron's surface is clean.) If you use a

Boyce combines tricot, soft-backed, brocade feather tissue, pleated, brocade, and tissue lamés (shown here clockwise from top right) with cottons, silks, and velvets for special effects in her garments. The two soft-backed lamés at top left have been fused with cotton woven interfacing.

Detail of kimono entitled "Games People Play." Designed and constructed by Kimberly Long Masopust, of Somis, CA, using tissue lamés. Photo by Richard Billings.

regular home iron, wet the press cloth. I have a VaporSimac iron, which is available mail order through Treadleart (see "Sources," page 103). After having thrown out an iron every year when it started to leak and spit, I decided to indulge myself in this high steam/continuous steam iron, which will fuse through a dry press cloth, saving time and frustration. After the bonded lamé is dry, cut it to shape or into strips with scissors or a rotary cutter.

Fusible webbing is a see-through spider-web-like fabric. Sold under the trade names Jiffy Fuse and Stitch Witchery, it is available by the yard in an 18-in. width. You can use it to sandwich the bonded lamé to the background or base fabric before you appliqué, but I rarely do this—once in place, the piece is almost permanently positioned, and to reposition or remove it, you must apply a lot of steam. The webbing also leaves a glue residue, which sometimes distorts the color of the background fabric.

Fusible webbing can be fused to the appliqué piece and background fabric at the same time. If you want to fuse only one side of the fabric, you can use No-Stick Appliqué Press Sheet, a heat-resistant plastic sheet that is placed on the ironing board under the fabric and fusible webbing. This is especially good for complicated designs. The fabric, bonded on one side with fusible webbing, can be cut out into shapes, arranged onto its background, and fused in place on the background fabric later. The plastic sheet also keeps the fusible webbing from moving around under the appliqué pieces before they are fused together.

If I am appliquéing tissue lamés, I often fuse them, then cut them into shapes. When I use tissue lamés in patchwork, to retain their softness while still protecting them from raveling, instead of fusing, I lay the fabric on wax paper and apply a thin line of Fray Check around its edge. After the piece has dried thoroughly, I hold it up to the light to make sure that I've covered all the raw edges. I also use Fray Check on the edges of lamé pieces I'll be using in patchwork. The Fray Check bleeds about ⅛ in. to ¼ in. into the fabric edges, but this isn't a problem in patchwork, as the edges are sewn into a seam.

As a safeguard, Fray Check can also be used on the edges of fused lamés intended for appliqué. The combination of fusing the lamé fabric first and then applying Fray Check to the edges leaves only the slimmest possibility the fabric will fray in a garment that gets heavy wear or in a place where there is friction, such as under the arm. When the shape is appliquéd onto the background, the sewing-machine zig-zag stitches that I use for appliqué cover the Fray-Checked edges so they don't show.

I once overlocked the raw edge of a piece of lamé on my serger to prevent fraying. I thought this would be an easy solution. It wasn't. The line of overlock stitching pulled right off the fabric edge. What did work was this: I overlocked the edge, flipped the blade out of the way, turned the serged edge under, and then overlocked the edge once again to hold the first stitching in place. An even more secure method is to change the serger foot and plate to a rolled-edge attachment and serge a rolled hem. The serger rolled-edge attachment automatically rolls the edge under in one step, instead of your having to manually turn under the edge as you feed it into the serger blade. Again, flip up the blade and serge another rolled edge on top of the first one. The slight disadvantage to this method is that the finished seam edging is a little more bulky than it is when you simply overlock-stitch.

Another way to finish edges is to make French seams, but I don't have the patience for this. Seams Great, a sheer sewing tape, provides a better way to machine-finish raw edges. Follow the manufacturer's directions and machine-stitch the tape near the raw edge of the lamé. The tape will naturally roll over the raw edge to the opposite side of the fabric. Run a loose zigzag stitch over the tape's other raw edge to enclose the lamé edge. This tape finishes off the seams nicely, especially for a garment, and there's no bulk in the finished seam.

When sewing with lamés, be sure to use a new needle in your machine. An old needle may be dull or have a burr on the tip. A dull needle can cause skipped stitches, and a burr may pull a thread. This is also true for other woven fabrics—cotton, silk, linen, etc. As a general rule, for the best results, change your sewing-machine needle after eight hours of sewing, and if you sew into or over a pin accidentally, throw out the needle. This seems extravagant, but it's necessary to ensure even sewing and no pulling of threads. Use a size 11 in an American machine and a size 80 in a European machine. The lower the number, the thinner the needle. A thick needle will leave larger-than-thread-width holes in the fabric. For this reason, you should also use sharp, thin straight pins. I prefer the thin European glass-headed pins that come on a paper wheel. The glass heads make them easier to pick up. Silk pins are the thinnest, but I find them hard to handle.

Lamés and other fabrics—When a lamé fabric is incorporated in a garment with fabrics that are not as shimmery—silks, cottons, velvets—the finished look can't be duplicated. Lamés add excitement to the piece; they are eye-catching, they have pizzazz. I use lamé fabrics sparingly, however. If you overuse the glitz, the garment will end up looking as though it should be worn by a Las Vegas showgirl. When used as an accent fabric, lamé can enhance the colors of the other fabrics. I started out using silver and gold lamés. Lately I have been experimenting with lamés of the same color as the garment.

My favorite fabrics to combine with lamés are 100% cottons or silk noil. Silk noil, my newest discovery, has a slight sheen, a nubby texture, and dark, characteristic flecks throughout, which when dyed, blend into the fabric well. The fiber comes from the inner part of a silk cocoon, and the fabric is often and incorrectly referred to as raw silk. It handles like a heavyweight cotton and is easy to sew. It doesn't ravel, it takes machine washing well, it holds its color, and it doesn't wiggle around when you cut or sew it. Noil is available in two weights and many wonderful solid colors.

I have a fairly substantial cache of non-glitz fabrics, but seeing all the new fashions made from glittery, lavish fabrics and adorned with sequins, beads, or rhinestones, makes my creative ideas soar. I am off in serious pursuit of anything that sparkles, shines, or glitters. □

Ann Boyce, of Salem, MA, is a free-lance designer, whose creations have appeared in several magazines. In her spare time, she is a free-lance professional double-bassist and is required to wear black.

Sources

Aardvark Adventures
240 North I St.
P.O. Box 2449
Livermore, CA 94550
(415) 443-ANTS
Interesting array of threads and other treasures for embellishing garments.

Concord Fabrics
1359 Broadway
New York, NY 10018
(212) 760-0300
100% country cottons. Write for nearest supplier.

Fabric Arts
7 Pleasant St.
Gloucester, MA 01930
(617) 281-3305
Swatches, $2; silk noil.

Fairfield Processing Corp.
Donna Wilder, Director Retail Marketing
88 Rose Hill Ave.
P.O. Drawer 1130
Danbury, CT 06813
(203) 744-2090
Batting. Write for nearest supplier. Every year since 1979, The Fairfield/Concord Fashion Show, a juried, invitational show, has featured the work of about 50 designers. Last year's Starburst Show included garments with metallic lamé fabrics. 1986's Royal Star Show premiered in Houston in October and will travel throughout the country.

Folkwear Patterns
P.O. Box 3859, Dept. TD
San Raphael, CA 94912
(415) 457-0252
Color catalog, $1.

Imports by Clotilde, Inc.
237 S.W. 28th St.
Ft. Lauderdale, FL 33315
Catalog, $1. Olfa cutter, blades, and mat; Quickline by Nancy Crow; Fray Check; Seams Great; glass-headed pins; No-Stick Appliqué Press Sheet.

Jehlor Fantasy Fabrics
17900 Southcenter Parkway, Suite 290
Seattle, WA 98188
(206) 575-8250
Catalog, $2.50 (deducted from first order). Metallics, lamés, baubles, bangles, beads.

Newark Dressmaker Supply
6473 Ruch Rd.
P.O. Box 2448, Dept. TM
Lehigh Valley, PA 18001
(215) 837-7500
Free catalog. 100% woven fusible interfacing, Tear Away, Fray Check, clip-on rhinestones and rhinestone setter, metallic pearls.

Quintessence '84
Box 723544
Atlanta, GA 30339
Austrian rhinestones by the yard; unusual embellishments. Mailing list of upscale boutiques and owners for direct marketing of wearable art.

Treadleart
25834 Narbonne Ave., Suite 1
Lomita, CA 90717
(213) 534-5122
Catalog, $1. VaporSimac iron.

Getting into Leather

Methods for manipulating the world's oldest nonwoven fabric

by Arlene Handschuch

*l*eather has gone far beyond the basic black used for motorcycle jackets. It's available in many types, textures, weights, qualities, sizes, colors, and prices. If you'd like to try working with leather, start with a leather that's suitable for your project and a pattern that will fit on the skins you buy. I've been designing and making leather garments for several years and have found that almost any design is suitable as long as I select the leather characteristics to match the design.

Selection and purchase–If you're lucky enough to have a leather supplier in your area, you can see and feel the leather and make your selection directly from the shelves. If you don't have one, you can order leather from the suppliers listed on p. 107. To make your selection, you need to be familiar with some basic terms.

Leather is the tanned hide or skin of any animal. Tanning stops the hide's decomposition. *Vegetable-tanned* leather is usually firm, stiff, and water-resistant. It's good for shoes, saddles, and some jackets. Most of the leather you're likely to use for fine garments will be *chrome-tanned,* which produces a very soft, supple skin. It is not meant for all-weather wear.

Topstitching, covered buttons, and bound buttonholes are fine details in this lambsuede suit designed and constructed by Arlene Handschuch. The skirt pattern pieces fit on the small skins because the skirt has princess lines and a horizontal band at the hem.

A *hide* is leather from a large animal, such as a cow; large hides may be cut in half and sold as *sides*. A *skin* comes from a smaller animal, such as a lamb, calf, or young deer. *Splits* are created when the hide or skin is split into different thicknesses to yield thinner pieces or to even out irregular skin thickness. *Grain* is the smooth, outside surface of the hide or skin, from which the hair has been removed. The most common grain leathers come from cows and goats. *Suede,* the napped, inside surface of the hide or skin, is often created from splits. Most suede comes from lambs, pigs, deer, and cows.

Leathers differ in weight per square foot, strength, size, and the colors in which they're available. Hides and skins range from ¾ oz. to over 12 oz./sq. ft. The weight indicates thickness: Each ounce represents ¹⁄₆₄ in. of thickness (4 oz. = ¹⁄₁₆ in.). In general, the thinner the skin, the softer and more drapable it is. Lighter-weight skins usually come from younger and smaller animals. Thickness isn't particularly a measure of quality, which is determined by the type of animal, its environment and food source, and the processing. A deersuede and a lambsuede of equal weight, for example, may not have the same strength.

Leather prices vary from $1.50 to $5/sq. ft. You must buy an entire skin, hide, or side. The square footage is usually marked on one end of each skin with a number like 061, 062, or 063, which means 6¼ sq. ft., 6½ sq. ft., and 6¾ sq. ft., respectively. For quick reference, I've listed the weight and square footage per skin for common suedes and grain leathers in the table on p. 106.

Leathers are available in many colors; those sold for high-fashion apparel come in the greatest variety. Lambsuede and pigsuede come in luscious colors that follow the same trends as the fashion-fabrics market. There are also many embossed, perforated, and foiled leathers (see photo at right), as well as exotic snakeskin, lizard, turtle, and frog.

As with fabrics, you should examine skins carefully before purchasing them. Skins are seldom perfect and may have irregular shapes, scars, holes, wrinkles, and uneven thicknesses. Animals are rarely grown specifically for leather, and many skins are obtained from animals raised for meat. Size and color may vary from skin to skin even when the skins are from the same type of animal and color lot. Expect some flaws, but make sure you can live with them.

To figure out how many skins you need for a particular design, calculate the square footage of the pattern pieces. The most efficient way to do this is to make a paper duplicate of the skin you intend to use. You can then place all your pattern pieces on the paper skin and count the number of skins it will take. If you already know how many yards of fabric you need, convert the yards into square feet: 1 yd. of 36-, 45-, 54-,

Fashionable leathers are available in smooth or suede textures, a wide selection of colors, embossed and metallic-imprinted designs, and many different weights.

or 60-in.-wide fabric equals 9, 11, 13, and 15 sq. ft., respectively. Add at least 20% to the total footage to account for irregular skin shapes and imperfections.

When you choose your leather, the skins or hides ideally should be large enough for your individual pattern pieces. If your skirt-front pattern is 28 in. long, for example, it may not fit an average 6-sq.-ft. lambsuede skin; the skin is irregularly shaped, and the largest piece you would be able to fit in the middle of the skin is about 18 in. wide and 25 in. long. Check with your leather supplier to see if it has a pattern-layout service that allows you to send in your pattern so you can get the correct number of skins.

Design – Choose leather based on the type of garment you plan to make and the cost per skin. For high-fashion items, you can use weaker suedes and grains than for jackets or pants, as they'll receive less wear. For dresses and shirts and for soft skirts, jackets, and vests, I use 1- to 1½-oz. leathers. Many are buttery soft and supple, which drape beautifully, even for cowls and ruffles. For coats and pants and for vests and jackets that I want to have a more structured appearance, I choose 2- to 3-oz. leathers.

While many designs are possible, I recommend those that allow a shirt, blouse, or scarf to be worn underneath. This protects the leather from body oils and perspiration and reduces the need for frequent cleaning. I also like to line my leather pieces to prevent the suede from shedding onto garments worn underneath.

Also consider colorfastness when designing apparel that combines leather with other fabrics or that combines many colors of suede and leather. Even dry cleaners will have difficulty cleaning a multicolor garment if the colors run.

Small skins require small pattern pieces; select patterns with yokes, peplums, princess lines, center-back seams, and color-blocked pieces. You can also make smaller pattern pieces by cutting apart patterns and adding seam allowances, which may be straight or curved. Curved seamlines are very attractive and aren't hard to stitch in leather. Leather doesn't react well to steam and heat, so avoid pressed pleats. You can, however, use topstitching to hold folds flat. No matter what pattern I use, I make a muslin to check the pattern's fit and construction sequence before I cut the leather.

My greatest challenge has been the design and construction of a two-piece, lined suit from plum-colored lambsuede (photo, facing page). Since the skins were small, I had a hard time creating a jacket and skirt design with pattern pieces small enough to fit on the individual skins. I had to incorporate more vertical and horizontal seamlines than is usual for a relatively conservative suit. I settled on a jacket with a peplum and set-in waistband to get the length I wanted. The skirt has stylized princess-line panels and a horizontal band and panel at the hemline to achieve a mid-calf length. Creating attractive locations for these seams was critical to the success of the design.

Layout and cutting—Before laying out pattern pieces, check the skins for color consistency, flaws, holes, and thin spots. I held each of the 12 plum lambsuedes for my suit up to the light to locate holes. I reinforced thin spots and tiny holes by gluing a small piece of matching suede behind the area with rubber cement. Rubber cement, a thinner version of Barge Cement, an industrial glue that is used for shoes, is drycleanable. I then paired up the skins with a similar thickness and color so I could cut out the right front and left front of the jacket on skins with a similar appearance. The color of the plum skins varied even though they were from the same batch.

After checking the leather for flaws, lay out the pattern pieces on a single thickness of leather. I make separate patterns for the right and left sides so I don't cut out too many lefts or rights. You can use the center of the skin, or backbone, as a grain line for the major pattern pieces and fit smaller pieces, like facings, onto the remaining portions. For my suit, I laid some of the small pieces slightly off-grain to achieve the most efficient layout. For suedes, you may have to follow a "with-nap" layout.

My set of pattern weights (see photo below) is very useful in holding the pattern pieces securely while I cut them out with a rotary cutter or scissors; pins leave permanent holes. I like rotary cutters for cutting curves and for edges that need to be particularly neat and even.

Construction—Before I start work on a garment, I stitch a few practice rows on a suede scrap to check for skipped stitches or difficulty in feeding the leather into the needle. I'm always surprised by leather's stretchiness. When working on suede, I often cover the bottom of the presser foot and the top of the throat plate with cellophane tape to prevent the leather from sticking to the sewing machine. An even-feed presser foot may be useful.

To help alleviate problems with skipped stitches during the construction of the suit, I used a smooth polyester or nylon thread and a leather needle with a wedge point. I also switched to a single-hole throat plate. This prevented the stretchy leather from being pulled into the machine.

I like to use lightweight woven interfacing for collars, cuffs, button and buttonhole areas, waistbands, peplums, and front openings. To hold the interfacing in place, I permanently "baste" it with small dabs of rubber cement or small circles of Stitch Witchery. To minimize skipped stitches, I avoid placing the glue directly under areas where the needle will stitch. For temporary, removable basting I use paper clips or hair clips. Straight pins don't easily penetrate leather, but if you use them, be careful not to create holes that will be visible on the outside of the finished garment. For my suit, I applied twill tape to the front shoulders, front edges, and armscyes at the same time that I stitched the seams to keep the leather from stretching.

To sew seams, I set the stitch length at eight to ten stitches per inch; the needle holes from smaller stitches tend to split the skins. I hand-tie threads at the end of a seam rather than backstitch; backstitching puts too many holes in the skin and may cause it to split along the seamline. I wanted my suit to look conservative, so I used plain seams. To hold my finished seam allowances flat, I topstitched the seams and applied rubber cement to the seam allowances.

For sportier garments and for designs with curved seamlines, like my outfit in the top photo on the facing page, I use lapped seams. I remove the seam allowance on one side; lap it over the other, being careful to match seamlines; and topstitch close to the edge. Sometimes I add a second row of topstitching to give the appearance of a flat-felled seam.

The outer edges of the upper collar and undercollar can be joined without seam allowances. Remove the seam allowances from the outer edges of both pieces, and topstitch the collar sections together ⅛ in. from the edge.

On a pliable skin I seldom have problems stitching any type of seam or setting the sleeve into the armscye, even though the sleeve cap might be 1 in. larger than the armscye. With stiff leather I might have to reduce the amount of ease called for on the pattern to no more than ½ in. larger than the armscye. I trim the height and width from the cap in the area between the notches.

Bound buttonholes are common on leather apparel and are usually constructed after the interfacing is applied and before further assembly. A bound buttonhole is easy to make because leather doesn't ravel, and it can be "basted" with rubber cement.

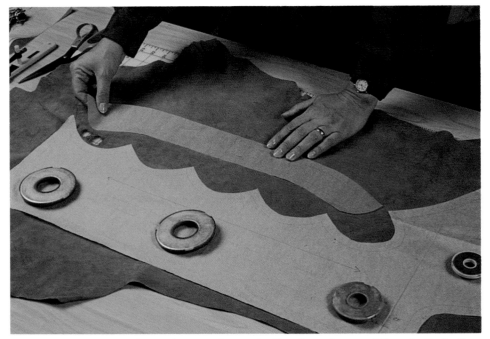

Handschuch lays out pattern pieces one layer at a time to work around flaws in the leather, and she uses weights rather than pins to avoid making holes.

Weights and sizes of common suedes and grain leathers

	Leather	Weight per sq. ft.	Size
Suedes	Pigskin	1-1½ oz.	10-12 sq. ft.
	Lambsuede (shirting suede)	1-1½ oz.	5-7 sq. ft.
	Deersuede splits	1½ oz.	5-7 sq. ft.
	Cowhide-suede splits	1½-2 oz.	8-10 sq. ft.
	Silksuede (sheep)	¾ oz.	4 sq. ft.
Grain leathers	Cowhide	1½-3 oz.	20-25 sq. ft.
	Goat (cabretta)	2-2½ oz.	8-10 sq. ft.
	Cow (plonge)	1½ oz.	25-35 sq. ft.

I like to use the window method for buttonholes in leather (bottom photo). Make a rectangular opening in the leather the length of the button and ⅜ in. wide. You can make the opening by cutting a hole directly in the leather or by stitching a rectangle through a thin piece of fabric placed on the right side of the leather, then slashing and pushing through the fabric and glueing it to the inside to form a faced opening. Next, cut two strips of leather, each 2 in. wide and 1 in. longer than the buttonhole opening. Machine-baste the strips together along the center, press the seam open, and glue the adjoining wrong sides together. Position the strips behind the window and glue them in place with the seamline in the middle of the opening. To finish the buttonhole, apply the facing (if any) to the backside of the buttonhole. Stitch around the window from the outside to secure all thicknesses. Cut out the buttonhole in the facing, being careful not to cut into the welts and remove the basting that holds the welts together.

Hemming a leather skirt is a joy. Blind catchstitching isn't necessary; I secure my hems and facings by topstitching or by using rubber cement. Be careful in lining up the surfaces, since it's hard to reposition the pieces after the initial contact is made.

Care—Leather isn't the easiest material to care for or to clean. Smooth leather may be wiped clean with a damp cloth, and suede may be cleaned with a soft brush. For serious cleaning, leather-apparel manufacturers usually recommend taking the garment to a suede-and-leather cleaner. The better the leather, the more likely it is that the garment will go through dry cleaning without a problem. Some leather suppliers suggest hand-washing certain suedes and leathers. Always try a test sample first. Use cool water and a mild detergent. Let the garment drip-dry away from heat and sunlight. When it's dry, you may have to work the leather with your hands to restore its soft texture.

Store leather apparel in a cool, ventilated area rather than in plastic. Avoid exposure to a combination of heat and moisture. If your garment gets wet, let it dry away from any heat source. If you must press leather, use a cool, dry iron, but first test it in an unseen part of the garment. Press the garment on the wrong side, or use a press cloth to prevent iron imprints. The cloth will also help keep the leather from stretching as you iron.

An excellent in-depth brochure is *Consumer Care of Leather & Suede*. It's available from local dry cleaners who belong to the International Fabricare Institute. Check the *Yellow Pages* under "Cleaners." ☐

Arlene Handschuch, a designer of historic costume reproductions, wearable art, and contemporary apparel, teaches at Framingham State College in Framingham, MA.

Suppliers

Berman Leathercraft
25 Melcher St.
Boston, MA 02210
(617) 426-0870
All types of leather.

Cinema Leathers
1663 Blake Ave.
Los Angeles, CA 90031
(213) 222-0073
All types of leather; $20 for samples of entire stock, refundable with first order.

Hermes Leather
45 W. 34th St., Room 1108
New York, NY 10001
(212) 947-1153
Chromed-tanned cowhide and pigsuedes; swatches on request.

Hide and Leather
595 Monroe St.
Napa, CA 94559
(800) 453-2847
All types of leather, including elk and deerskin; $5 for each set of samples; free catalog.

Iowa Pigskin Sales Company
Box 115
Clive, IA 50053
(515) 232-5024
Pigsuede and grain leathers; $4 for swatches, refundable with purchase.

Libra Leathers
259 W. 30th St.
New York, NY 10001
(212) 695-3114
All types of leather, prints, metallics; for swatches, send LSASE.

Prairie Collection
RR1 Box 63
Meservey, IA 50457
(515) 358-6344
Pigskin, cowhide, snake, fishskin; $3 and LSASE for swatches.

M. Siegel Company, Inc.
120 Pond St. (Rte. 126)
Ashland, MA 01721
(508) 881-5200
All types of leather, particularly beautiful, washable deersuede; catalog, $2.

Siegel of California
324 C State St.
Santa Barbara, CA 93101
Outside CA: (800) 862-8956
Within CA: (800) 932-8956
All types of leather, particularly deersuede; free catalog.

Leo. G. Stein Company
4314-4322 N. California Ave.
Chicago, IL 60618
(800) 831-9509
All types of leather; $3 and LSASE for color cards.

Tandy Leather Co.
Advertising Dept.
Box 2934
Fort Worth, TX 76113
Outside TX: (800) 433-5546
Within TX: (817) 551-9770
All types of leather and supplies; call for catalog and location of nearest store.

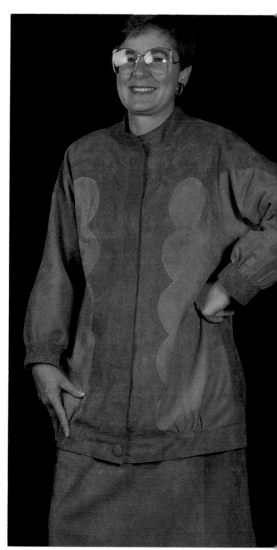

Curved edges in Handschuch's lambsuede suit are easily lapped and stitched.

Phases of a bound buttonhole: Cut a rectangular opening in the suede (center). Baste the welts together (in fingers). Glue the adjoining wrong sides of the welts together (right). Stitch the welts in place behind the rectangular opening, as was done for the buttonholes in the jacket waistband.

Custom Patternmaking

Ease and style turn a basic pattern into your own design

by Rosemary Ingham

as a theatrical costume designer and technician, I create clothing for actors of all shapes and sizes. Each custom-fitted costume begins with the actor's measurements, from which we make a basic fitting pattern (or set of slopers) that fits like a second skin. From this representation of the body, and with a design firmly in mind and on paper, costumers develop style lines and add sufficient ease to make the costume comfortable.

If you've made a basic fitting garment, perhaps using a pattern from a major pattern company, you're ready to begin designing simple garments and creating custom patterns. I'll introduce you to a direct, easy-to-understand version of this pattern-making method, called flat patterning or flat-pattern design, by describing how I developed patterns for two blouses. I'll guide you through the casual tee-shaped blouse that I'm wearing in the photo on the facing page and explain how I worked out the sleeves and pleats of the mannequin's blouse.

There are other methods of making patterns, such as draping and pattern drafting, but flat patterning is the most widely used method in this country and the easiest to learn. The theory of flat patterning is that no matter what fashion silhouette a design requires, as long as you start with an accurate basic fitting pattern that controls the fabric around your curves—bust, waist, hips, shoulders—you'll be able to develop a pattern for the design you want and also retain a good fit.

You can vary a blouse in a variety of ways; begin with these easy blouses, and try different fabrics and colors. As soon as you feel at ease with them, try something more complicated. Challenge yourself. There is nothing more satisfying, or more comfortable, than a lovely piece of clothing that really fits.

Tools of the trade—To begin custom pattern-making, you'll need a basic fitting pattern that has been customized for you (for information on fitting a basic pattern, see "Making Your Own Sloper," pp. 114-119). Adult-education centers, fabric stores, and sewing centers often offer courses on drafting and fitting a sloper or fitting a basic pattern, so check in your area, or try one of the sources of instruction on p. 112. If you're up to a challenge, check out the books on p. 112 on drafting a personal sloper.

The basic fitting pattern (drawing, facing page) includes a close-fitting, high-neck bodice with bust and waist darts and long, straight sleeves. The shoulder seam of the bodice back is ½ in. longer than the front shoulder seam; the extra length is eased in to allow for shoulder and arm movement. Between balance points (the sleeve and arm-hole notches on a commercial pattern), the sleeve cap is approximately 2 in. bigger than the bodice armhole. The sleeve cap fits around the upper arm and joins the bodice at the shoulder joint.

A sloper, or block, refers to the piece, or pieces, of the basic fitting pattern for a part of the body. The body sloper, or body block, has a front and back; the sleeve sloper, or sleeve block, is one piece. Slopers usually don't have seam allowances, which makes them easy to trace and manipulate.

Every time you begin to work on a pattern, you'll need to trace a fresh copy of your sloper; this copy is called a development pattern, and you use it to shift darts and draw style lines. Neither the tissue paper of a commercial basic fitting pattern nor the craft paper of a custom-drafted pattern will endure repeated tracing without tearing or fraying at the edges, so before you begin, copy your slopers on oaktag. Cut the pieces out, cut out the darts, and punch one hole at the bust point and one at the top of the sleeve. If you can't get oaktag, put your sloper pieces on cardboard or illustration board, and brush a layer of shellac around the edges so they won't disintegrate when you draw repeatedly around them.

Label your slopers clearly and date them. Because our bodies change, you'll need to update your slopers every two years, or after a weight loss or gain of 10 lb. or more.

Brown, medium-weight craft paper that's 25 in. to 30 in. wide is good for making development patterns, as well as final patterns; white paper with 1-in. squares, made especially for patterning, is also good. Newsprint is too pulpy and tears easily, but butcher paper is fine. Also, you'll need a clear plastic ruler (I use one called C-Thru) that's at least 18 in. long, a flexible curve (available at art-supply stores), and Scotch Removable Magic Tape or tape that can be removed from paper without ripping it. To trace the new patterns, you'll need a needlepoint tracing wheel, available from the tailoring suppliers listed on p. 112. A spiked tracing wheel can be used, but a smooth wheel cannot. And last, you'll need a work surface that you can pin into, some tacks, and long quilting pins or T-pins.

Design first—To make a successful pattern, you must know exactly how the garment will look. Even for simple garments, you need a good photo or detailed drawing from which to work. I never begin to work on a pattern unless I have an image of the design—whether the design is mine or someone else's—pinned to the board over my cutting table. Even when I'm making a pattern for a tee shirt, I do a quick drawing first.

If you don't think you can draw a human body, find a photo or drawing of a normally proportioned, standing nude female figure, and make a dozen photocopies of her. "Dress" this figure in the blouse you've tried on, can't afford, and want to copy, or in the perfect blouse you can imagine but can't

From *Threads* magazine (October 1989) 25:62-67

With her personal sloper (on wall), Rosemary Ingham made patterns for the blouse she wears and the formal one on the mannequin.

find in the commercial pattern catalogs. For ideas, start a clipping file of styles that you'd like to copy.

Before I begin to make a pattern, I study a photo or sketch of the garment and write down a detailed description. How low is the neck in relation to the bustline? Where do the shoulder seams fall? How long are the sleeves? Locate every seam. Where is the opening? If you're working from a drawing or photo that doesn't give a back view, you'll have to decide how the back will look and describe it.

Decide how you'll finish the inside. Think about facings, zippers, hems, and pockets. Make a list of the details you must remember.

A clipping from a catalog inspired me to make the short-sleeve blouse. In my list of details I note that it's loose-fitting without any stitched darts and made from striped material. The front yoke extends below the bust point and includes the sleeves. The neckline is about ½ in. below the base of the neck. Center-front buttons extend to the yoke bottom. The sleeves fall to just above the elbow and are cuffed with a contrasting fabric. I couldn't see the back of the blouse, but I decided to add a yoke with the same horizontal stripes as the front, only 3 in. longer. I'd stitch a bias facing to the neck edge and an on-grain finish on the bottom edge with the same contrasting fabric I'd use to cuff the sleeves.

A basic tee—I make development patterns from my bodice sloper, being careful to include all darts and the bust point. Even though this blouse has sleeves, they're developed as extensions of the bodice, and I don't need my sleeve sloper.

The style of the blouse determines where the fullness of the bust dart should be shifted. Not many garments these days are so fitted that they need a stitched bust dart, but the fabric fullness must still be in the final pattern; otherwise, the blouse will pull across the bust. I don't want to leave the fullness in the side or shift it to the waist, because I want the side seams to be straight. I decide to move the fullness to the shoulder (drawings, pp. 110-111). I like to fold the dart closed, but you can also slash the legs of the dart on the fold line and overlap them. Don't worry if the development pattern has a little wrinkle around the bust point when the dart is folded; as long as all pattern edges lie flat, it's okay.

After you've shifted darts, pin the development pattern to craft paper; then add seams, style lines, and wearing ease. The yoke line falls 3½ in. below my bust point, so I draw a line across the development pattern perpendicular to the center front for the yoke seamline. Using a flexible curve, I mark the neck edge ½ in. lower on the

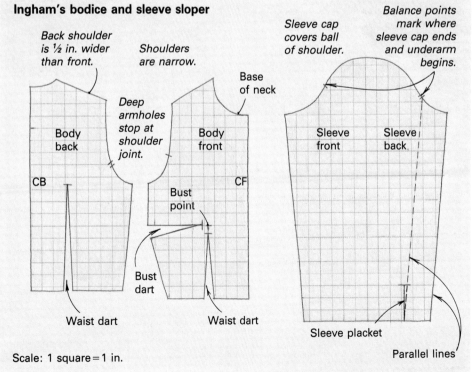

Ingham's bodice and sleeve sloper

Back shoulder is ½ in. wider than front.

Shoulders are narrow.

Base of neck

Balance points mark where sleeve cap ends and underarm begins.

Sleeve cap covers ball of shoulder.

Body back

Deep armholes stop at shoulder joint.

Body front

CB

CF

Bust point

Bust dart

Waist dart

Waist dart

Sleeve front

Sleeve back

Sleeve placket

Parallel lines

Scale: 1 square = 1 in.

development pattern, then roll the needle-point tracing wheel over the curve to transfer it to the paper underneath.

To decide how long my blouse will be, I study myself in a full-length mirror while wearing my most becoming blouse. I measure its length and, using a yardstick, I extend the center-front pattern line to the desired distance.

Next, I have to decide how much ease to add to the blouse so it will be comfortable— not too tight and not too baggy. There are two kinds of ease in clothing: wearing ease, which allows you to move freely; and style, or design, ease, which the designer adds to give the garment its characteristic look. When you're the designer and patternmaker, you can add exactly the right amount of ease. To find out what the right amount is, measure your favorite blouse, subtract your actual circumference measurements at the hip, bust, and waist, and divide the resulting ease equally between the pattern parts. If you like 6 in. of ease around your hips, for example, and your pattern has a one-piece front and back, you add one-fourth of the ease to each side seam. If you can't decide on your ease, you can use the following suggested minimum amounts: 2 in. to 3½ in. at the bust; ½ in. to 1 in. at the waist; 2 in. to 3 in. at the hips.

I add my hip ease, which is 6 in., to my hip measurement and divide by 4 to determine the front-pattern width. I measure this width out from the center front at the level of the bust point and draw the side seam. I then join the center-front line and the side seam to form the blouse bottom. I use my hip ease but check it at my bust level to make sure that I've added enough to satisfy both areas.

To determine how far to extend the shoulder line for the sleeve, I measure my arm from where the neck edge of the blouse will fall to just above my elbow. I draw the shoulder line so it meets the outside edge of the shoulder dart; this raises the shoulder and gives the front of the blouse fullness for the bust. By using my own shoulder slope, rather slightly adjusted for the dart, I ensure that the fabric cross grain will fall parallel to the floor and perpendicular to the center front, and the blouse won't bag at the neck or under the arm. For the bottom of the sleeve, I draw a line perpendicular to the extended shoulder line. The sleeve will have a 16-in. circumference, so I make the sleeve front 8 in. wide. The lower line of the sleeve is parallel to the upper sleeve line and intersects the top of the side seam. The cuff is about one-fifth of the total sleeve length, so I draw in a cuff line one-fifth up from the sleeve bottom.

A clean pattern—While the development pattern is pinned in place, roll a needle-point tracing wheel over all the lines of the new pattern, including style lines of parts.

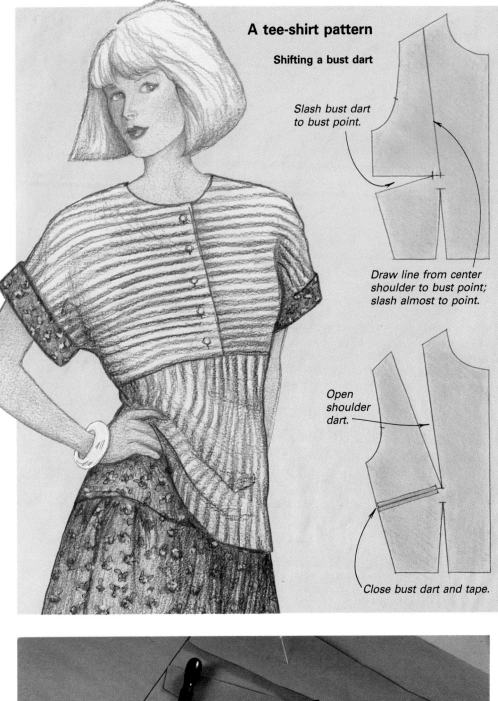

A tee-shirt pattern

Shifting a bust dart

Slash bust dart to bust point.

Draw line from center shoulder to bust point; slash almost to point.

Open shoulder dart.

Close bust dart and tape.

A new pattern starts with a copy of Ingham's sloper that has its bust dart shifted to the shoulder. Ingham transferred the yoke line to the final pattern with the needlepoint tracing wheel; here, she uses a flexible curve to draw smooth, curved lines.

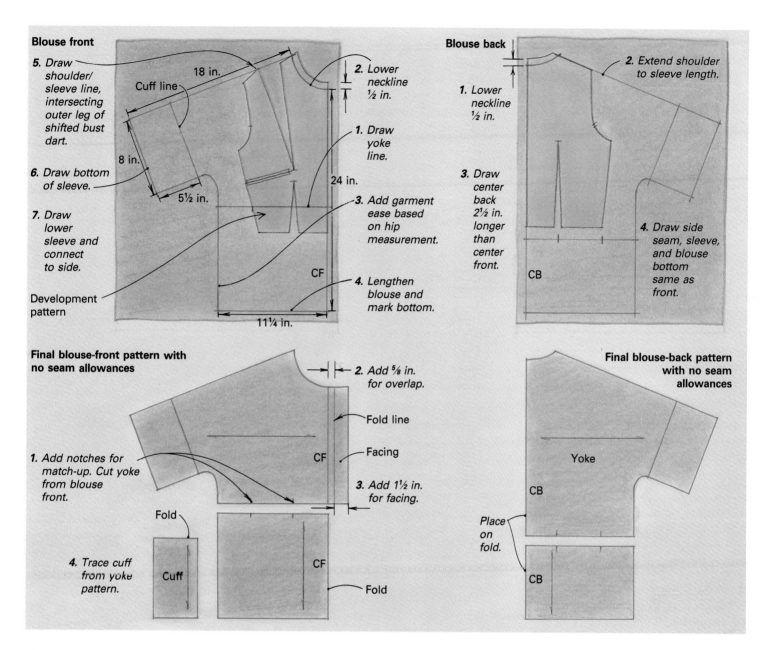

Blouse front

5. Draw shoulder/sleeve line, intersecting outer leg of shifted bust dart.

Cuff line

18 in.

6. Draw bottom of sleeve.

8 in.

5½ in.

7. Draw lower sleeve and connect to side.

Development pattern

11¼ in.

2. Lower neckline ½ in.

1. Draw yoke line.

24 in.

3. Add garment ease based on hip measurement.

CF

4. Lengthen blouse and mark bottom.

Blouse back

2. Extend shoulder to sleeve length.

1. Lower neckline ½ in.

3. Draw center back 2½ in. longer than center front.

CB

4. Draw side seam, sleeve, and blouse bottom same as front.

Final blouse-front pattern with no seam allowances

1. Add notches for match-up. Cut yoke from blouse front.

Fold

4. Trace cuff from yoke pattern.

Cuff

2. Add ⅝ in. for overlap.

Fold line

CF

Facing

3. Add 1½ in. for facing.

CF

Fold

Final blouse-back pattern with no seam allowances

Yoke

CB

Place on fold.

CB

The sharp points leave fine holes in the paper. With a permanent pen, I make smooth lines over the perforations, using a ruler and a flexible curve.

After I've traced the new pattern, I stand back and look at what I've drawn. I concentrate on seeing and feeling where each part of the pattern piece will be on my body. The underarm sleeve curve begins at my bust point, which should give me plenty of room for movement and a comfortable drape. The armscye of a tee shirt needs to be lower than that of a sloper by an average of 2½ in. to 3 in. for ease of movement, which we got automatically on this pattern, but is a good thing to check for. I check the lengths again and remeasure anything that doesn't look right. If I have to draw a new line, I cross out the old one.

Before you cut a pattern apart, mark seamlines with notches for matching later on, as I did with the yoke line. I mark the center front of the bottom and note that this edge will be placed on a fold.

The blouse has a closing at the center front and needs an overlap for buttons and a facing. A ⅝-in. overlap is suitable for buttons no larger than ⅝ in. When you use larger buttons, increase the distance to the fold line, as well as the width of the facing. To make sure the facing has the same curve as the neckline, I fold the pattern on the fold line and cut out the whole yoke.

The back pattern is almost identical to the front; the development pattern needs no dart shifts. I lower the neckline ½ in., then pin the development pattern to craft paper. The center-back length of most basic patterns is longer than the front because the neckline is higher in back; I add 2½ in. to the center-front length to find the back length (photo, p. 112). To draw the sleeve, I extend the development pattern's shoulder line to match the length of the front, then finish the sleeve bottom, lower sleeve, and side seam the same as the front. The only difference is that I lower the yoke line 3 in. according to my style preference.

At this point, some people like to redraw their pattern pieces and add seam allowances. I usually add seam allowances on the fabric just before, when I cut out my garment. You can measure the seam allowances quickly and easily with the transparent ruler or a ⅝-in.-wide tape measure and draw them in with chalk or a marking pen.

If this is your first venture into flat patterning, I recommend making a mock-up. I like to use inexpensive gingham with woven checks so I can determine the accuracy of my grain lines at a glance. If I make alterations in the mock-up fitting, I transfer them to my paper pattern. Don't use cloth patterns to cut out your garment fabric; they can easily stretch out of shape. Before you start to work on your actual blouse, take a few minutes to list your construction steps in a logical sequence.

Now for something formal–I wanted a simple, long-sleeve, high-collar classic blouse. Since nothing in the pattern catalogs was quite right, I sketched the blouse that I envisioned (drawing, p. 113) and made a pattern. It has ten narrow pleats in the front and set-in sleeves with gathered caps, bloused at the bottoms over narrow cuffs. The shoulders and shoulder pads are extended slight-

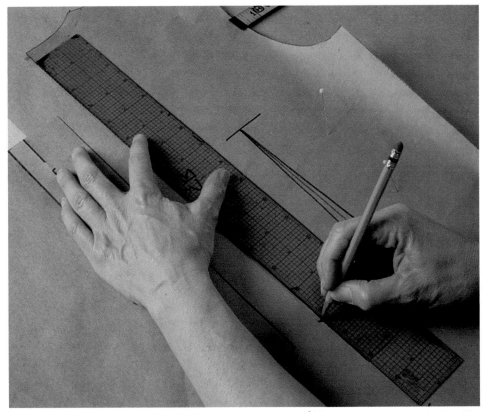

To determine the back-center length, Ingham lays the front 2½ in. below the back-neck edge. She draws the center-back seam to that length. The back of Ingham's bodice needed no dart shifts.

ly. Since this blouse has set-in sleeves and the body is loose-fitting, I shifted the bust-dart fullness in the development pattern to the existing waist dart. Then I marked the pleat lines and drew a match-up line across the pattern piece. I cut the strips apart and spread them out on a clean sheet of paper, leaving ½ in. between each strip. I made sure the match-up line remained perpendicular to the center front.

To allow room for the shoulder pads, I raised the shoulder line at the shoulder edge, then extended the shoulder seam. Whenever you extend the shoulder, you must lower the armhole; otherwise, the garment will restrict your arm movement. Before I drew the new armhole curve, I added an extra 1½ in. of ease at the side of the front pattern piece. The underarm point has now been dropped 1 in. and extended 1½ in. I connected the extended shoulder line with the lowered and extended underarm point, creating a larger and more shallow armhole curve, common in today's loose-fitting styles.

The pattern piece was ready to be cut out, but before I cut the neck edge, I had to true it so I'd have a smooth curve when the pleats were folded. I scored each pleat line with the tracing wheel and folded the pleats in the direction I wanted them to lie. Then I cut the neck curve. When the pleats are unfolded, the neck edge is jagged, but when they're folded, the curve is smooth.

I created the pattern for this sleeve by slashing and spreading the development pattern. First I drew a match-up line across the sleeve cap perpendicular to the straight grain line. The three slash lines are located within the sleeve cap, above the balance points; I cut the sleeve apart on these lines.

On a clean piece of paper, I drew a line that would extend from the top of the new sleeve pattern down the straight grain line. Working from the top of the sleeve cap, I spread the two center sections apart on each side of the centerline and secured each piece with a single pin in the top. I spread out the two remaining pieces and pinned them in place. Using the pins as pivot points, I spread the pieces farther apart at the bottom to create some flare.

To achieve a more graceful back drape at the sleeve bottom, I lengthened the wrist edge at the back of the arm and raised it in front, using a flexible curve to draw the curves smoothly. The apex of each curve should occur below the front and back balance points on lines approximately parallel to the underarm seams. I lowered the underarm sleeve curve so it would match with the underarm bodice changes, and I blended the curve. Using a tracing wheel and pen, I drew a clean sleeve pattern, marked the top of the cap, and identified the back and the front with balance points.

The sleeve I've developed from the sloper is a full sleeve with blousing. Even though I didn't lengthen the sleeve pattern, I had sufficient blousing because the blouse has extended shoulders and sleeve cuffs. ☐

Rosemary Ingham has been designing theatrical costumes for over 30 years. She teaches in the Department of Theatre and Dance at Mary Washington College in Fredericksburg, VA.

Books

Hollen, Norma. *Pattern Making by the Flat-Pattern Method*, 6th ed. New York: Macmillan, 1987.
Patternmaking, using commercial patterns to make slopers.

Ingham, Rosemary, & Liz Covey. *The Pattern Development Handbook.* Charlottesville, VA: Great Jones Books, 1988.
How to draw personal slopers and develop a variety of patterns from them.

Kopp, Ernestine, et al. *Designing Apparel Through the Flat Pattern*, new. 5th ed. New York: Fairchild, 1981.
Pattern drafting with basic slopers.

Supplies

Greenberg & Hammer
24 W. 57th St.
New York, NY 10019
(212) 246-2836
Needlepoint tracing wheel, C-Thru rulers, fabric with dotted grid; $10 minimum order.

William Wawak Co.
Box 59281
Schaumburg, IL 60159-0281
Within IL: (312) 397-4850
Outside IL: (800) 654-2235
C-Thru rulers, needlepoint tracing wheel; $15 minimum order

Instruction

Sloper drafting and fitting (S)
Basic pattern fitting (B)

Katherine Davis (S)
802 Janice Drive
Annapolis, MD 21403
(301) 268-1843

Eastern Michigan University (B)
Dept. of HECR
206 Roosevelt Hall
Ypsilanti, MI 48197
(313) 487-1217

Florida Community College (S)
3939 Roosevelt Blvd.
Jacksonville, FL 32205
(904) 387-8255

G Street Fabrics (B)
11854 Rockville Pike
Rockville, MD 20852
(301) 231-8998

Lake Washington VoTech School (B)
11605 132th Ave., N.E.
Kirkland, WA 98034
Judy Barlup: (206) 828-5600

Milwaukee Area Technical College (S)
60th St. & Bradley Rd.
Brown Deer, WI 53209
(414) 354-6662

Sewing Workshop (B)
2010 Balboa St.
San Francisco, CA 94121
(415) 221-7397

Sew Magnifique (B)
3220 Paces Ferry Place
Atlanta, GA 30305
(404) 237-0955

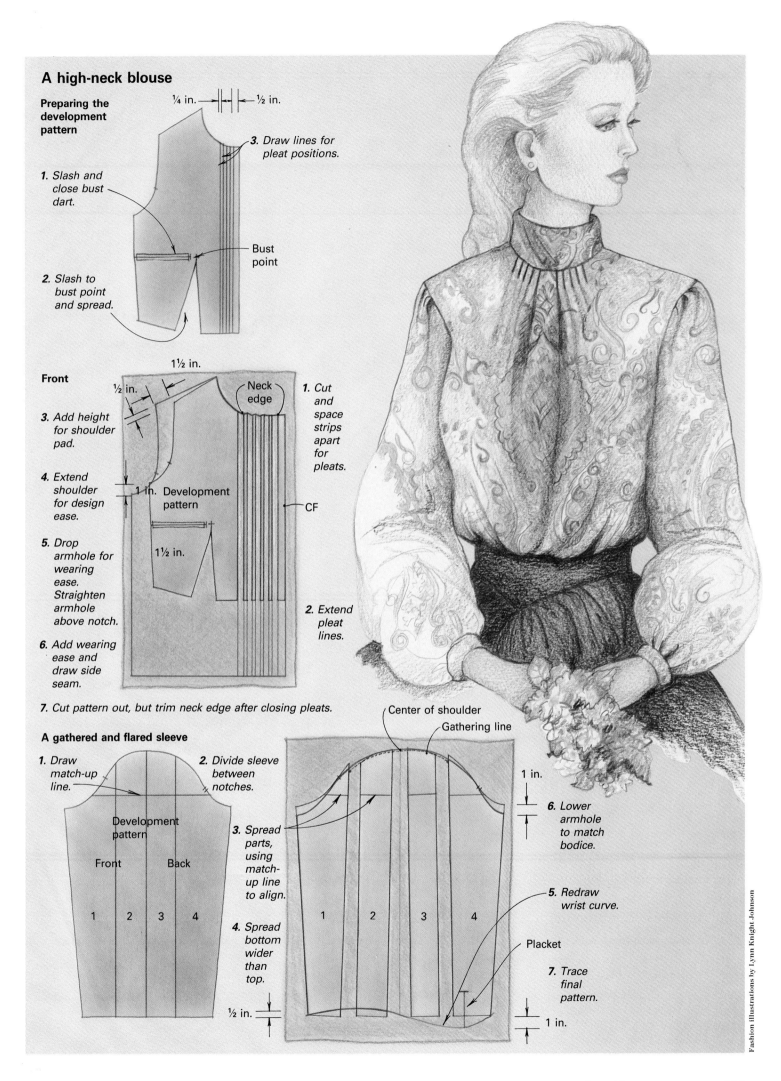

A high-neck blouse

Preparing the development pattern

¼ in. | ½ in.

3. Draw lines for pleat positions.

1. Slash and close bust dart.

2. Slash to bust point and spread.

Bust point

Front

1½ in.

½ in.

3. Add height for shoulder pad.

4. Extend shoulder for design ease.

1 in.

Development pattern

1½ in.

5. Drop armhole for wearing ease. Straighten armhole above notch.

6. Add wearing ease and draw side seam.

Neck edge

CF

1. Cut and space strips apart for pleats.

2. Extend pleat lines.

7. Cut pattern out, but trim neck edge after closing pleats.

A gathered and flared sleeve

1. Draw match-up line.

2. Divide sleeve between notches.

Development pattern

Front   Back

1   2   3   4

3. Spread parts, using match-up line to align.

4. Spread bottom wider than top.

½ in.

Center of shoulder

Gathering line

1   2   3   4

1 in.

6. Lower armhole to match bodice.

5. Redraw wrist curve.

Placket

7. Trace final pattern.

1 in.

Fashion illustrations by Lynn Knight Johnson

Making Your Own Sloper

You can learn a lot about fit by customizing a commercial fitting pattern

by Mary Galpin with Linda Faiola

To fit her own sleeve, Mary Galpin first bastes the cap and pins the armscye. Since she is right-handed, she must fit the left sleeve so she can mark it accurately. After she makes the obvious corrections, she can fine-tune the fit.

Several years ago when I lived in New York City, I took some patternmaking classes at the Fashion Institute of Technology. In one class, we draped muslin directly on a dress form to get front and back bodice and skirt slopers (basic garment shapes that are used for flat patternmaking). In another, we measured the dress form and then drafted slopers, following rigid and rather intriguing mathematical formulas.

All very interesting, I thought, but I wanted a sloper that fit me, not a dress form. I could have taken the basic draped sloper and adjusted it for my body, or I could have measured myself and drafted a sloper, but it occurred to me that the "basic fitting patterns" sold by some of the pattern companies were essentially slopers, and it might be easier to start with one of them. These patterns for a basic fitted dress with a waistline seam are intended to be used as fitting masters: After making up the pattern in muslin, you adjust it until it fits you, note where and by how much you altered it, and make the same changes to other patterns you buy from that company. I thought I could alter the pattern for myself, then use it for my own patternmaking.

To make my sloper, I worked with Linda Faiola, an experienced patternmaker who has led many people through the challenge of constructing a sloper from a fitting pattern. She makes minimal corrections to the pattern prior to fitting—only those necessary to ensure that the muslin will fit loosely around the body. She fits the skirt separately from the bodice. And, she makes fitting corrections to just half the muslin, then duplicates the corrections to the other half, ensuring a symmetrical pattern.

Even if you don't go on to design your own patterns, the process of making a sloper is valuable for what you'll learn about measuring, fitting, and altering patterns. But getting a garment to fit properly is not easy. It takes a lot of time and involves a good deal of hand basting, ripping out, and resewing, even for those experienced at evaluating and correcting fit. If you understand before you begin that making a custom-fitted sloper is a major project, you'll be less likely to get frustrated and give up.

From *Threads* magazine (April 1988) 16:56-61

The tools you'll need to make your sloper include a basic fitting pattern, a measuring tape, a large work surface you're not afraid to scratch, a gridded plastic ruler, a hip curve and a French curve, pins, needle and thread, a soft, sharp pencil, other colored pencils or markers, ¼-in. elastic, several yards of medium-weight muslin, and, if you're fitting yourself, a back-view mirror. A needle wheel (available from Wawak, Box 59281, Schaumburg, IL 60159), like a tracing wheel but with sharp points to puncture paper, is helpful. Don't wash the muslin before using it, but straighten the grain. You'll also need about two days to make your sloper: one to baste the muslin and one for fitting.

One other "tool" is almost a must—a sewing friend who can provide an extra pair of hands and a second opinion on fitting. You can fit yourself, but if you're not experienced at making fitting evaluations and adjustments, it can be very frustrating. Ideally, each of you should be making your own sloper so that neither sits idle, impatiently waiting while the other rebastes a seam.

The pattern

To make a sloper, a cardboard pattern with no seam allowances, you start with a commercial pattern in a size that best matches your measurements. After measuring the pattern within the seam allowances, you adjust it to go around your body with adequate ease and draw new seamlines and 1-in. seam allowances. Then you cut out the muslin, baste and fit it, and transfer your fitting corrections to the pattern tissue. Finally, you transfer the corrected seamlines to cardboard to produce the sloper.

Buying the pattern—To get a basic pattern that's the right size, measure yourself and then compare your measurements with the pattern company's standard body measurements. Don't just get your regular pattern size; it won't necessarily work for the basic fitting pattern. The basic pattern is "fitted"; i.e, it includes much less ease (extra fabric relative to your body) than most other commercial patterns, so there is little latitude regarding fit. Take the pattern company seriously when it says a 32½-in. bust needs a size 10 fitting pattern.

To measure, wear your usual undergarments or tights and a leotard. Breathe normally, and don't pull the tape tight. Measuring too snugly now could cause fitting problems later on. Keeping the tape measure horizontal, measure your bust and hips at their widest and your waist at its narrowest (even if you prefer your waistband elsewhere). Record these measurements on a chart like the one at right.

Don't assume that where you consider your hips to be or where the standard hipline is (9 in. below the waist) is actually your fullest part. Many women are widest just above their thighs. The purpose of finding your largest measurement is to deter-

mine how big the skirt must be to go around your body. Measure in several places until you find out where you are widest. Hold the tape measure so the 1-in. mark is at your side. After getting your hip circumference, let go of the long end of the tape, and, still holding the 1-in. end against your body, measure up to your waist. (Bend slightly to the side; where you indent is your waistline.) This tells you how far below your waist the widest part of your hips is. Record both measurements.

Next, compare your measurements with the pattern company's standard measurements. Choose the size that will be easiest to adjust. Since the bodice is usually more complicated to fit than the skirt, select the size with the closest bust measurement.

Only Vogue and Butterick sell basic fitting patterns suitable for making a sloper. McCall's fitting pattern has no waistline, so it can't be used for a bodice and skirt sloper. Vogue has two versions: one for $9 (#1000) and another for $25 (#1001). The $25 version comes in a plastic carrying case and includes a paper tape measure and cardboard curve. The pattern is made of a gridded, nonwoven material (like stiff interfacing) that you can fit directly to yourself. The Butterick pattern (#3415) costs $4.50. But the backbone of the patterns—the actual pattern lines—is exactly the same on all three, except that the Vogue pattern includes the option of a slightly longer sleeve. My advice is to buy the Butterick pattern. You don't get much for the additional cost of the others.

Measuring the pattern—Pattern in hand, your next step is to measure the pieces, compare the results with your body measurements, and make preliminary corrections to the pattern. Smooth out the pattern pieces with your hands to eliminate wrinkles (an iron could distort the tissue). Measure the pattern from seamline to seamline, excluding the widths of darts, pleats, or tucks. The lines on the pattern are thick, and the measurements can vary by ⅛ in., depending on whether you measure between the inside or outside of the lines. Be consistent.

To measure the **bust,** lay a gridded plastic ruler along the bustline marked on the bodice-front pattern, with one end at the side seamline. Measure to the bust point; then pivot the ruler and measure to the center-front line. On the back, measure along the bustline from the side seamline to the first stitching line of the waist dart. Note the measurement. Move the ruler to the other side of the dart so the measurement excludes the dart (see the top-left photo, page 116). Note the measurement at the center-back seamline. Total the front and back bodice measurements, multiply by 2 (because you measured only half the pattern), and enter the result in the chart.

Measure the **waistline** on either the bodice or skirt in the same way, from seamline to seamline, leaving out the darts. Hold the ruler on its edge and bend it to follow the curved waistline. Add front and back measurements, multiply by 2, and enter the result in the chart.

For the **hip** measurement, first draw new hiplines on the front and back skirt pattern pieces at the distance below the waist where your true hip is and parallel to the old hiplines. Measure the new hiplines on the skirt front and back, add them, multiply by 2, and enter the result in the chart.

Next, determine whether the pattern allows enough ease, and correct it if necessary. The right amounts of ease for this sloper are 2 in. in the bust, 1 in. at the waist, and 2 or 3 in. at the hip. Subtract your body measurements from the pattern's measurements. The differences are the ease amounts. If a pattern measurement is actually smaller than your body measurement, you'll get a negative number. Enter the ease amounts in the chart.

Correcting the pattern—Now correct the pattern so that each area has the specified amount of ease. The purpose of these preliminary adjustments is to ensure that the muslin shell will fit around you comfortably, not to make it fit right, which you can do only when you have the muslin on. It is not as critical to correct too much ease; you can do that during fitting.

Measurement adjustments					
	Your body	Pattern	Ease (pattern minus body)	Desired ease	Adjustment
Bust	33 in.	34½ in.	1½ in.	2 in.	+ ½ in.
Waist	25 in.	26 in.	1 in.	1 in.	—
Hip	35⅝ in.	36½ in.	⅞ in.	2 in.	+ 1⅛ in.
Waist-to-hip distance	9 in.	9 in.			—

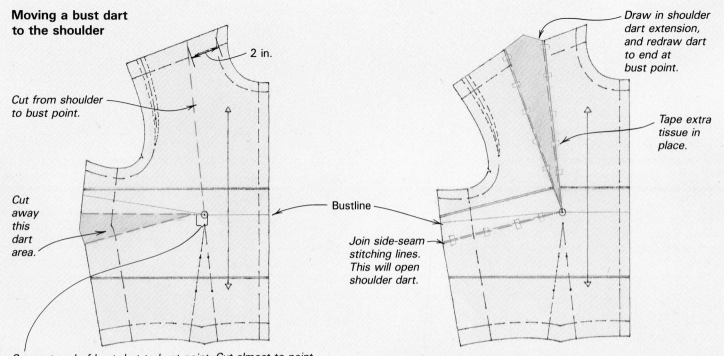

Moving a bust dart to the shoulder

2 in.

Cut from shoulder to bust point.

Cut away this dart area.

Connect end of bust dart to bust point. Cut almost to point.

Bustline

Draw in shoulder dart extension, and redraw dart to end at bust point.

Tape extra tissue in place.

Join side-seam stitching lines. This will open shoulder dart.

Illustration by Mark Kara

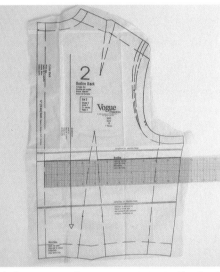

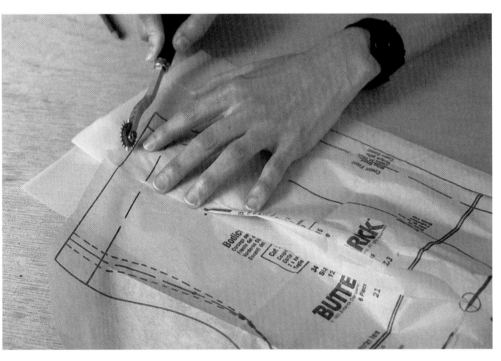

This is how Galpin measured the bodice-back bustline—from seamline to seamline, omitting the area inside the waist dart (above). She folds the shoulder dart closed and uses a needle wheel (right) to prick out the new dart extension.

Galpin re-marks a curved line by laying the gridded ruler with the correct measurement tangent to the curve and placing a mark at the ruler's edge (above). Shifting the ruler along the curve, she'll repeat this at intervals. Faiola draws a smooth hipline with a hip curve (right).

Expert advice on fitting a sloper

by Linda Faiola

The first step in understanding how to use a basic pattern is to understand what it isn't. This basic is not usually used for a garment pattern. You would have a basic if you took your skin off and laid it flat. Making a basic teaches you about your shape in relation to pattern pieces and garment construction. In the process of making this basic pattern, you learn about fitting. Measurements begin to have meaning. Every garment you make—from this basic, from a stylized pattern you made from this basic, or even from a commercial pattern—will give you a pattern that could be used as a basic for a future stylized pattern.

Why bother to make a basic pattern? The process is time-consuming and tedious; it takes patience and skill and usually a helper. The rewards are many, but I honestly don't believe that one of the rewards is to use the basic to "correct the fit" on other commercial patterns. I've come to the conclusion that most people who invest their time in my class are ready to make their own patterns, design their own clothes, and experience the luxury of garments that fit.

To learn about fitting, you must go through the process of making a well-fitted basic. Reading and observing are not enough. When you begin to use some of the information to make your own stylized patterns, you will be that much ahead. For example, you will know what you are adding to when you want the basic longer and wider. You will know what you are cutting away from if you want a lower neckline, a V-neckline, or a square neckline. If you want a skirt that measures 85 in. at the hem, and your basic skirt is 44 in., then 41 in. is the amount that you should add; if you

need a lower armhole (and wider) because you want to wear a bulky sweater under the garment, then you'll know what you are taking away from and adding to.

How do you go about beginning to fit a basic muslin? Or for that matter, how do you go about fitting any garment if it needs it? Here are some guidelines:

Fitting questions—Take a good look. Changes can be made not only because the fit is off but because something is aesthetically displeasing, such as waist darts of a skirt being too close to the center front. The following are just some of the things you should look at and for.
- Are the darts too long?
- Are the seams where you want them?
- Are there puckers or folds of fabric?
- Are the vertical seams perpendicular to the floor?
- Can you move your arms?
- Can you bend your elbows?
- Could you drive your car?
- Could you make that bottom step of a bus?
- If you overate, could you still breathe?
- Does the neckline gap away from your body?
- Does the bodice pull too tight across your bust?

Fitting suggestions—Be neat. A good motto is: "Aim for perfect because you'll never get it; aim for mediocrity, and you'll get a mess." Crooked stitching causes problems; always cut and stitch carefully and neatly.

Pin the closing together in the same place because the garment has to be put on and taken off many times during the fitting and making.

Remove the stitching of a seam or dart if you don't like the placement or if it looks wrong and you can't figure out why. Repin it, juggling around placement and amounts. Make the darts skinnier, wider, longer, shorter, observing just through the pinning how the changes affect the fit. In other words, fool around with the fabric until you get something you want to try in basting. You can't hurt a muslin by pinning and hand-basting over and over.

When pinning, pick up small amounts of fabric only, and don't use too many pins. Explaining what I mean is difficult, but try putting a lot of fabric into each pin, and put in lots of pins, and you'll see. Often excess fabric in a closely fitted garment indicates that the garment is too tight, not too big. For example, on a skirt, if there are wrinkles parallel to the waist between the waist and hip, it isn't because the body is short-waisted. The skirt is probably too tight at the hips. Open the side seams from a few inches below the waist to below the widest part of the hips, and see what happens.

Experiment with fit in muslin test garments, whether you're making your own patterns or using commercial ones. The more you learn about designing, fitting, and patternmaking, the fussier you should become. Knowledge does not mean speed. The more you know, the more you realize can go wrong. Skill comes with practice; certainly that's not a new concept. You must be willing to make some mistakes—and use lots of muslin.

Linda Faiola is a patternmaker and clothes designer in Winchester, MA. She teaches patternmaking and specialty-clothing classes, as well as knitting design, at the Cambridge Center for adult education.

Before making width adjustments, you should change the bust dart in the side seam to a shoulder dart, as shown in the drawings on the facing page. It will be easier to adjust width in the bodice side seams with the dart out of the way. A shoulder dart also tends to fit more smoothly.

To move the dart, first mark the shoulder seamline 2 in. from the neck seamline. Then draw a straight line from this point to the bust point, and cut the pattern along this line. Next, draw a line from the point of the bust dart to the bust point. Cut away the dart area on the bust dart; then cut along the line from the bust dart almost to the bust point, leaving about $\frac{1}{16}$ in. to keep the piece from separating.

Now bring together the sides of the bust dart at the side seamline. Let the pattern lie flat, with the side-seam length unchanged. Some paper will overlap, and the dart points won't quite match.

Tape tissue under the new shoulder dart. To redraw the dart extension, bring the stitching lines (cut edges of pattern) to-

gether for about 2 in. from the shoulder seamline, and fold the dart as you would press it—toward the center. Holding the dart closed with one hand, run a needle wheel along the shoulder seam (top-right photo, facing page). When you open the dart, the punctures show the stitching line for the dart extension. Add a 1-in. seam allowance by drawing in the cutting lines parallel to the stitching lines.

Now you can make width corrections. Divide the amounts you have to add by 4 (because you will correct at both sides of the two side seams.) Thus, to add 1 in. to the bust, redraw the front- and back-bodice side seams $\frac{1}{4}$ in. outside the original seamlines, and then draw new cutting lines 1 in. beyond. Don't change the center-front and back lines. Even if you need to add to the bust only, draw the new line parallel to the existing seamline. Tapering the seamline is tricky, and the excess is easy to pinch out during fitting. My bodice was long enough, but many people also have to add length at this point.

If you need to add to the waist, correct the side seams of the bodice and the skirt. To add to the waist or hip measurement on the skirt, redraw a curved line. Mark several points equidistant from the existing line, measuring with the gridded ruler (bottom-left photo, facing page). The sharper the curve, the closer the marks should be. Join them with a hip curve (bottom-right photo, facing page). Then redraw the cutting line the same way. The pattern allows a 2-in. seam allowance at the skirt's side seams. However, if you've measured accurately and honestly, a 1-in. seam allowance will do.

After making the corrections, extend the grain lines on all the pieces to the top and bottom edges and mark them with arrows. Pin the pattern pieces to the muslin along the lengthwise grain. Cut out the pieces, and mark the seamlines in pencil, or use a tracing wheel. Hand-baste the bodice and skirt darts, then the side seams, the center-back seam of the bodice, and the center-front and back seams of the skirt, leaving the back seam open for about 8 in. from

Faiola has improved the bodice fit by moving in the side seams and shifting the darts a bit.

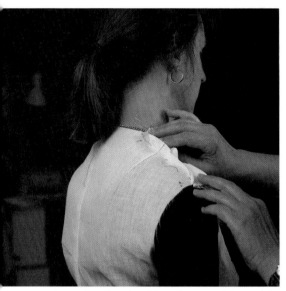

To make the shoulder fit smoothly, Faiola moves the shoulder seam forward.

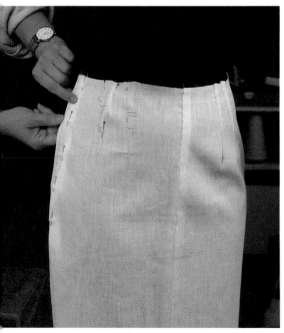

Having simplified the skirt darts, Faiola adjusts the side seams.

the waist. Thread-mark the seamlines of the bodice center front and the skirt center back so you'll always pin exactly on the same lines. Leave the sleeves until later. For ease of removal, hand-baste with stitches about ¼ in. long and no knots; backstitch ends at least three times. You'll repeatedly undo and rebaste these seams and darts.

Fitting

Fit the bodice and skirt separately. After fitting the bodice, fit only one sleeve, unless your arms or shoulders are asymmetrical.

Put on the muslin shells right sides out, but pin the bodice closed at the center front, with this seam allowance outward. Pin closed the open part of the center-back skirt seam by folding one seam allowance in along the stitching line and pinning it over the other stitching line.

When you're fitting the muslin, one side should be your "master"—the side on which you make and mark all corrections when you have the garment on. To make adjustments, pinch the fabric to take it in, and pin. After you take off the muslin, turn it inside out, and mark both edges of the fabric at the pins. Then transfer the corrections to the other side.

To make corrections to the side you didn't mark, take out all basting that will be changed or will interfere with new seams, and align the marked side over the unmarked one, right sides together. Stick pins through the new marks to copy. Use a curved ruler to redraw all curved seamlines.

Bodice fitting—We began my fitting session with the bodice. Linda pinched in the side seams with her fingers to see if she could take them in. She was able to take in about 1 in. Always make sure you can pinch an equal amount on both sides.

Then Linda looked at the darts. The front shoulder dart should point at the bust point, ending just above it; if it doesn't, adjust it. The fullness of the darts was okay, and their positions were fine for the moment. Linda usually finds that the back waistline dart is too wide and long, which was the case, so she opened and repinned it. This meant the side seam had to come in a bit more.

With the side seam thus refined, Linda looked again at the front darts, undid the waist dart, and repinned it smaller, placing the bottom pin at the waistline. She also moved the point of the dart about ¼ in. toward the center front and, with a cross mark at the dart point, indicated that the shoulder dart should do the same.

The first bodice fitting was over. I took the muslin off and marked the adjustments before removing the pins. Since the side seam is straight, I had to mark it only at the top and waistline. Then I transferred the corrections to the left side of the bodice. After rebasting the pieces along the new lines, I was ready for my second fitting.

The bodice looked much better—smoother and more natural. Having made basic cor-

rections, we could now refine the fit. We pinned the side seams in another ¼ in. and decided that the front shoulder dart should end slightly higher (top photo).

It wasn't clear why the shoulders didn't look right, so Linda undid the shoulder seam and repinned it smooth (center photo). This moved the seam toward the front.

Next, Linda clipped into the armscye seam allowance to eliminate the puckers near the front notch. Always start with shallow clips, less than the width of the seam allowance. This was the end of the second fitting. It's important not to overfit. Remember, a sloper is just the basic blueprint for designing other garments, each of which will require its own fine-tuned fitting.

I made the second group of corrections to the muslin on both sides and tried it on a final time for the neckline and waistline fitting. The natural position of my necklace indicated the back-neck stitching line. Linda marked the back with pencil, then several points of the rest of the neckline curve and clipped into the seam allowance. Finally, we pinned elastic snugly around my waist, joining it just off the center front, on the left side. Linda placed pins at the center front and back, at the side seams, and at several places between and marked the curve below the elastic at the pins.

Skirt fitting—I put the skirt on, pinning it closed at the center-back opening. Like the bodice, the skirt fit reasonably well, but not as smoothly as we wanted. We first attacked the darts. The fewer the darts, the easier a sloper is to use, so Linda undid the two right-front darts and repinned them to one smaller dart. She temporarily pinched the excess fabric into the side seam and did the same to the back dart. She then repinned the side seam to center it (bottom photo). Although slightly curved darts can make a skirt fit better, a sloper requires straight darts.

After I'd made these corrections, the new side seam bulged a little below the hip and angled in toward my body instead of hanging straight. Linda opened the seam from the bulge down to let the skirt hang as it wanted, then repinned it. Once I corrected this problem, the skirt fit. We pinned elastic snugly around my waist, with the join just to the left of the center back, and marked the lower edge of the elastic.

Sleeve fitting—Even though we had corrected both the shoulder and side seams, we hadn't made any preliminary corrections to the sleeve, because sleeves often fit anyway. I basted the elbow dart and the sleeve seam, then put the bodice on and pulled on the sleeve, right side out.

Linda pulled the sleeve up so the underarm was smooth and relatively tight. She pinned the sleeve to the bodice only at the front and back notches, letting it fall into position. Then she pinned it at the shoulder seam. She aligned the straight grain between shoulder and elbow perpendicular to the floor and checked to see that the cross grain was straight with the bodice. I took the sleeve and bodice off and pinned the sleeve cap in several more places, easing in the fullness. I then checked the fit of the sleeve underarm to the lower armscye and found that the sleeve seam needed to come in just ⅛ in.

This method is not recommended for the novice or for self-fitting. Instead, before you try on the sleeve for the first time, pin the basted sleeve to the bodice on the outermost stitching line, as you would if you were going to sew it in—right sides together, basting and easing the sleeve cap. Place the pins lengthwise to the seam. Try on the bodice and sleeve, mark any obvious corrections, as shown in the photo on page 114; then make the corrections, and baste the sleeve into the armscye for further fitting.

After basting the underarm, I tried the sleeve on again. Linda adjusted the pins and marked on the bodice where the armscye needed to come in slightly. The elbow dart was in the right place, but the sleeve was ½ in. too short, so we marked the lower edge of the sleeve "+½ in."

The sloper

Once you have a muslin bodice and skirt that fit you, like the ones shown in the photo below, you must transfer their new shapes back to the pattern tissues. Then you transfer the corrected lines to cardboard, and you have your sloper.

Transferring corrections to the pattern—Before taking the muslin apart, mark the seamlines and dart positions on all pieces of the master side, including unchanged seamlines. Mark seamlines and dart stitching lines on the right side by making small marks on both adjoining edges with a pencil or fine-tipped marker in a new color. Wherever stitching lines cross, mark the intersection. Mark the waistline of the bodice and skirt below the elastic, wherever it is pinned to the muslin, and put a cross at dart points.

Undo the stitching on all the pieces and remove the elastic. Press the pieces flat, always pressing with the grain. To transfer the markings from the muslin to the pattern, lay the pattern tissue on top of the master side of your muslin and trace the marks with a colored pencil, or lay the muslin on top of the pattern and transfer the corrections by running a needle wheel along them. In either case, stick push pins through the two layers and into the table to keep the pieces aligned. If there isn't enough tissue, lengthen or widen a pattern piece, and make a note at the seamline.

Next, with a sharp pencil and straight and curved rulers, draw the final stitching lines on the pattern tissue. You don't have to draw dart extensions or cutting lines, because your sloper won't have them. Use a French or hip curve to draw the neckline, armscye, waistline, and hiplines. Wherever seamlines intersect, they must meet at right angles to produce a straight line or smooth curve. Even a curved line, such as the neckline, intersecting with a straight line, such as the center front, must make a right angle for a short distance in order for the final line to be a smooth curve. Make sure side seams and dart edges are equal in length.

Drafting the sloper—The final step is to transfer the lines of the corrected pattern to a clean sheet of heavyweight paper or light cardboard, such as bristol board. Anchor the pattern tissue over the paper with push pins. With the needle wheel, mark all seamlines and darts where stitching lines intersect. On a straight edge, mark only the ends. Make a cross at dart points. Then draw in the lines with straight and curved rulers. Label each new pattern piece, put the date and the wearer's name or initials on it, and write "no seam allowances." Draw in the straight grain lines. Cut out the pattern along the stitching lines, cutting out the dart flaps, and you're done.

Now that you have a custom-fitted sloper, what do you do with it? Admire it. Then think about the shapes of some garments you've sewn and how they relate to these pattern shapes. For other ways to reshape a basic pattern, see "The Drafter, the Draper, the Flat Patternmaker" on pp. 45-49 and "Playing with Darts" on pp. 16-19. I plan to use my sloper to design a perfect skirt. □

Mary Galpin is a former associate editor of Threads. *Photos by Roger Barnes, except where noted.*

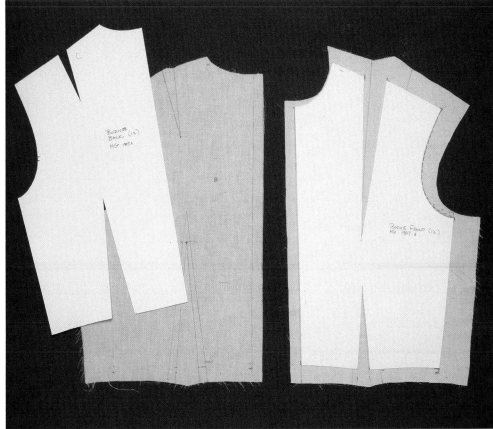

Her muslin fitted to her liking, Galpin (left) is ready to mark the seams and transfer them back to the pattern tissue. Galpin's back and front bodice sloper (above) took two days to make. The pressed fitting muslin is laid below the sloper. (Above photo by Michele Russell Slavinsky)

Bodybuilding for a Better Fit

Making a styrofoam copy of yourself

by Verena Gelfand

O ur bodies have as many distinguishing features as our faces. Despite obvious variations in size, shape, proportions, and posture, patterns and clothes come in "standard" sizes. One way you can adjust patterns and fit clothes perfectly is to compare them against a dress form that's a duplicate of yourself.

What follows is an inexpensive way to make a dress form that has all the critical dimensions and the posture necessary for successful pattern adjustment. It takes just $15 to $20 of readily available materials, some common tools, a bit of elbow grease, and 15 to 20 hours of your time. Two people need to work together to take each other's measurements, make body profiles, and share materials and tools to minimize costs. So call a friend, and let the fun begin.

The dress form is made from 2-in.-thick polystyrene-foam insulation, shown in the photo on the facing page, which is sold at building-supply or insulation-supply houses. You'll need an 8-ft. x 2-ft. sheet; two people can split an 8-ft. x 4-ft. sheet. Polyvinyl or polyurethane rigid foam is also suitable but is about five times as expensive as polystyrene. Avoid foam that has been treated with chemicals to prevent insect or weather damage.

The idea is to stack up oval-shaped layers of styrofoam into a shape that roughly re-

From *Threads* magazine (August 1989) 24:34-38

Custom dress forms (left), made from $15 to $20 worth of styrofoam insulation, batting, and knit fabric, match individual body shapes.

sembles you from neck to hips. You smooth and refine the shape with a serrated knife or a file—with measurements and body profiles for guidance—then cover it with batting and knit fabric, which is convenient to pin fabric onto. (For another method, see "Cloning your body," p. 125.)

When you're ready to begin, wear a leotard with your regular bra underneath for the measurements. The leotard shouldn't flatten your bust or change your dimensions. A soft-cup bathing suit or body stocking is another option. Don't wear a girdle unless you usually do. Tie a piece of string, elastic, or twill tape around your waist to mark your waistline. If your hair hangs below your neck, pin it up.

Me and my shadow—To make templates that will guide you when you're cutting the ovals and shaping the styrofoam stack, trace the front and side profiles of your body on a sheet of ¼-in.-thick foam-core board (available at art-supply and office-supply stores); later, you'll cut out the profiles. You can compare these templates against the body form as you carve the styrofoam, and they're handy places to record circumference measurements (top drawing, p. 122). Foam core is easy to cut, yet stiff enough to be held against the styrofoam stack as a guide. Paper is too limp, and corrugated cardboard will bend.

First, the model's body needs to be marked for reference to match the profiles. A person is usually narrowest at the waist, so the waist is a convenient height to place the edge of one styrofoam layer. Place a piece of masking tape down the center back of the model, from the hairline to below the widest part of the hips. Mark the masking tape at the waistline. With the tape measure, determine the widest part of the model's body below the waist near the hips, and place a mark on the masking tape at this level. Place another piece of tape down the model's side perpendicular to the floor for a side-seam reference, beginning at the underarm. If the model's posture is very stooped, the side seam may not coincide with the center of the side profile. Extend the side seam on the outside of the arm above the armscye and on the neck.

To figure out how many layers of styrofoam will be above and below the waist, hold a yardstick perpendicular to the floor and measure the model from the waist down to the widest point at the hips and from the waist up to the hairline. Divide these lengths by 2 (for the styrofoam thickness) and round off the result to the next largest number. If the division yields 5½ layers below the waist, for example, round off to 6.

Tape the foam core, marked with horizontal lines spaced 2 in. apart, to the wall with the long edge parallel to the floor. Mark the waist on the foam-core board, and match the waistline on the board to the height of the mark at the waist. Note the top of the layer that comes closest to the model's hairline, and label that line as the top of the dress form.

Trace both side and front profiles on the same foam-core board, as in the drawing on p. 122; position the model to allow for a 2-in. to 3-in. margin around each tracing. You can trace the profile by guiding one leg of a dressmaker's square around the body's contours, while keeping the other leg flat against the board or by using a slide projector placed 25 ft. away and just tracing the shadow. If you don't have a square, use a yardstick with a pen or pencil taped to the end, but be careful not to tilt the yardstick; a profile that's too thin or too wide will result. With either method, the person being traced can't shift position.

Trace the front profile while the model stands with normal posture (not an exaggerated shoulders-back, stomach-in stance) with her back against the board. If the model stands more erect than normal, the profile will be distorted. With the model's arms slightly raised, trace from the underarm down. With the model's arms down, trace the outline from the chin, down over the shoulder and arm, to the level of the armscye. After the model has stepped aside, connect the arm to the underarm with a horizontal line. Smooth out the tracing. If the two sides look very different, check the model visually to verify the difference.

Repeat the procedure while the model is standing sideways with the side of her arm and hip touching the board. Trace the back, then the front from the neck (or chin, if the model has a pronounced dowager's hump) down. Make sure the model's back stays aligned with the back outline while you trace the front.

Leave the foam core on the wall, and number the layers in the profiles from the bottom up. Using the square, transfer the height of each line to the masking tape on the model's back (left photo, p. 122). A small bubble level taped to the flat side of the square helps keep the marks level with those of the profile. Also transfer the heights of the bottom and top of the profiles. On the profiles, mark the positions of the bust points and navel for future reference.

Measurements—To make the paper patterns for each styrofoam oval, you'll need both full-body circumference and side-seam-to-side-seam-around-the-back measurements. Take these measurements at each marked level on the tape, starting at the lowest mark. Record them on the profile, using a *C* after the total circumference and a *B* for the back-only measurement. The model can help keep the tape measure level in front. At the armscye, take measurements with and without the arms. Repeat for all the marks. Be sure to get a measurement at bust level.

Take the foam core off the wall, and label both inside and outside the front profile with *left* and *right*. Draw the side seam on the side profile to match the tape of the model.

The widths between the front-back and side-to-side lines of the profiles define the depth and width of the styrofoam ovals. Draw perpendicular lines (red lines in top drawing, facing page) between each pair of horizontals; each vertical line contacts the widest point of the profile. Measure the dis-

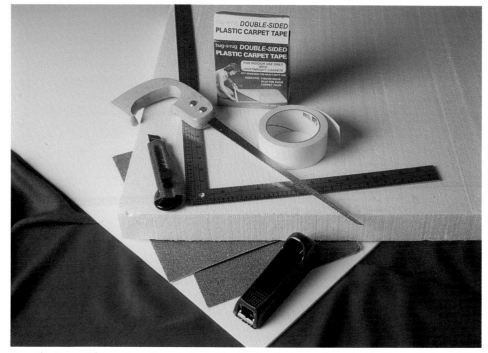

Supplies for making a dress form include 2-in.-thick polystyrene-foam insulation, a 30-in. x 40-in. sheet of ¼-in.-thick foam-core board, a keyhole saw, a square, a razor-blade utility knife, a Stanley Surform file, coarse sandpaper, and double-sided carpet tape.

Profiles and measurements

Foam-core board, 40 in. x 30 in.

Cut along profile to make templates.

Front template

Back template

Layer	D	BD
#12	6 13/16 D	3 5/16 BD
#11	5 15/16 D	3 7/8 BD
#10	7 1/2 D	4 1/4 BD *(Side seam)*
#9	9 1/8 D	4 1/2 BD
#8	9 13/16 D	4 5/8 BD
#7	9 1/2 D	4 1/8 D
#6	9 13/16 D	3 13/16 BD *(Back depth (BD))*
#5	10 D	3 1/4 BD *(WAIST)*
#4	9 1/2 D	2 9/16 BD
#3	11 D	3 1/16 BD *(Front-to-back depth (D))*
#2	11 7/8 D	4 9/16 BD
#1	11 1/2 D	4 13/16 BD

Shoulder template — R, L — Plumb lines — **Shoulder template**

Right — Left

Side template — **Side template**

Mark widest part of each layer with vertical lines.

Layer	W	C	B
#12	6 1/4 W	18 3/4 C	10 B
#11	14 1/2 W	36 1/2 C	18 1/2 B
#10	17 3/16 W	41 C	21 1/4 B (R ... L)
#9	18 3/16 W	55 1/2 C	18 B
#8	12 3/16 W	35 C	16 1/4 B *(Bust points)*
#7	11 1/8 W	31 1/2 C	15 B
#6	10 5/16 W	30 1/2 C	13 1/4 B
#5	10 1/2 W	31 C	13 B *(WAIST)*
#4	11 5/8 W	34 1/2 C	15 1/4 B
#3	12 13/16 W	36 1/2 C	17 B *(Width of profile (W))*
#2	13 1/2 W	38 C	16 B *(Back only (B))*
#1	14 W	39 C *(Circumference (C))*	20 B

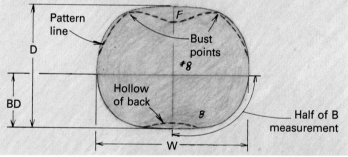

Patternmaking for layer #8

Use visual clues (bust points, shoulder blades) and C and B measurements to determine shape of each oval pattern. Label front and back, and number.

Pattern line — F — Bust points — D — BD — Hollow of back — #8 — B — Half of B measurement — W

After the model's profile has been traced on 1/4-in.-thick foam-core board, the level of each styrofoam layer is transferred to the masking tape on the model's back. A square is used for accuracy (left). At right, Gelfand cuts styrofoam ovals with a keyhole saw; each oval is labeled with the layer number, front, back, and sides. It's hard to remove styrofoam crumbs from carpeting, so work outdoors or in a garage.

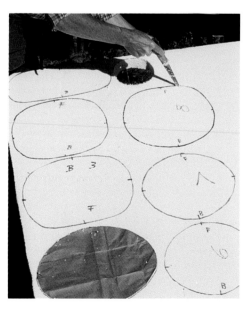

tance between verticals and record it on the foam core (*D* for depth, *W* for width).

Patterns and styrofoam cakes—It's better to cut a pattern too large than too small, so when in doubt, cut big.

On opened and flattened grocery bags or brown wrapping paper, draw two lines that cross at right angles (patternmaking drawing, facing page). The vertical line represents body depth; the horizontal line, the width. Refer to the front-view and side-view profiles for the depth, width, and back-depth measurements, and transfer them to the crossed lines.

Divide the back seamline-to-seamline measurement by 2, and distribute each half in an arc between the center back and the side-seam points. Subtract the back measurement from the circumference and distribute the remainder around the front of the oval. Use visual clues from the model to create the proper shape. Label the pattern with *front, back,* and the layer number inside the cutting line; you won't recognize them later. Repeat for all layers.

Crumbled, static-ridden styrofoam is almost impossible to remove from carpeting or fabric surfaces, so work in an uncarpeted room, in a garage, or outside, preferably with a vacuum and a dust mask handy. Anti-static spray makes the process less messy.

Secure the patterns on the styrofoam sheet with pins, trace around the patterns, and mark center front, back, and sides *inside* the cutting lines with a wide felt-tip pen by lifting the edge of the patterns. Number the styrofoam layers immediately. Cut out the layers with a keyhole saw, being careful to keep the blade perpendicular to the styrofoam (photo at right, facing page).

Stack the layers by lining up the front, back, and side-seam marks, and stick them together with 1½-in.- to 2-in.-wide, double-sided carpet tape (photo at top left). You can use epoxy or white glue, but avoid glues with solvents (rubber cement or airplane glue), which will dissolve the styrofoam. Glue must set overnight, as the styrofoam acts like a water barrier and slows down evaporation. The layers *will* slide apart if you start carving before the glue is set.

To stick two layers together, mark the position of the smaller layer on the larger layer with a felt-tip pen. Stick four pieces of carpet tape to the larger layer, keeping the tape at least 1 in. inside the positioning line in order to avoid gumming your carving tools. It's difficult to pry layers apart once they've been joined with tape or glue, and it's damaging to the styrofoam. From the waist up, you may have to look from underneath or pick the form up to check that all points are aligned. Be sure of the positioning before removing the slick surface from the top of the tape and sticking the next layer to the form. Proceed in the same manner for all layers up to the top of the form.

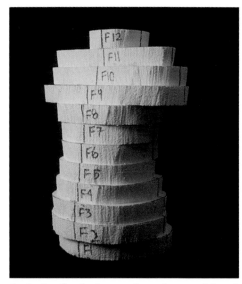

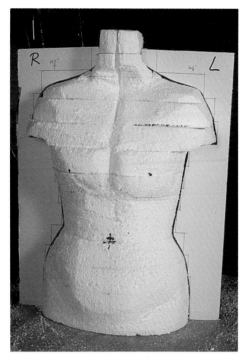

A stack of polystyrene-foam layers (above) already resembles a human form. The carved form (right) matches the body profiles and is ready for sanding. Veréna Gelfand (below) removes styrofoam with a serrated knife.

Sculpting the final shape—Sculpting may take some perseverance. Rely on visual and tactile clues for information about the model's shape, in addition to the measurements. Have the model wear the leotard or bathing suit with her waist marked for reference.

Before you carve, prepare the profiles as your guides. On the left- and right-side templates, draw several vertical plumb lines in the space outside and above the shoulder line; these will help establish the position of the shoulder once it has been cut loose from the rest of the tracing. Cut along the outlines with the utility knife. Save what was inside the tracing (the body), and reserve the pieces around it as templates. Separate the shoulder templates from the side templates at the armscyes.

Don't worry about cutting off too much styrofoam. You'll be sanding down the final circumference measurement for each layer by ½ in. to ¾ in. less than the actual measurements to allow for the thickness of the batting and knit covering. If you've really taken off too much, you can stick a replacement piece of styrofoam on the form or pad it with batting. Nothing short of intentional mayhem is irreparable, so don't worry. You'll be relieved and astonished when suddenly, despite all doubts, your shape begins to emerge from the anonymous ziggurat.

A good sculpting strategy is to carve the form's sides and centers until all four templates fit and then use the circumference measurements and visual clues to sculpt the areas in between, from the bottom

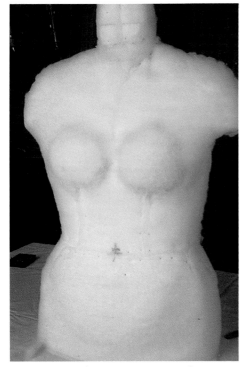

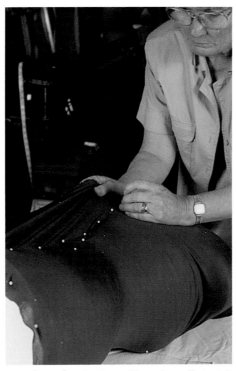

Flat-headed pins anchor the batting edges smoothly at seams and darts. Masking tape underneath the batting marks where over-carved areas were padded.

Working with the form "face down," stretch knit fabric tightly around to the back and pin it in place with glass-headed pins, which are easily seen.

up. Hold the front and side body profiles upright on the work surface between wood blocks for quick reference (bottom photo, p. 123). The knife is most useful for carving large chunks; the file is good for smoothing. When using a profile to check the contours, hold its bottom flat against the work surface; a small tilt can make a big change in the profile. Keep the work surface clean.

Mark the waistline or navel of the form. This gives you a reference point for measuring. With a yardstick, measure from the waist up and mark the bust points, making sure they're the proper distance apart.

Begin by carving off the "steps" between styrofoam layers. Note how the legs fit into the body at the hips and crotch; note also the shape of the stomach's contours. If you're carving a form for yourself, feel the contours of your body; then feel the form, and match them. The sides of the hips may be flat or slightly curved. The circumference from the waist to the bust may not change much. Note where the bottom curve of the bust starts. Sculpt out the cleavage until your bra fits properly on the form.

Work from the bust up to the shoulders. On the model measure the distance between the bust points and where the shoulder meets the neck (where the garment shoulder seam would meet a crewneck edge). Duplicate the relationship on the form. For example, if the model's measurement from bust point to shoulder-neck point is 10 in., but 11 in. on the form, lower the top of the shoulder at the shoulder-neck point by carving more.

Use the neck-shoulder-upper-arm profile to re-create the proper slope of the shoulders and the curve of the upper arm. Take your time to get the shoulder area perfect; proper fit and hang of garments depend to a large extent on duplicating the model's shoulder width, slope, shape, and posture. Your eyes and your fingertips are the most important tools you have to create the final shape. Trust yourself.

Keep the plumb lines on the shoulder template vertical while fitting the shoulder pattern to the top of the shoulders. Have the model kneel so you can get a bird's-eye view of the shoulder area. Note the extent or absence of protruding shoulder blades.

If you've carved too much foam, and the circumferences are too small, pad the "dented" areas with extra batting and masking tape. After you've achieved the desired shape and dimensions, use a Stanley Surform or sandpaper to file evenly all over the surface of the body form. Reduce the final circumference measurements by ½ in. to ¾ in. less than the model's to make room for the batting and the outer knit fabric.

Batting and knit fabric—To cover the foam, you'll need 1 yd. of 8-oz. bonded polyester batting, split into two layers (enough for two forms); long, flat-headed straight pins; and 1 yd. of knit fabric. A two-way-stretch knit is easier to stretch tightly over the form than a one-way-stretch knit. Choose an opaque fabric so areas that might have to be patched with additional foam and masking tape don't show through.

Fit the batting by layering it around the body and anchoring it with flat-headed straight pins. Cover the area below the waist separately from that above the waist.

Cut a piece of batting about 2 in. longer than the form from the waist to the lower edge and as wide as the circumference of the bottom layer. Fit the batting around the core, beginning at the lower edge, cutting out darts where necessary to fit the batting smoothly over the styrofoam. Pin completely around the waist, down the sides of all darts, and around the bottom of the form, as was done in the form in the photo at left.

Cut another piece of batting long enough to cover the form from the waist to the neck and wide enough so you can wrap the widest point at the shoulders. Cut, stretch, and/or ease to fit the batting as necessary. You may have to add a separate piece to cover the neck. Cut a piece of knit fabric wide enough to wrap around the entire body form at its widest—at the shoulder or hips—plus a few inches for adjustments; it should be the length of the form plus 6 in. for tucking under at the lower edge and for adjustments at the top.

Mark the center of the piece lengthwise. Lay the form on a table "face up." Place the fabric over the form with the marked centerline down the center front of the form, allowing about 2 in. for tucking under at the lower edge. Hold the fabric in place by pushing pins straight into the form along the center front from the neck to the bottom edge. Carefully turn the form over without ripping out any pins. Pull one selvage around the form, and pin it in the center back (right photo, above).

Adjust the amount of pull in order to eliminate wrinkles. Later, you may have to cut off excess as you determine how much fabric is actually needed to cover the form. Create a slight overlap in the center back by pulling and adjusting the other selvage around the form to match the first half. Turn under a neat edge along the center back and handsew it in place. Turn under excess fabric below the form and pin it in place or glue it; pinning gives you the option of changing the form's dimensions at a later date. Finish off the shoulder and neck areas by pulling and adjusting fabric as needed, avoiding seams as much as possible. There should be no wrinkles when you're finished.

Most of the time I use my form while it sits on a worktable; but to fit dresses, coats, jackets, and long tops, I put the form on the stand of a greeting-card display rack that was discarded by a local store. The rack has a wide base and a pipe that fits into a hole in the center bottom of the form. A similar stand may come your way, or you might create a different one, but in any event, you're done. Enjoy!

Veréna Gelfand designs and weaves warp-painted garments in Seattle, WA. As a member of the Seattle Weavers Guild, she came across the concept for the dress form and developed it to use in her own work.

Cloning your body: The home sewer's moment of truth

by David Page Coffin

I recently allowed myself to be taped inside a plastic bag and then wrapped, from hips to neck, in surgical plaster— the kind doctors make casts out of. When the plaster mold was cut off and I got a good look at it, I had a moment of revelation that I believe every sewer should have: I saw for the first time what shape I am.

I'm no stranger to mirrors, and I've been making clothes for myself fairly successfully for a long time, but based on what I saw that afternoon in damp plaster, I realized that I'd been working in the dark.

I got an even better look the next day, when I made a form in the mold out of polyurethane foam. The main surprises for me were the shape of my shoulders and back, the angle of my neck, and the slope of my waist from front to back. I've known for years that one of my shoulders is lower than the other, but it has never been obvious to me; now it is inescapable. Since I completed the form and put it on a stand, I'm even surprised at how tall it is whenever I go into my sewing room.

However you come by it, I'm certain that, if you're sewing for yourself, you'll never regret the trouble you take to get a custom-made dress form. Your mental body image, no matter how you've scrutinized yourself, is still the work of your imagination and needs to be replaced with the hard truth. Besides, you can actually drape cloth on a form. It's tough to drape on a mental image.

The form I made and the red one in the bottom photo were put together with the help of a kit (about $50) from Carol Stith Zahn (Box 8004, Salt Lake City, UT 84108). It includes an instruction booklet and all the supplies but the foam (Carol gives sources), utility shears to cut the mold, and the stand. There's also an excellent videotape, *My Twin Dress Form,* in which Carol demonstrates the process; it's very reassuring and, I think, essential. It's available from Clotilde (1909 S.W. First Ave., Ft. Lauderdale, FL 33315; 305-761-8655) for $25.60 ($3.20 for booklet only). You'll need helpers, so why not make several forms and split the cost of the video? Rita Buchanan (top photo) and I spent an entertaining weekend, with help from our spouses, making a pair of forms. We found that Carol's instructions left very little out, but we did make several observations that may help if you decide that a plaster body cast is the way to go. I think it's the most accurate method.

Neither Rita nor I found standing still and being wrapped for about 45 minutes uncomfortable or difficult, but some people do, and that's the main argument against this method. The plaster is only skintight when you inhale fully; most of the time, it feels a bit loose. We both wish we'd spent more time cutting and taping the plastic wrap underneath the plaster to fit more smoothly around necks and armholes, because when the foam came out, these areas looked more like bunched-up plastic than bodies. I should have wrapped as high as possible around my neck; it seems a little short to me now.

One thickness of plaster bandage is never enough. Use two layers on all parts of the body; plenty came with our kits. All the edges at openings in the cast (neck, armholes, and at the bottom) need an additional layer of reinforcement, particularly the shoulder areas just above the armhole; otherwise, the edges are too fragile.

By all means, wear the plastic gloves in the kit, and old clothes, when mixing and pouring the foam; it doesn't clean off. Although the foam didn't smell awful or bother us at the time, our noses and throats were slightly irritated from its vapors for a day or two. It would be better to mix and pour the foam outdoors. Also, when you sand the few places that need smoothing out on the form, wear a dust mask to avoid inhaling crumbs of irritating foam dust.

You pour the foam in from the hip end of the mold, and it billows up like a soufflé, so to even off the base, we balanced each form on a table and tried to hold it so its posture exactly matched that of its future owner. Then we drew a pencil line around the bottom as close to the table as possible, holding the pencil on a block of wood to keep it parallel and equidistant to the table top, to indicate where to cut it off. Sawing the foam was easy enough, releasing jillions of static-clingy crumbs that went everywhere, but they vacuumed up easily.

We followed Carol's instructions for the plywood base and used inexpensive (about $20) microphone stands to hold the forms at the right height. We screwed a short fitting into the metal flange that Carol describes attaching to the plywood; the forms slid right over the end of the metal pipe from the stand. We didn't have to cut the stands down, but it would have been easy to do with a hacksaw. Both of us decided to buy colored knit ribbing to cover the forms, instead of using the white knit in the kits. Counting the kits, the foam (there's enough left to do two more forms), the cloth, and the hardware, we each spent about $110 and three days to make perfect duplicates of ourselves, and we both agree they're fantastic tools. □

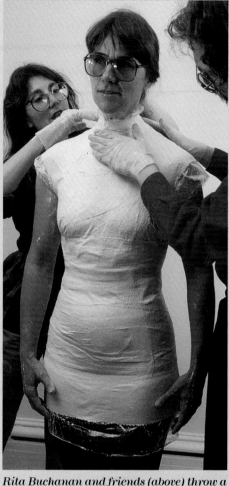

Rita Buchanan and friends (above) throw a plaster party. Rita's plaster body mold will be cut off when it's dry and filled with foam to make the customized dress form in red below. Even though Rita measures a perfect size 12, the exact shape of her body is as unique as her fingerprints. Comparing her form with a standard industrial model, it's obvious which will be more helpful to her when she's trying to solve her personal fitting problems.

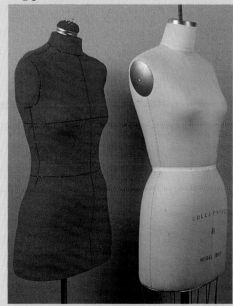

Index